To Cynthia,
With love,
Charlie
10/25/19

THE
NORTH
ATLANTIC
CITIES

To Daniel Rose and Edward Rutkowski
Thinkers and doers
Builders of cities and people

© Charles Duff 2019
Published by Bluecoat Press, Liverpool
Book design by March Design, Liverpool
Printed in China by Latitude Press

ISBN 9781908457530

BLUECOAT

THE
NORTH
ATLANTIC
CITIES

Amsterdam – Baltimore – Bath – Birmingham – Boston – Bristol
Delft – Dublin – Edinburgh – Glasgow – Leyden – Liverpool
London – Manchester – New York – Philadelphia – Richmond
Rotterdam – The Hague – Washington

Charles Duff

BLUECOAT

CONTENTS

Opposite. The Royal Crescent Bath.

FOREWORD

By Alexander Garvin

The North Atlantic Cities, by Charles Duff, is a book on urban development and urban life masquerading as a book on architecture. It is a fascinating study of four hundred years of architecture and urban development in four countries: the Netherlands, Great Britain, Ireland, and the United States. But it is not a typical book about a few great buildings and a few great men. Unlike most writers who care about architecture, Duff is not dazzled by famous monuments or illustrious designers, though he gives them their due. He shows cities in full.

Duff starts with a kind of building that few writers have ever considered seriously, the row house. And he sees – and helps us to see – that this innocuous-seeming housing type is the key to understanding why many of the world's great cities look and function as they do.

The story begins in the Netherlands in 1600. Duff makes a good case that the Dutch in the generation of Rembrandt and Vermeer built the first modern country: a middle-class business society with religious toleration and a respect for serious, practical analysis. They also invented the modern row house and built the first row house cities. Dutch cities, as Duff notes, are the most pleasant cities in the world, and the row house would remain the symbol of serious, tolerant, middle-class society for centuries.

And what centuries they were! The row house cities on both sides of the North Atlantic built the modern global economy, with all its goods and all its evils. Along the way, these cities transformed themselves continually and very creatively. They built the first public parks, the first mass transit systems, and the first all-business Downtowns.

Duff is the first writer I know of who has noticed that the row house cities of the world form a region. Amsterdam and London have row houses while Paris and Vienna do not. Brooklyn and Baltimore have them while Denver and Los Angeles do not. This is a very important observation and should be taken seriously by anyone who is trying to understand a row house city in any nation.

For years I have unsuccessfully tried to convince people from outside the United States that although Americans from all parts of the country dress in the same jeans, drive the same cars, drink the same Coca Cola, and eat the same breakfast cereals, the way of life and personal characteristics of the residents of Chicago, Los Angeles, Miami, and every large American city are significantly different from one another. Duff finds that these differences are rooted in the history of American settlement and expressed in the design of buildings and cities.

There is a lot of history in this book, but it is not a "history book". Duff takes us through the growth of a dozen cities for the purpose of preparing us to understand what is happening in our cities right now. He is a practical man, a successful real estate developer. He has been working for decades, with considerable success, to rebuild large parts of a tough North Atlantic city. He has come face to face every day with what works and what doesn't, and he has a good nose for what works.

His fundamental idea is sound, and it is new. He believes, and shows by example, that the North Atlantic tradition, which by now includes apartment buildings and 24/7 Downtowns as well as row houses, is a good way, perhaps the best way for us to avoid suburban sprawl, urban decay, and even the worst catastrophes of global climate change. I believe that American cities outside the North Atlantic region would profit greatly from studying this book.

I already loved the cities in this book before realizing that they formed a specific region. Now that I have read this book and looked at its beautiful pictures (some of which, in the interest of full disclosure, I took) I love them even more. I predict that you will too.

INTRODUCTION

When I walk out of the front door of my house and look across Lanvale Street, I see a row of houses. Although they are not identical to each other, they are connected to each other, and they form a continuous wall along the street. Casual observers usually assume that they were all built by the same people at the same time, though in fact they result from eight separate construction projects over a period of more than thirty years.

Lanvale Street.

What is the right name for houses like this? On average, Americans tend to call such houses row houses, while the British speak of them as terraced houses. But it is more complicated than that. My New York cousins invariably call them brownstones. The wise Patrick Shaffrey in Dublin calls them street houses. People who are trying to sell them, on both sides of the Ocean, routinely call them town houses, a phrase that apparently adds to the price. The Dutch, who invented them, simply call them houses.

Whatever people may call these houses, I can see a lot of them from my front door, and that is fine with me. If I look straight ahead, or turn my head to the left, the houses I see are three stories tall and date from several decades of the nineteenth century. If I turn my head to the right, and squint a bit, the houses are a story shorter and were built in my memory. Whichever way I look, the view is very pleasant, and I sometimes wonder how I came to be lucky enough to live in so beautiful a place.

I would probably have a similar view, and similar feelings, if I lived in London, or Amsterdam, or Dublin, or Brooklyn, or Bristol, or Philadelphia. Row houses are a common building type in those cities, as they are in hundreds of cities and towns on both sides of the North Atlantic Ocean. But my view would be very different if I lived in Paris, or Vienna, or any of the major inland cities of Europe, beautiful as they are. These are cities of apartment houses, many of them palatial, and row houses are virtually or absolutely unknown. Nor would I see row houses in Houston, Minneapolis, Los Angeles, or most American cities west of the Appalachians. These are cities of free-standing houses, each house surrounded on all four sides by unbuilt land. When I was growing up, in a city with hundreds of thousands of row houses, I assumed that every city had row houses. Not until I began traveling as a young adult did it dawn on me that the row house was a regional phenomenon.

This was not entirely my fault. The row house region is large enough to seem infinite. It includes several countries, in whole or in part, and it spans the North Atlantic Ocean, so that half of it is three thousand miles away from the other half. The European half includes the Low Countries, the British Isles, and Ireland, with some outliers among the smaller

Hanseatic cities of Germany. The American half lies mainly within about fifty miles of the East Coast of the United States, with some outliers among the older cities of the Midwest and Canada. The ocean that divides the two halves of the row house region has served more often to unite them. As a result, I find it useful to speak of the row house cities as *the North Atlantic cities*.

These cities are some of the most important places in the world. To measure their impact, try to imagine what the world would be like if London, New York, Amsterdam, and the other North Atlantic cities had never existed. For starters, we would have to live without railroads, steamships, telegraphs, toilets, factory production, surgical anesthesia, and representative democracy. And the importance of these cities is not merely, or even chiefly, historical. New York and London still guide the world's economy. Washington, for better or worse, still sets the agenda for the world's politics.

The North Atlantic cities have invented many of the things that make modern cities work. To them we owe public parks, mass transit, and central business districts, not to mention plentiful supplies of clean water and the sanitary disposal of human waste. To them, also, we owe the invention of year-round middle-class suburbia, a nineteenth-century innovation that would later prove nearly fatal to many of them.

It has taken a lot of work to build these cities, and their story features some heroic architects and builders. Jacob van Campen in Amsterdam, Inigo Jones and Christopher Wren in London, and Charles Bulfinch in Boston sparked revolutions in architecture and in the building of cities.

But the real shapers of the North Atlantic cities are, and have almost always been, their people. Most of us have never been employed in architecture or building, and our involvement in the shaping of cities has generally been infrequent and unsystematic; but it is we who have usually determined what architects and builders would get paid for creating. We have sometimes exercised this power directly, by hiring experts to design and build buildings to meet our needs and fulfill our dreams. More often we have exercised it indirectly, as consumers, by deciding what kinds of buildings we would, and would not, buy or rent – or as citizens, by setting standards, creating parks, and building or failing to build vital pieces of municipal infrastructure. Without emperors or dictators to tell us what to build, we anonymous amateurs have made most of the crucial design decisions in our cities – whether a piece of ground should have a house or a church or a skyscraper, a row house or an apartment building or a park – leaving it to architects to devise subtle improvements for our ideas.

On the whole, this loose-limbed system has worked rather better than one might expect. It has been a great pleasure to me to walk every city and town that I mention in the following pages. We have done good work surprisingly often, and we have created more than our share of urban masterpieces.

And somehow, for more than four hundred years, we have built row or terraced houses. This is a fact that needs some explaining. How did millions of people in a number of different countries hit on the row house way of building and stick with it for centuries – even though most of their neighbors failed, or refused, to follow their example?

This book started as an attempt to answer that apparently simple question, and I am still surprised that no one has attempted to answer it before. I cannot possibly be the first person who ever noticed that London resembles Brooklyn more than it resembles Paris, or that Brooklyn looks more like London than like Houston, and that row houses are the reason. Perhaps I am merely the first person who thought these things were important.

If so, well, good for me. These things are important. It is not merely a matter of appearance. Row house cities are cities of moderate density, halfway between the high densities of continental Europe and the low densities of continental America. If I lived in Paris, sharing an acre of urban ground with two hundred families, my apartment would be small and somewhat on the dark side, but I could meet most of my needs and many of my friends in short strolls. If I had a big lawn on the outskirts of Houston, my house would be large and sunny, but I would have to drive several miles to buy a tube of toothpaste. As it is, with the moderate population densities of a row house neighborhood, my neighbors and I can have houses as big as in Houston on much smaller pieces of land, and we can usually walk or bike or take public transit to a reasonable array of things to do and things to buy. A well-functioning North Atlantic city offers people the best of both worlds.

Given that the North Atlantic cities are a type of city, denser than Houston and more spacious than Paris, it should be obvious to city planners that they should plan for the North Atlantic cities in specific ways. Nonetheless, too many planners have tried to treat the row house cities of the North Atlantic as if they were apartment house cities like Paris or sprawling cities like Houston. This has resulted in a fabulous waste of money, a great deal of preventable environmental damage, and a lot of unnecessary pain to large numbers of people.

All this matters today for two reasons. The first is that most of our cities are still working their way out of the urban crisis that pushed them to the wall in the late twentieth century. They are still trying to deal with the challenges posed by the automobile, the high-rise building, low-density sprawl, de-industrialization, and racial and ethnic diversity. Many cities are still fighting to survive, while some have gone from failure to success so suddenly that many of their people can no longer afford to live in them. The experiences of the past century have called many of the North Atlantic traditions into question and are forcing us to decide which traditions we should keep and which we may discard. Since that is our assignment, it would help us to understand just what our traditions are, how they came to be, and to what extent they can still be useful to us.

We have not yet begun to do this. Although the North Atlantic region is international, there is no international dialogue about what works and what doesn't work in shaping our family of cities. As I have researched this book, I have found that each of our cities has solved some problem that is important to all of them, but each city is singing in the shower with no one to hear. I hope that this little book will start the dialogue that we so desperately need.

That is one reason. But there is, unfortunately, a second. The second reason to care about the North Atlantic cities, and the habits of building and living that arose in them, is that global climate change is a real and terrifying threat. We need to find ways of living satisfying lives with a much lower carbon footprint. Since living closer together is the easiest way of consuming less energy, we are lucky to have home-grown traditions of building and living at adequate density. While most of us will never want to be as crowded as Parisians are, or most New Yorkers, we don't need to be. We can get there by developing along North Atlantic lines, with a mixture of apartment buildings and row houses and generous public transportation. We can even retrofit much of America's post-war suburban sprawl.

I hope that you will enjoy reading this book as much as I have enjoyed writing it. And I hope it will help you to take delight in beautiful places, as I do when I walk out of my front door.

Gardens and borrowed views behind Lanvale and Bolton Streets.

PRELUDE

THE URBAN REVOLUTION OF THE 1600s

A bi-lingual person, visiting Paris and London in 1600, would have had trouble telling them apart. In each of the two cities, a few dozen noble families lived in palace compounds, while almost everyone else lived in ramshackle houses made of wood or half-timbering, the rotting and sagging ancestors of today's masonry row houses.

The town palaces of nobles are best thought of as castles on compressed lots. Each had walls, guards, and interior courtyards, taking up an acre or more of urban land and housing a few score of knights, pages, ladies-in-waiting, and other household officers.

The richest commoners lived in houses that were four or five stories tall and twenty feet wide, with workshops on the street front, a heavy iron-bound door to ward off robbers and rioters, and a scattering of family members and servants bedded down haphazardly amongst piles of merchandise. Poorer people – the vast majority of the people in London, Paris, and all other cities – had smaller houses, less personal space, and even less construction quality. We might call their houses shacks. Add large amounts of filth, disease, and crime, and it is not hard to understand why people, noble and common, wanted to make their cities better. By 1600, the Italian Renaissance was showing them how.

The Three Elements of a Renaissance City

In 1600, Italy was at least two hundred years ahead of Northern Europe in architecture and city design. After 1600, northerners set to work bringing the Renaissance to their own cities by introducing three revolutionary elements: classical architecture, straight streets with aligned buildings, and dignified public places.

Classical architecture, derived from the architecture of ancient Rome, began to be revived in Florence around 1420 and began to affect the design of Florentine houses in the 1440s. From that time until the middle of the nineteenth century, classical architecture was the only kind of serious, intentional, "capital-A" Architecture in Europe, and the use of classical principles in the design of houses – not just for churches or palaces – was the clearest indication that people were taking the design of houses seriously.

The first true Renaissance house, Palazzo Rucellai in Florence, showed architects how to marry the grandeur of the ancient Romans to the basic building practices of contemporary Italy and sparked countless thousands of imitations. Each country in the

Opposite. Via Giulia, Rome. The first street in Europe to embody the design principles of the Renaissance. It is straight, and the buildings that frame it are properly aligned – that is, their facades form a smooth and continuous wall. Via Giulia does not look in any way extraordinary today, a measure of its success.

A nobleman's palace. The Hotel du Maine in Paris.

Houses for rich commoners in the City of London before the Great Fire of 1666.

*Palazzo Rucellai, Florence
Designed by Leone Battista
Alberti in the 1440s, Palazzo
Rucellai is a fairly normal
Florentine palazzo in everything
except its decoration; but its
decoration, derived quite
closely from the Roman
Colosseum, was revolutionary.*

North Atlantic world would eventually build its own home-grown version of Palazzo Rucellai, usually a brick house five bays wide with flat pilasters on the façade: the Coymans house in Amsterdam, Lindsey House in London, the second house for Harrison Gray Otis in Boston. Wherever such a house appeared, it announced that people in that city were ready to approach the design of houses with full architectural seriousness.

The other two elements of a Renaissance city, straight streets and dignified public spaces, required heavy public investments and the collaboration of many different property owners, and were in consequence much longer coming. Not until 1508, more than a generation after Alberti's death, could Pope Julius II, not unfairly called the Warrior Pope, cut the first modern street, the via Giulia, through a tangle of private and public properties in Rome; and not until the 1580s did Pope Sixtus V lay out the magnificent Roman avenues that mark the birth of modern city planning. But this long gestation was over by 1600, and the nations north of the Alps took notice.

France and the Court Societies

The first Northern Europeans to apply the lessons of the Renaissance on a grand scale were the kings of France, the masters of the largest, richest, and most powerful state in Early Modern Europe. They were lucky in their timing. Italian art was entering its Baroque phase in 1600, and artists were judged by their ability to inspire reverence by displaying a parallel universe – usually Heaven – of overwhelming grandeur and glory. It did not take the French kings very long to realize that Baroque art, designed to inspire reverence for God, could also inspire reverence for *them*.

Everything came together in the long reign of Louis XIV, from 1643 to 1715. The Sun King, as his people called him, presided over the embellishment of large parts of Paris, and it was in his time that Paris began to find its modern form. But Louis XIV did not like Paris, and his greatest work – the greatest work of the French Baroque – was a gigantic palace at Versailles, in deep country about twenty miles from the capital.

Versailles dwarfed the scale of papal palaces. Even before it was finished, it had room for ten thousand courtiers, and limitless enfilades of rooms and limitless parterres of topiary gardens led courtiers on and on beyond their reckoning. As befitted the palace of a supremely aggressive monarch, Versailles was a model of world domination.

The kings and princes of inland Europe followed Louis's example. Even his most determined enemies, like the Holy Roman Emperor in Vienna, built the grandest baroque palaces they could afford, and their nobles followed suit with private palaces. The great historian Norbert Elias speaks of these seventeenth-century societies as "court societies". In a court society, according to Elias, kings set fashion, nobles imitate kings, rich commoners imitate nobles, and so on down the line.

The Chateau de Versailles in 1668.

Not surprisingly, then, the nobleman's palace became the model for middle-class housing in the court societies of Europe. Although middle-class people could not afford to build private palaces, they could rent suites of rooms in palatial buildings with courtyards and carriage entrances. They invented the apartment house, and courtly capitals like Paris and Vienna, and the secondary cities that followed courtly fashions, became cities of apartment houses.

The North Atlantic Alternative

The exact opposite happened in the Netherlands and the British Isles. There, noblemen abandoned their palaces and adopted the middle-class row house. People of all classes, in one city after another, learned to translate the ramshackle medieval row house into an elegant classical vernacular of brick and stone.

In the years and centuries that followed, a family of cities grew up on the two coasts of the North Atlantic Ocean. Though sometimes divided by politics and war, they have usually found that blood – and commerce – are thicker than water. The North Atlantic cities remain a family today, with all the varieties of love and rivalry that families are made of. Their story begins in the Netherlands.

Chapter One

MAKING REALITY BEAUTIFUL

Dutch cities may well be the pleasantest cities in the world. They are quietly busy, unpretentiously lovely, and just clean enough. Pedestrians and cyclists maintain a neighborly feel in the historic city centers, and cars are refreshingly scarce. There are street trees and lovely little patches of urban greenery, and miles and miles of charming houses.

For most of this we should thank the Dutch of the seventeenth century, the Golden Age, the age of Rembrandt and Vermeer. The neighbors and patrons of the great painters could take a bog with a scraggly little river and shape it into an elegant canal, rippling with light and framed with buildings of perfect scale. They could take a scrap of back-alley land and shape it into a magical little courtyard, with tiny houses, perfect spatial relationships, the right touch of greenery, and a profusion of flowers.

All this is reason enough to stroll and explore in the cities of the Netherlands. But there is more. Here, on these old streets, we can come face-to-face with one of the great ages of the past. Surely, we think, as we watch the light of a spring evening fall on the old bricks and play on the slow water of the canals – surely, we are almost there. We know what Dutch cities were like in the Golden Age, thanks to the greatest realistic painters in history; and simply being in one of these cities today, walking the streets that Vermeer walked, going from room to room in Rembrandt's house, seeing the buildings and the light as Berckheyde and van der Heyden painted them, gives us one of the strongest and happiest senses of connection with people who are no longer alive.

Think of Vermeer's painting The Little Street. Looking at it is not like looking at a picture in a frame. It is like looking out of the window. There it is, a real alley, in all its everyday realness, with a real brick building and a pair of real unromantic women, all in the everyday light of Northern Europe. For anyone who wants more, Vermeer's little city of Delft is there every day, a whole reality of quiet little streets, of mellow bricks in a soft light, of unromantic people living, still living, there.

But is it still Vermeer's Delft? The city today has very few buildings that Vermeer would recognize. Almost every building has been built or drastically rebuilt since his day. Even his Little Street, which looks like so many little streets in Delft today, is not exactly like any one of them. Vermeer's model for *The Little Street*, now determined by scholars to be 40-42 Flamingstraat, has been changed beyond recognition.

If we are not seeing what Vermeer saw, then, just what are we seeing? Not the world

Johannes Vermeer,
'The Little Street'.

that formed Vermeer and Rembrandt and their great generation, but something immeasurably better: the world they formed. Dutch cities are as much a product of the Golden Age of Dutch realism as Rembrandt's *Night Watch* or Vermeer's *Girl with a Pearl Earring.*

These are the world's first realistic cities. Their builders, like the great painters, brought something new into the world by discovering how to make everyday reality beautiful. Just as Dutch painters, with their unsentimental eyes, revealed the fascinating personhood of ordinary people, so the builders of Dutch cities built houses and streets that revealed the fascination of ordinary life without romanticizing or falsifying it. Like the burghers and burgheresses in the portraits of Hals and Rembrandt, the buildings of Dutch cities are satisfied and satisfying, self-confident without pride, dignified without pretense, individual without oddness.

The Dutch in their Golden Age invented what we now call the row house or the terraced house. They were the first people to dignify the ramshackle houses of medieval commoners by building them of durable materials – usually brick – and touching them with the seventeenth century's magic wand of classicism.

How did this happen? In a century when fashions were set by kings and popes in silk and ermine, how did the middle-class men and women we see in Dutch portraits create the most beautiful cities in Europe? Look at the people in portraits by Rembrandt or Hals. There they are, sitting quietly in black suits or black gowns. They are much poorer than princes or prelates; and architecture is a very expensive art. How did they do it?

A New Kind of Society

For one thing, they were richer than they looked. The men who commissioned Rembrandt's portraits built a commercial empire that circled the globe. They dominated the grain and timber trade of the Baltic and sent ten thousand men every year to hunt whales in the Arctic. They beat the Spanish and the Portuguese in spectacular sea battles, took the Mediterranean trade from Venice and Genoa, and conquered both Indonesia and Brazil. Along the way, without much fanfare or capital investment, they established a settlement in North America, New Amsterdam, to facilitate the fur trade in the Hudson River Valley. Because they could live on imported Baltic grain, they were free to go to sea instead of plowing fields, and their tiny country never had any trouble manning powerful fleets.

But they remained middle-class people. Their frame of reference was always the house, not the palace. While Louis XIV and his rivals were dreaming of world power and bending the arts to serve their purposes, the Dutch were cobbling together an oddly-shaped republic with no king, a weak nobility, and a tolerance for religious diversity.

This was very unusual. Even the other two large seventeenth-century republics,

Venice and Genoa, had Dukes (Doges), hereditary nobles, and state pageantry to rival any court. There was none of this in the Dutch Republic. Only one Dutch nobleman, the Prince of Orange, had the income of an English earl or a French duke, and this level of wealth was exceptional enough to give the House of Orange a unique position in Dutch society. The national assembly, called the States General, was an alliance of town councils, and its rulers tended to dress, spend, and think like town councilors. At their best, they were serious and practical. They wasted little money or blood on glory, and they avoided the religious bigotry that turned much of seventeenth-century Europe into a murderous snake pit.

The Golden Age was an urban age, as might be expected in a nation ruled by town councilors. More than half of the Republic's population lived in towns and cities by 1600, a proportion that England, the next nation to reach it, would not match until 1850; and what was true of the Republic's population was even truer of its wealth. One city, Amsterdam, paid an astonishing fifty-seven percent of the total national tax bill.

Of the many causes of Holland's greatness, perhaps the most telling was the willingness of the people to trust each other and work together. We still see the evidence of their respect for common effort in the group portraits that the Dutch – and no one else – commissioned by the hundred in the Golden Age. While painters in other countries were glorifying generals and field marshals as uniquely-favored individuals, Rembrandt painted a whole military unit in *The Night Watch*, and any member who wanted to appear in the picture had to pay his share of the artist's fee. Every museum in Holland is full of pictures of groups of Dutchmen caught in the act of doing unspectacular things together. Rembrandt's *Syndics of the Cloth Guild*, which rivals da Vinci's *Last Supper* for the honor of being the most famous group portrait ever painted, shows nothing more dramatic than the officers of a trade association conducting a meeting around a table. These great pictures are monuments to trust and collaboration.

Trust turned out to be good business. The black-suited burghers of the Golden Age made huge amounts of money out of their willingness to collaborate and trust each other. No kind of business requires trust and teamwork as much as seafaring, and the Dutch were first and foremost a nation of seafarers. Because they trusted each other, they could become the first Europeans to form simple ship-owning partnerships. If a voyage was successful, they shared the profits fairly. If a ship went down, no one lost too much.

Eventually, the Dutch transcended the narrow limits of trust among friends and business partners. They recognized the importance of social trust, of trust between strangers, of trust as a general rule. They created habits of trust and, finally, turned trust into a saleable commodity. Their confidence in each other was so great that they were able to create the first impersonal joint-stock corporations, the East India and West India Companies. Thousands of small investors funded these global enterprises by trusting

Rembrandt, Syndics of the Cloth Guild.

their money to men they did not know personally. The greatest monument to social trust was the Bank of Amsterdam. Founded in 1609, it still excited the admiration of Adam Smith in 1776. It never lost a depositor's penny, and its reputation for absolute trustworthiness allowed Dutch merchants, for almost two centuries, to trade in more places, at lower rates of interest, than any of their competitors.

Social trust was also key to the shaping of Dutch cities. Earlier merchants, and merchants in other countries, stored their trade goods in their houses because they feared neighbors and competitors; and the wives and children of merchants shared their private lives with burly men who moved bales and barrels endlessly up and down the stairs of their houses. Because Dutch merchants trusted each other, and their employees, they could store their goods outside their houses in public warehouses, and their family life, at home, could be just that, family life. From our point of view, as we try to understand why and how the Dutch were suddenly able to build beautiful houses and cities, this was the most important innovation of the Dutch Golden Age. The brick row houses of Golden Age Holland were the first city houses in history that we would recognize as houses, the first city houses that were not primarily warehouses, offices, or shops. It is no accident that Witold Rybczynski's book *Home: the History of an Idea* begins in Holland in the seventeenth century.

Trust and realism were two of the glories of the Dutch Golden Age, but there was a third: religious toleration. Like every European nation in the seventeenth century, the Dutch Republic had an official state religion, the Reformed Church. It was a Calvinist church, like the powerful and bigoted Calvinist churches in Scotland, Geneva, and New England at the same time, and it would have been glad to establish a religious monopoly. But it was not powerful enough for its bigotry to be dangerous. The town councilors, the black-suited patrons of Rembrandt and Hals, controlled church funds, and they were usually tolerant. Though their ministers often objected to toleration, often at great length and in public, the councilors could usually afford to ignore fulminations from their own official pulpits.

This was unique. At a time when Queen Elizabeth and King James were hunting and executing Catholic priests in England, something like twenty percent of the Dutch remained openly faithful to the Church of Rome. Though Dutch Catholics could not worship publicly, no one bothered them if they worshiped in private, and worship they did. Vermeer's rich Catholic in-laws kept him and his family in middle-class comfort, and two of the five Syndics of the Cloth Guild in Rembrandt's group portrait were Catholics.

And there was more. At a time when the Spanish and the Portuguese were burning Jews at the stake, the Portuguese Jews of Amsterdam were building a synagogue that ranks high today among the glories of that beautiful city. It is vast and radiant with light. Strong stone columns support its lofty roof, and the ark is a masterwork of classical design. This large building is not hidden, like the Catholic churches. It is bold and public, the outward and visible sign of a community strong enough to produce, if ultimately to reject, the great philosopher Spinoza.

Taken altogether, the Dutch Republic in the Golden Age of the seventeenth century was something new. Rich, powerful, tolerant, – above all straightforward and trustworthy – this was the society that invented the row house. The people in the portraits by Rembrandt and Hals built the buildings and cities of the Dutch Golden Age and founded the North Atlantic tradition.

Dutch Cities in 1600

In 1600, however, the Netherlands must have seemed an unlikely spot for a revolution in architecture and city design, if only because Dutch cities were so small. Amsterdam, the biggest of them, had only fifty thousand people, only a fifth as many as London or Paris. The other Dutch cities – Delft, Leyden, Haarlem, Utrecht and the rest – had populations

The only surviving wooden house in Amsterdam.

of between fifteen and thirty thousand, comparable to provincial cities like Norwich and York in England or Verona and Vicenza in the Venetian Republic. Size alone would not make them remarkable in the eyes of visitors.

Nor would magnificence. Dutch cities had none of the splendors that visitors in 1600 expected to see on their travels, the palaces, the cathedrals, the gilded coaches and splendid processions of prelates, noblemen, and sovereigns. The most impressive buildings in each city were the town halls, and even these were less impressive than town halls in many other countries.

Nor would religion make them remarkable. Processions and masses were usually the main source of color and lawful excitement in a seventeenth-century Catholic city, and Lutherans and Anglicans provided music that still delights us, but the Dutch Reformed Church was no fun to watch or to listen to, except of course for Dutch-speaking believers. It offered black robes, long sermons, and, usually, no music. Seventeenth-century paintings of church services show dogs running through the congregation. As for religious architecture, the Reformed Church had inherited magnificent Gothic churches built for Catholic worship, but only after Protestant mobs had burned the pictures and smashed the statues and stained-glass windows. By 1600, the polychrome interiors had all been whitewashed. All the magic was gone. The best that could be said for these church interiors, stripped bare and glaring in unfiltered light, was that they were luminous. It took great painters like de Witte and Saenredam to make them look beautiful.

And, of course, almost all houses were still made of wood, as in the Middle Ages. Wooden houses cannot have held up well in so damp a climate. They must have sagged and cracked, at least as badly as they did in London and Paris, and they were horrible fire hazards. The wooden house that survives today in Amsterdam's Begijnhof is far more carefully maintained than the average house would have been in 1600. Even so, it is architecturally far inferior to its lovely brick neighbors. A whole city of such houses would have seemed very dull.

Not surprisingly, then, visitors from other countries wondered what they were supposed to look at. Black-suited merchants and gable-fronted houses? Every European city had those, but only Dutch cities had nothing else. Where were the jeweled nobles, the courtly pageants, the monuments and festivals of church and state that were the boast and fun of great cities? Dutch cities were like the background of a picture without the foreground. Visitors from courtly countries felt as city-dwellers often feel today when they go to automotive suburbia: they saw lots of people, lots of work, lots of money, and lots of things to buy, but they felt lost and looked in vain for the things they were used to thinking of as the signs of a good community.

Dutch cities did have one feature that most visitors envied. They had canals. Anyone

who has walked along Dutch canals knows how beautiful they are and how enjoyable it is to walk along them. Some of them are narrow, some wide: some are bright, some shadowy; some have their walkways almost at the level of the water level, and some have cliffs ten or fifteen feet high. The canals of Delft are straight and clear, like boulevards. Those of Utrecht are twisting and intimate, with small surprises around each bend. The Rapenburg in Leyden and the great canals of the Canal Belt in Amsterdam present a baroque synthesis of sweep, surprise, and grandeur.

In 1600, the canals lacked their present charm, bordered as they were by small wooden houses. Nonetheless, most of the canals existed, flowing as they flow today, and they were everywhere. They were the streets that every European city dreamed of in 1600: broad, straight, orderly, open to the sky. They gave a firm structure to towns and cities in all corners of the country, ready to be ennobled by the taste and wealth of a Golden Age.

The beauty of urban canals was a happy accident. Like everything else in this practical country, canals were made for practical purposes, of which the most important was drainage. Canals are the urban segments of the rivers and drainage ditches that criss-cross the Dutch countryside. Without them, the cities of the Netherlands would still be

Lingelbach, The Market on the Dam. This chaotic open-air market was the ceremonial center of Amsterdam. The crooked little building at center was the City Hall of Rembrandt's city.

A Dutch canal, the Rapenburg in Leyden.

unproductive bogs. Canals were also the urban sections of the rivers that carried most goods across the country. Safer than the sea, quicker than the wretched roads, and cheaper than both, the inland network of Dutch rivers was an essential ingredient in Golden Age prosperity. Most Dutch towns and cities were built where two or more trade routes came together, or met the sea, and most of their original main streets were canals.

Dutch urban canals seem to have excited even more admiration in the seventeenth century than they do today. There were both practical and aesthetic reasons for this. On the practical side, canals carried the stinking waste and garbage that Londoners and Parisians dumped onto their streets. Dutch pedestrians could walk without soiling their shoes, and housewives could keep their floors clean without armies of servants. All visitors to the Netherlands wrote home about the mania for cleanliness in Dutch houses, and travelers were amazed to find the most powerful men walking through the streets, rather than riding on horseback or sitting in closed carriages. Contemporary visitors often ascribed the walking habits of powerful Dutchmen to bourgeois simplicity or republican fellow-feeling, and there was truth in what they said; but it was also true that Dutch notables walked through their cities because, unlike their equivalents in England or France, they could.

On the aesthetic side, seventeenth-century visitors noticed that canals had already given Dutch cities, more or less by accident, the two most difficult elements of Renaissance city design. They were broad, properly-aligned streets, and they were dignified public places. Each of them was at least as wide as the widest seventeenth-century boulevards in Rome or Paris. They were bright and airy and quiet, and even the biggest houses could present their windows directly onto the street, with no need for a forecourt. Because most goods came and went by boat, there were few wagons on the streets and few dangers to pedestrians. Besides, Dutch city governments had long required that all houses be set back a uniform distance from the canal bank, and these requirements had been enforced. And there were what we would call street trees, giving shade and pleasure as they do today. They were the first street trees in European history and excited the envy of King Henri IV in Paris.

The result, in town after town and city after city, was an established pattern of city planning and city building that fit almost exactly the dreams of the age. Not until the second quarter of the nineteenth century, at great expense and with great controversy, would the French state succeed in straightening even short streets in the center of Paris and aligning all building fronts evenly with the street. All in all, Dutch canals were the first streets in European history that functioned as dignified public places.

The Dutch Palladios

Of the two things that Dutch cities lacked at the beginning of the seventeenth century, size and grandeur, size would not be a problem for long. Dutch cities grew smartly between 1570 and 1670, as farmers left the land to become craftsmen or seamen, and Protestants and Jews sought refuge from war and persecution in Flanders, France, and Germany. Most historians agree that foreigners brought a vivid energy to Dutch society and the Dutch economy. Some argue that they sparked the Golden Age, which sputtered out when their children and grandchildren assimilated.

Grandeur would prove harder to achieve. When seventeenth-century Europeans spoke of grandeur, they meant the bright foreground of princes and prelates, palaces and processions. How could middle-class Dutchmen create seventeenth-century grandeur?

They did it through the arts of architecture and city design. Since the canals had solved the two most difficult problems of Renaissance city design: straight streets and polite public places. That left architecture. Although architecture is a notoriously expensive art, an Italian architect, Andrea Palladio, who died in 1580, had already discovered ways of creating great buildings on a middle-class budget.

Palladio had done most of his work in and around the city of Vicenza, a provincial backwater on the Venetian mainland where even the greatest families had relatively modest incomes; and he had become the first architect in history to build houses that were small, cheap, and convincingly grand. If you think this is easy, think of America's McMansions. The Netherlands needed to bring forth a generation of home-grown Palladios.

Fortunately, they did. Though some of these remarkable architects are locally famous in the Netherlands, we know painfully little about their lives and personalities. Unlike court architects in Italy or France, who rose on princely favor and had their biographies written by the likes of Vasari, the Dutch Palladios were middle-class people who worked for middle-class clients. They were hired and paid like lawyers or cabinet-makers and were no more likely than other useful citizens to attract biographers in their own day. Considering how many years of archival research it took John Montias to establish the basic facts of the life of Vermeer, it is perhaps little wonder that scholars have not uncovered more facts about the lives of the Dutch Palladios.

The first of them, and the best-known, was Hendrick de Keyser (1565-1621), the City Architect of Amsterdam. He is a famous man in the Netherlands today, and the nation's premier Preservation organization, the Dutch equivalent of the National Trust, is named after him. Like many Italian architects, he trained as a sculptor and built his reputation with a chisel before turning to architecture. Unlike the Italians, however, he was not trained to imitate the sculpture of the ancient Romans, which was little known in Holland in his youth. His greatest work of sculpture, the monument to William the Silent in Delft, is fundamentally a Gothic piece of work with some classical ornament.

De Keyser's first buildings were similar. Even his magnificent double house at Herengracht 170-172 in Amsterdam, now the headquarters of the national preservation organization that bears his name, is no more classical than the house in Vermeer's *Little Street*. But he aspired to classicism, and he worked at it for decades. When he started, he thought of Roman architecture as a grab bag of decorative elements. Gradually, however – in part through close personal contact with Inigo Jones, the father of classicism in English architecture – he won his way through to an understanding of Roman architecture as a complete system of proportion and structure. We can trace his evolution by looking at two large Amsterdam churches that he built over a period of twenty years.

The first of these, the South Church, begun in 1603, gets credit for bringing the Italian Renaissance to the Netherlands, and a very early Renaissance too. It has a simple arcaded nave like Brunelleschi's San Lorenzo in Florence and is a strong piece of work. But San Lorenzo was almost two centuries old by 1603. No Italian would have designed, or admired, a version of it in the seventeenth century, and the facades of the South Church would have been beneath Italian notice. It is the work of a talented beginner.

By the time de Keyser got his next church commission, eighteen years later, he had deepened his understanding. The West Church in Amsterdam, begun just before his death in 1621, has an interior that is positively thrilling. Suddenly, more or less out of nowhere, de Keyser knew how to use the Roman Doric order consistently to form clear, self-confident spaces. Everything is tall and bright, strong and solid; and the light is wonderful. The walls are a plain white, the bold Doric columns and the generous mouldings a calm grey in a stone like Florentine *pietra serena*.

De Keyser's two great churches are not only the beginning of the Renaissance in the Netherlands. They are also the beginning of Protestant religious architecture. He was the first architect who ever had the chance to design a big, expensive, church for Protestant worship, and, in the West Church, he responded to the challenge with huge, clear windows – a necessary thing in word-centered Protestant worship – and a masterful handling of light itself as a sculptural element in architecture. Here began the tradition of Protestant classicism that the British would develop fully and make the official style of their first empire, from Sir Christopher Wren's City Churches in London to the white clapboard meeting houses of New England. The same is true of de Keyser's spires. He was the first architect to translate gothic steeple forms into Latin, a skill that Wren learned fifty years later and made the English standard. Paul Revere looked for lanterns in a Boston descendant of a de Keyser spire.

Hendrik de Keyser, 170-72 Herengracht, Amsterdam.

Dying as construction began on the West Church, de Keyser was unable to try his new language in the design of houses, but it was obviously in the design of houses that Dutch architecture would rise or fall. This bourgeois society would need to find a way of turning the flimsy and inelegant gabled house of the Middle Ages into great architecture with durable materials, all on a modest budget. This the Dutch Palladios would do.

The greatest of them – many say the greatest architect in Dutch history – was Jacob van Campen, and the little that we know about him is tantalizing. He was, for one thing, a landed gentleman, with an estate in the Province of Utrecht, and he apprenticed to a painter. It seems to have been very uncommon for landed gentlemen in the Netherlands to apprentice to artisans of any kind, and it is typical of our ignorance that we have no idea why such an arrangement was made for the young van Campen. Nor do we know where he spent a crucial decade of his young manhood (Italy, perhaps, but there is no evidence,) or how he became a designer of buildings. Much less do we know how he very suddenly emerged with the richest clients, the biggest commissions, and the most original ideas in Amsterdam. There are suggestions that he was hard to work with, but there are such suggestions about most architects. The one surviving portrait of him, an engraving, makes him look like a sly toper out of a painting by Frans Hals. And that is all we know.

Be that as it may, he burst very suddenly onto the architectural scene in 1625 with a house on the Emperor's Canal (Keizersgracht) in Amsterdam for a pair of rich merchant brothers named Coymans.

Hendrik de Keyser, West Church, Amsterdam.

Coymans house before renovations.

Left. Jacob van Campen, Coymans House, Amsterdam.

Judging from literary records, the Coymans house was an astonishing thing in 1625. "Those who examine our Town without seeing or noticing the beauty of this building," wrote Salomon de Bray, "they neither have seen all the splendor of our Town, nor understood Architecture." According to old pictures (the attic was enlarged in the 19th century, changing the proportions considerably,) the Coymans house was a fairly crude attempt to create the façade of an Italian palazzo. It imitates the worst features of Palladio's city palaces, notably their odd high-waistedness, without catching Palladio's ability to marry the freedom of wall space to the order of columns and architraves. The second floor is cramped, particularly the little pediments over the windows (now removed) that seem to be squashed by the entablature above. But these are quibbles of connoisseurship. From our point of view, as we try to understand the birth of a new kind of city, the important thing about the Coymans house is that two clients and a novice architect, in Amsterdam in 1625, realized that their society needed to be able to build classical houses on a bourgeois scale – and made a pretty good first stab at it.

Two innovations in the design of the Coymans house would turn out to have revolutionary impact throughout the North Atlantic world. The first was the great size of the windows. Here van Campen broke away from Italian classicism, which dealt with a hot, bright climate by keeping windows small. His big windows suited the cooler, greyer, less abundant light of Holland and would become a hallmark of Dutch architecture thereafter. The second was more basic, and more important: the house was built of red brick.

There was no Italian precedent for this. Brick was an ignoble building material in Italy, a mere structural background that architects veneered with stone when their clients could afford it and with stucco when they could not. That the Coymans brothers built their big Italianate building in brick was in itself a statement of independence from foreign models. It was not quite, however, a statement of fellowship with their fellow citizens. Brick was still a luxury item in Holland in 1625, used more for churches and town halls than for houses. At least, however, it was a local product, unlike stone, and it could potentially be mass-produced and made inexpensive with the technology of the time, as it rapidly was. The brick facade of the Coymans house created a fashion for brick architecture and paved the way for middle-class people to build in durable materials.

If the Coymans house has the look of a test piece, within a decade van Campen and two other architects, Arent van 's-Gravensande (that is not a typographical error) and Phillips Vingboons, were ready to build brick classical masterpieces.

Van Campen's Mauritshuis of 1634, built in The Hague for a member of the House of Orange and now a national museum of Golden Age painting, is domestic in scale but as grand as any building in the world. It is a complete work of art, perfect in form, in balance, in texture, in color, rising up in warm red brick and tan stone from a tranquil little lake in The Hague.

Like the Coymans house – or, for that matter, Palazzo Rucellai – it is a masonry box overlaid with classical columns and architraves. This creates an intentional ambiguity: did van Campen build the brick walls first, and then overlay them with columns and architraves? Or did he start with a Roman temple and fill in the spaces between the columns? The two facades have pediments like the facades of a Roman temple. The two sides, like the sides of a temple, have rows of columns without pediments. The entrance façade, on the street side, is rhetorical and rich. The back façade and the two sides, rising from the lake, are calm and quiet. From any angle, the building is effortless and satisfying. To have brought so much variety together in so firm an order, on a modest scale and with no impression of hard work, was an achievement of European significance.

Within five years the little court village of The Hague could boast two more mature masterworks of brick classicism. Van Campen's house for the learned Constantijn Huygens, has been destroyed, but the Sint Sebastiansdoelen, a meeting and banqueting hall for the local militia, built directly across the street from the Mauritshuis, survives as the Historical Museum of The Hague. Of its architect, Arendt van 's-Gravensande, we know even less than of van Campen; and the building is less famous and somewhat less beautiful than the Mauritshuis across the street. But it was simpler, and cheaper,

*Jacob van Campen,
Mauritshuis, The Hague.*

and thus much more influential. It became the prototype for an almost infinite number of English country houses and American public buildings.

A man who could build grandly on a middle-class budget was plainly going to be a useful citizen in the Dutch Golden Age. Within a few years, van 's-Gravesande had become City Architect in Leyden, a booming center of cloth manufacture, and there his talents flowered. In little more than a decade, he built a series of public buildings that made classicism the default approach for public architecture in the Dutch Republic and the North Atlantic world. Leyden today boasts of the charming little library, the Thysiana, that he built near the University; and his Marekerk, the first domed church in the Protestant world, is the most remarkable building in the city.

*Avove. Arendt van 's-Gravensande,
Bibliotheca Thysiana and the Marekerk.*

*Right. Arent van 's-Gravensande, Sint
Sebastiansdoelen, The Hague.*

The Marekerk is relatively small, with a simple light-filled interior of white plaster and grey stone like that of de Keyser's West Church. Its originality comes mainly from its shape: it is octagonal, not long like traditional Dutch churches or round like the Italian churches based on the Pantheon. For all its classicism, any one façade of the church, seen from a distance, looks like the apse end of a Gothic church – proof that classicism did not need to exclude the other traditions and practices of a proud people.

By 1640, then, van Campen and van 's-Gravesande had shown that Dutchmen could build honest and unaffected public buildings in a classical idiom. The two architects had brought about a successful fusion of ancient grandeur with the traditions and materials of their native land, and had produced public buildings of convincing grandeur on relatively modest budgets. Important as this achievement was, however, it was not enough. If the two men had been content to design public buildings, the Dutch classical movement might have resulted merely in special-occasion architecture for public buildings. Dutch cities today might be quaint and lovely in a pre-classical way, like nearby Bruges in Belgium, but the Dutch would not have created a new type of city. The Dutch Palladios needed to renew the effort that van Campen had begun in his house for the Coymans brothers. They needed to bring good, serious design – capital-A Architecture – to urban housing.

Arent van 's-Gravensande, Houses on the Rapenburg, Leyden.

Two architects rose to the challenge. One was van 's-Gravesande himself. He was lucky that Leyden in his day was an industrial boomtown, the biggest cloth-making center in Europe, with capitalist employers who could build ample if not palatial houses along their city's broad canals. His houses– no one seems to know whether house design was part of his job as City Architect, or whether he was moonlighting – made it possible for successful commoners to have the architecture of the princely Mauritshuis at reduced scale and reduced cost (and often with over-exuberant ornament).

The second architect, Phillips Vingboons, who worked in Amsterdam, had a far greater talent and a far greater influence. Barred by his Catholic faith from competing for official commissions, he was free to concentrate on houses, in which field neither Catholicism nor anything else prevented him from finding rich clients. In short order, and with panache, he solved both of the problems that faced classical house architects in his generation: wide houses and narrow houses.

For his richest clients in the 1640s, Vingboons built a collection of wide, five-bay houses that make van 's-Gravesande's little palaces in Leyden seem cramped and labored. Vingboons's wide houses have a Palladian assurance without any slavish copying. On those rare occasions when one of his big houses comes on the market today, his name is displayed prominently in the advertisements.

Phillips Vingboons,
Poppenhuis, Amsterdam.

But only the super-rich among Dutch citizens could afford to buy forty-five or fifty feet of canal frontage to build five-bay houses. Even middling-rich clients usually had to settle for houses with a width of thirty feet or less, as their ancestors had done; and the merely prosperous were happy with twenty feet or less. Vingboons met their needs in an original way, by re-imagining the gable of a medieval Dutch house front as the entrance front of an Italian baroque church, a perfectly well-accepted form of classicism in his generation.

His house called *The King of Poland* set a precedent that would be followed throughout the country, with charming variations (bell gables, neck gables, etc.) for a hundred and fifty years. Rich people often added sculpture to their gables, and it is great fun to look up at garlands, volutes, pediments, even slippery-looking dolphins and tritons high above the canals. Poorer people followed the lead of the rich, as usually happens

Phillips Vingboons, The King of Poland, 168 Herengracht, Amsterdam.

in the expensive art of architecture. They built more plainly, but in similar ways, and with an almost unerring sense of proportion.

Late in his career, around 1660, Vingboons was instrumental in the creation of a new architectural language that Dutch historians call The Flat Style. In this approach to architecture, Vingboons and others, notably Adriaen Dorstman, stripped away columns and pilasters and developed an architecture based on classical proportions without classical ornament. Though the theory of this was not new – architectural writers had long spoken of the classical orders as a system of proportions, and Italian architects had occasionally built classically-proportioned buildings without columns or pilasters – it was Vingboons and the other Flat Style architects in Amsterdam who first put a purely proportional classicism into practice.

Phillips Vingboons, Houses for Weavers.

Right. Amsterdam Gables.

The result was a kind of house façade that could frame the sweeping views of Dutch canals clearly, calmly, and without fussiness. Flat Style architects, building beside canals that were, in effect, the first wide streets in the world, realized that most spectators would never see the kind of architectural ornament that gave pleasure in the narrow, twisting streets of medieval cities. Vingboons and Dorstman relied instead on rhythm and proportion, and their success paved the way for two centuries of building on the wide streets that were to characterize the North Atlantic cities.

It was the Flat Style that banished the medieval gable altogether and brought the classical cornice and roof to the architecture of narrow houses. Though Vingboons' earlier idea of turning a row house into a baroque church would linger on as a local tradition throughout the eighteenth century, with charming results, the Flat Style would eventually predominate and would bring the design of average Dutch city houses into the mainstream of European classicism, in which house tops had straight cornices and did not resemble churches. When Berckheyde painted *The Golden Bend*, he was celebrating a triumph of modern architecture. His fellow citizens could build great classical urban environments without palaces.

Bringing it all together in Amsterdam

Gerrit Berckheyde, The Golden Bend, Amsterdam, 1672.

Amsterdam was to the seventeenth century what New York would be to the nineteenth, a rich city without the marks of social hierarchy, a parvenu city envied for its success but sneered at for its philistinism and dullness. And dull it was, at least for visitors: a Calvinist city without theatre or music, a republican city without splendor or ceremony, a stay-at-home city without a social season, a private city without galleries or frescoed churches to show off the skill of its artists. Great its painters may have been, but their works were locked up in houses and guild halls, invisible to the public.

Fortunately, the physical beauty of Amsterdam made up for many of its other deficiencies. Visitors noticed this without grudging, and the beauty of this very man-made city gave an important legitimacy to the social and political innovations of the Dutch Republic. Everyone loved the canals, which were much more numerous than they are today (after the twentieth-century mania for filling them in and driving over them). In fact, since canals carried the sewage that most Europeans were dumping onto their streets, and most walking in Amsterdam took place along one canal or another, visitors were usually enjoying things that they had never experienced before in any city: clean streets, extensive views, plenty of light, and a canopy of trees overhead.

And the architecture was good: the Dutch Palladios had discovered how to build grandly on a modest scale. Year after year, decade after decade, from the 1630s on, they studded the older canals and lined the newer ones with well-proportioned brick houses, fanciful gables, and Flat Style rows. At a time when most cities were squalid places with isolated bits of beauty, Amsterdam was becoming a beautiful place with bits of squalor.

Then, too, Amsterdam was no longer small. By 1670, with more than 150,000 people, it was big enough to seem infinite to anyone who tried to walk or row around it. Such rapid growth is usually a recipe for urban disorder. In Amsterdam, however, the city councilors put the quiet force of the particular Dutch genius – foresight, patience, planning, cooperation – to bear on the problem of urban expansion. They sensed early that the boom of the late 1500s would make Amsterdam too big for piecemeal additions, and they had both the breadth of vision and the financial resources to conceive and carry out the largest planned urban development ever attempted in Europe, not to be equaled until the rebuilding of Paris two and a half centuries later. They called it "the Canal Belt," a new set of canals in concentric rings around the city.

Begun before 1600 and pursued steadily for a century, the Canal Belt was planned in advance, and it was planned in detail. Three new canals were projected: the Herengracht (Gentlemen's' Canal,) Keisersgracht (Emperor's Canal,) and Prinsengracht (Prince's Canal,) each to be wide and tree-lined, with broad, well-defined vistas. The land area of the whole Belt was very large, far exceeding that of the whole city in 1600. Only baroque Rome was planning at comparable scale, and the results in Amsterdam were arguably better than Sixtus's diagonal streets – and were finished two hundred years sooner.

The city fathers of Amsterdam made no effort to regulate the design of individual buildings on their great new canals. This left the Dutch Palladios with the task of creating urban grandeur at the greatest conceivable scale by organizing thousands of individual facades, most of which would be only twenty feet wide. The whole thing could easily have degenerated into a hodgepodge. Each house could have proclaimed its individual message too loudly, as would often happen in the late nineteenth century. But the builders of Amsterdam were the people who commissioned portraits from Rembrandt. They valued their membership in a good society at least as much as their individuality. Although almost every house in the Canal Belt is unique, there is as much harmony along a great canal as there is in a gallery of Golden Age portraits. Amsterdam is the only great city in the world whose postcards feature private houses.

The Canal Belt from the Air.

Remarkably, the city fathers set the depth of most house lots in the Canal Belt at a very generous one hundred sixty feet and required that each property owner keep a full eighty feet at the back of each lot open in perpetuity. A hundred sixty feet is very deep for a row house lot, and eighty feet is very deep for a row house garden, but the Canal Belt proved that it works. The library of Amsterdam's Municipal Archives overlooks several dozen of these gardens. They are still there, as the law still requires, each a private paradise of flowers and trees, delighting residents and helping to maintain the high status that they helped to create. The average Canal Belt density of seventeen houses per acre would become the North Atlantic standard for prosperous neighborhoods in centuries to come (including the nineteenth-century American neighborhood in which these words are being written).

The Canal Belt embraced more than five hundred acres, each of those acres made by human hands and planned in a central office. Using the unique breadth of power that Dutch city governments possessed, the councilors of Amsterdam condemned private property and used public funds to create streets, canals, and building sites. And they stuck with it: the Canal Belt was under construction for almost a hundred years, and finished according to the original plans. Neither London nor Paris could boast an entire planned urban district of such scale in the seventeenth century. Even the grandest seventeenth-century developments in those larger cities, like the Place Royale in Paris and Covent Garden in London, were, by comparison, small, one-shot affairs, ten or fifteen acres at most, islands of intention in a sea of habit.

As important as any of the other aspects of municipal regulation in the Canal Belt was a set of limitations on the uses to which land could be put. Artisan work and retail trade were flatly excluded, something that mattered a great deal in the seventeenth century, when every independent businessman, from the humblest shoemaker to the most opulent financier – not to mention Rembrandt and Vermeer – worked at home. This meant that beauty was not the only result of these municipal ordinances. There was also residential segregation by income.

This is something that we take for granted today. Although we do not always celebrate it, at least in public, we usually look for it when shopping for a house or an apartment. Like it or not, it was revolutionary in the seventeenth century, and it was born in Amsterdam. The large lots and lovely back gardens of the Canal Belt intentionally excluded any buyers who could not afford to leave a large piece of hand-made ground without an income-producing use, and the ban on artisan work and retail trade confirmed this. Only the richest people in the city – wholesale merchants, professionals, and people of independent means – could buy and use land on the new canals.

Why did the rest of the people of Amsterdam allow their city government to use their tax money for an immense development that excluded them? Mainly because they were Europeans in the seventeenth century, and the notion of economic equality never crossed their minds. But there was more: to put it simply, the Dutch system worked for them. They were better off than any national population in Europe. They lived in peace, they had plenty of work, and, thanks to their monopoly of the Baltic grain trade, they were the only Europeans in their century who never starved. As for the inequality that the Canal Belt made visible, it was small by the standards of the day. The Amsterdam rich (with a tiny number of exceptions) were nowhere near as rich as the landed aristocrats whose carriages attracted crowds in London or Paris. Rembrandt's patrons walked the streets like other citizens, dressed in sober middle-class black, worked every day, and fell into poverty when their ships hit rocks or their deals went bad. Many had been born poor; not a few would die poor; and even the richest of them enjoyed no legal privileges that they could pass on to their children.

They even lived in the same kind of houses as their poorer neighbors. Bigger their houses and lots might be, but size was the only difference. The canal houses of rich Dutchmen did not differ in kind from the houses of the mass of the people, as French hotels differed from the proto-row houses of the common people; nor did they differ in style and materials, as the stone classicism of a French hotel differed from the creaky colombage of an ordinary family. It is easy to notice the consistency of architecture in any Dutch city, but it takes practice or a tape measure to notice differences in size between one house and another.

The simplicity of the Flat Style meant that even working-class people could afford good Flat Style architecture, and small houses came within the orbit of serious architecture for the first time in recorded history. Often, in fact, the simplicity and restraint of the Flat Style fitted small houses better than large ones. Vingboons himself led the way when he designed more than two hundred identical houses in a city-funded development for immigrant weavers in 1671. These were small houses indeed, and unfashionably located on the very outskirts of seventeenth-century Amsterdam, but

Vingboons and the Flat Style made them Architecture. Visitors today think that there is nothing special about them. They look like houses in any Dutch town, or like houses in any old city or town in England or Ireland or the American Middle Atlantic states. That, of course, is what makes them special. They were prototypes for the architectural vernacular of the North Atlantic world.

And there were enough houses for everyone. Despite the immense labor involved in creating buildable land, Amsterdam opened up new neighborhoods for working-class people while it was building the Canal Belt. The Jordaans, a working-class quarter now much sought-after, was part of the Canal Belt plan. It was all very different from Paris, where most new construction was for noblemen, and the rest of the people were left to cram themselves more and more densely into old neighborhoods.

Many people, in fact, believe that the greatest triumph of Dutch city-building was not the rearing-up of splendid canal houses for successful merchants but the delicate shaping of tiny sanctuaries for the poor. A society of seafarers will have a lot of poor widows, and every Dutch city made charitable provision for housing them. These settlements are called *hofjes*, a word that means little courts, or courtyards. Sometimes, the street fronts of *hofjes* are treated architecturally, never more so than in van 's-Gravensande's microscopic baroque temple for the van Brouckhoven hofje in Leyden. Most *hofjes*, though, are too plain to be noticed from outside. The true genius of the hofje has nothing to do with public presentation; it lies within, in the courtyards from which the *hofje* takes its name. These are the most peaceful, the most comfortable urban spaces in the western world.

An economy that worked, a culture built on social trust – hence the most interesting thing about the houses of the Canal Belt and all other Golden Age houses: they were not fortified, or defensible in any way. At a time when French and Italian noblemen were building palaces with oaken gates, iron bars, blank walls, and detachments of armed guards – when artisans in Paris were fitting their ground floors with doors and shutters stout enough to withstand criminals and rioters – Dutch citizens, rich and poor alike, were building houses with flimsy doors and glass windows on the ground floor; and men went to the Exchange, or to sea, without fear for their possessions, their wives, or their daughters. The Dutch Republic was built on social trust, and the buildings and cities of the Golden Age are realistic representations of the society that built them.

Even the Dutch, however, could succumb to the flattery of success. There was little realism in the planning of Amsterdam's new City Hall, begun in 1648. For once, the black-suited rulers of Amsterdam allowed their ambitions to get ahead of reality.

To be sure, in Amsterdam in 1648, the temptation to show off was very strong. The Netherlands had just won its eighty-year war of liberation against Spain, and the councilors of Amsterdam had used the peace treaty to impose their will on their

Arendt van' s-Gravensande, The van Brouckoven Hofje, Leyden.

Van' s-Gravensande achieved baroque grandeur in a façade less than 20 feet wide. The small car indicates the scale, as does the resident reading in the courtyard.

Jacob van Campen,
Amsterdam City Hall.

commercial rivals in Antwerp and their political rivals in the House of Orange. This was the apogee of the city's power, the ideal moment to show the world that a society of merchants and commoners could look kings in the eye.

Jacob van Campen, the first and greatest of the Dutch Palladios, won Amsterdam's City Hall design competition with an immense, brilliantly planned structure in a sober classical style, and the city put it up in only seven years, finishing the work in 1655. While we may quibble with van Campen's proportions – it would probably look better without the two lower stories – the important thing, the thing that contemporaries noticed, was that a bourgeois city had built the greatest palace in Europe. Neither the Pope nor the King of France could yet match it. It was twice as big as the city needed, but city fathers were confident that they would soon need the space.

Alas, they never did. If the city fathers had known what was to come after 1648, a generation of uneasy success followed by catastrophe and stagnation, they might have built more modestly. Van Campen's City Hall stood half-empty for a century and a half, a somewhat depressing reminder that the city and its people had fallen short of their goals. Eventually, it came to symbolize what it had been designed to defy: when the Netherlands became a monarchy in 1813, the City Hall of Amsterdam became, as it remains, a Royal Palace.

An Amsterdam Canal.

The Silver Age and the Dutch Legacy

It is hard to tell a tale of progress in an age of decline. By 1655, when the city fathers of Amsterdam dedicated their new City Hall, the West India Company had already lost Brazil to the Portuguese. The same poorly-managed company would lose New Amsterdam to the British in 1664. Hals would die in 1666, Rembrandt in 1669, Vermeer in 1675. And nothing in politics or painting would counterbalance those losses. Unnoticed at first, the slippage of the Dutch Republic became obvious in 1672, when Dutch militiamen like those in Rembrandt's *Night Watch* ran from the invading French, and much of the country fell to the enemy. Though the Republic survived, the Golden Age was over. The next age would be silver.

Dutch historians are still wondering whether their national Silver Age was good or bad. It lasted a long time – from 1672 until the end of the Republic in 1795 – and there is plenty of evidence for both views. Fortunately for us, everyone seems to agree that architecture and the design of cities were among the Silver Age strengths. Silver Age people had only to work within the Golden Age tradition, and they did. Did they realize how great van Campen, van's-Gravesande, Vingboons and the rest had been? Or did they merely follow Golden-Age practice out of plodding habit in an artistic backwater? Historians debate these questions in hopes of deciding whether the Dutch Republic was, or was not, a great country in its Silver Age.

A Silver Age Street in The Hague.

Interesting as that question may be, the important thing for us is that the architects and clients of the Silver Age, not their more celebrated predecessors, created most of the architectural beauty and harmony that we admire in Dutch cities today. After a long walk through the Canal Belt, it can be a bit of a shock to look in the *Amsterdam Canal Guide* and learn that most of the four thousand buildings in that incomparably coherent district were built, or substantially rebuilt, long after the official end of the Golden Age in 1672. Although there is no comparable guide to the canals of Delft or Leyden, even an amateur eye can learn to trace the same pattern without difficulty.

Working in a country whose population and economy were stagnant at best, the architects of the Silver Age had few new neighborhoods to embellish and fewer large commissions than van Campen and Vingboons had enjoyed. Most of their assignments involved renovations to private houses, far from exciting work in any age. But they had a lot of such work, in the course of a century and a quarter, and they did it well. Little by little, fifteen or twenty feet at a time, they turned wood into brick, gables into cornices, random windows into well-proportioned fenestration. They took advantage of the Flat Style, the cheapest form of classicism ever devised, to carry the principles of good design far beyond the realms of wealth and fashion. Whole cities, and a nation of brick classical towns, are their monuments. Together, Gold and Silver, the Dutch made the pleasantest cities in the world.

Chapter Two

HOW LONDON BECAME LONDON

England in 1600 must have seemed an unlikely choice for the country that would continue the Dutch revolution in architecture and city design. To all appearances, the realm of Elizabeth I was an absolute monarchy like France, not a merchant republic like the Netherlands. It was no surprise that London and Paris were such similar cities, with palace compounds for noble households and the ramshackle ancestors of row houses for everyone else, or that the two cities were growing in almost identical ways.

Queen Elizabeth I.

And they were growing fast, their growth fueled by the expansion of government and the centralizing of power. It was in the reign of Elizabeth, and of her French contemporary, Henri IV, that Paris and London became, for the first time, capital cities in the modern sense. Unlike earlier sovereigns, Elizabeth and Henri presided over bureaucracies that were too big to move. Nobles and high officers of state came to the palace, or to other government buildings, every day, and the monarch was often in residence. Very quickly, in both cities, the two royal residences exercised a gravitational pull on the top end of the housing market, drawing fashionable development westwards towards the seats of power – towards Westminster outside London and the Louvre at the west end of Paris – a pattern that still shapes the development of both cities today.

Anyone in 1600 would have expected England to borrow more from France than from any other country, as it had done for centuries; and the England of 1600 desperately needed foreign influences in the arts of architecture and city design. Except in literature, Shakespeare's England was a provincial backwater. Though we may have grown up on stories about Drake and Raleigh cutting gallant swaths on the high seas, Elizabethan England as a whole was a stay-at-home place, sluggish in trade and free from warfare on the Continent. Even the educated and the well-born were painfully ignorant of basic European geography. Shakespeare could frighten a court audience by producing a bear on the seacoast of Bohemia.

As it happened, though, France influenced England less and less as the century rolled on, and it was in this century that London and Paris began to take different paths. Paris took the path of baroque Rome, London the path of row house Amsterdam. By 1700, Parisian nobles had built entire neighborhoods of palaces around the city's densely-packed core, while Londoners of all classes, including the very highest, were living in brick row houses that fronted directly onto the street. Paris got steadily more crowded, while London maintained a moderate density by spreading broadly across the countryside.

How did this happen? How did the people of monarchical England decide, in the course of a mere century, to build and rebuild their capital city in a way that made sense for a republic like Holland? And how was it that London spread at moderate density, Dutch-style, with row on row of houses, while Paris remained locked within its traditional boundaries and packed more and more people into taller and taller buildings?

It was not because London was small or slower-growing. A continuous tide of ambitious migrants swelled London's population from 150,000 to 500,000 in the course of the century, despite hideous plagues in almost every generation and an overall death rate that far outpaced its birth rate. Paris, the larger of the two cities for centuries, grew much more slowly after 1600, and London has outranked its French rival ever since.

Closer to home, London's pre-eminence among the cities of seventeenth-century England was almost inconceivable. Unlike Amsterdam, a "first among equals" that was only two or three times bigger than Leyden or Haarlem, London was twenty times bigger than Norwich and Bristol, its nearest rivals. London had more people than all the other cities and towns of England combined.

London's wealth was even more disproportionate than its population. A commercial as well as a political capital, London dominated all the sophisticated elements of the British economy – overseas trade, banking, even manufacturing – and grew faster than any other English town, or England as a whole. Unlike the smaller British cities, which drew most of their migrants from nearby, London drew from the whole country, and young people from the countryside often returned home when they had mastered a trade in London or made a decent fortune. Shakespeare, who did well in London and set himself up as a gentleman in his home town a hundred miles away, is only the best-known of these temporary Londoners.

Almost all of London's astounding growth in the seventeenth-century was suburban – that is, it took place outside the walled City of London, which was already fully built-up by 1600. This was all the stranger in that all London suburban development, from one end of the century almost to the other, was illegal. The ban on suburban building went back to 1580, when Queen Elizabeth, fearing the disorder of a lordless urban proletariat, issued a Proclamation that outlawed the construction of any new buildings within three miles of the gates of the City. Any violating structure was liable to be pulled down without compensation. The Queen also forbade the subdivision of existing buildings. No house was allowed to contain more than one family. A homeowner could not legally rent a room to a lodger.

Applying as it did only to the suburbs, the Queen's proclamation was a clear sign that suburban growth was becoming both important and unpleasant by 1580. Her action did not represent a personal whim or respond to a temporary panic. Parliament made her proclamation a statute in 1592, and it was confirmed by repeated royal proclamations and Acts of Parliament for a hundred years.

If these draconian regulations had been effective, London would have developed in one of two ways. Either it would have remained a small city without large suburbs, as it had been before the 1570s, or it would have become a great deal denser within its historic boundaries, as Paris did after 1600. But neither of these things happened. London's growth was irrepressible, and Londoners did not want to live like Parisians. By hook and by crook – often, one suspects, the latter – Londoners found ways around Elizabeth's proclamation and the various statutes that echoed it. Though the metropolitan population reached 500,000 by 1700, the population of the City remained stable at about 80,000. The entire increase, 400,000 people or more, spread into the suburbs.

London's seventeenth-century suburbs were not leafy escapes from urban hardship. Most of them were shantytowns, the poorest parts of a pre-modern metropolis that was growing much too fast for its own good. Since most suburban dwellers were poor, and most suburban houses were at all times illegal and liable to be pulled down, builders had little incentive to build well; nor were the village and parish governments of London suburbia strong enough to provide streets or organize efforts to ensure health and safety. The result, by the middle of the seventeenth century, was a solid urban core – the City, with 80,000 people – surrounded by a vast corona of jerry-built slums, like a modern Brazilian city with its *favelas*.

The failure of so many proclamations and statutes raises some interesting questions. Why were the proclamations and acts not enforced? And why, if they were not enforced, did kings and parliaments keep reissuing them? Finally, what was there about Londoners that made them spread out beyond the city's walls, even in defiance of the law, while their contemporaries in Paris were staying within the walls and wedging themselves ever more tightly into a limited number of rooms and streets?

These are central questions. They bring us to the moment at which London swerved from the path that Paris was taking. By 1900, when the two cities attained their final form, Paris would have four times more families per acre than London. Most Parisians would live in apartments, most Londoners in houses. Eventually, apartment-dwelling Parisians would perfect the café and invent the restaurant, while Londoners would use their drawing rooms and dining rooms to perfect the dinner party and the kind of stand-up party that absorbed the attention of Woolf's Clarissa Dalloway. These and many other differences that shape every waking moment of the lives of millions of people, flow from decisions that were made and actions that were taken, consciously and unconsciously, in the seventeenth century.

To understand why London spread out while Paris bunched up, why repeated Acts and proclamations failed to stop London from gobbling up field upon field for a century, there is a strong temptation to blame the quality of London enforcement. Government regulation was more a concept than a reality at the time. Inspectors were often lazy and corrupt, and there were rarely enough of them to carry out their assigned duties. And royal proclamations may have been triggered by short-lived aggravations, like the "crime sweeps" that today's Mayors and Police Chiefs periodically launch, usually with more fanfare than follow-through. But it is hard to reconcile this explanation with what was happening in Paris at the same time. The Kings of France issued similar proclamations to restrict the growth of Paris, and public servants were no more zealous in France than in England; but Paris did not sprawl as London did. Some other factor is likely to have been at work.

Selective enforcement is one possibility. Elizabeth and her successors, James I and Charles I, seem to have paid much more attention to new buildings near their palaces in their suburb of Westminster than to development in less fashionable suburbs. Despite their proclaimed concern to prevent the creation of slums, it is possible that they just wanted to protect their own neighborhood. The Stuart kings (foolishly, as it turned out) feared the London mob less than Elizabeth had done, and the Elizabethan anti-slum language that they dutifully re-issued may have been merely an early manifestation of Not In My Back Yard.

It is unlikely, though, that law and enforcement explain the whole divergence between concentrating Paris and scattering London. When two cities get different results from similar ordinances, the causes of the difference usually have to do with things that are deeper and stronger than laws: family structure, business regulations, the market for land, or the ambitions, desires, and dreams of the people. In this case, all four of these elements were at work.

As to family structure, London had a culture of husband-and-wife nuclear families, while it was typical for multiple generations of Parisian families to live under the thumbs of their oldest and richest members. Young Londoners were far more likely to strike out on their own, forming nuclear families as soon as they could afford to (if not sooner). One would expect Londoners to seek a housing type that expressed their nuclear family structure, as the row house does. One would also expect Londoners to form smaller households and build smaller houses for single families, as they did.

Business regulation also seems to have played a role in defining where people wanted to live. Because the French court and the public markets of Paris were within the city walls, it was almost essential for artisans to live in the city and belong to one of the city's guilds. London was different because two of its three centers of economic activity were outside the walls, and thus outside the jurisdiction of the London guilds. To the east, much of the working waterfront and most of the shipyards were in suburbs like Stepney and Shadwell, which filled up with sailors, ship's carpenters, blacksmiths, and the like. At the other end of town, the western suburb of Westminster was home to the royal court, the nation's biggest market for luxury goods and the ultimate mecca for tailors, upholsterers, goldsmiths, and cabinetmakers. Once the suburbs became more

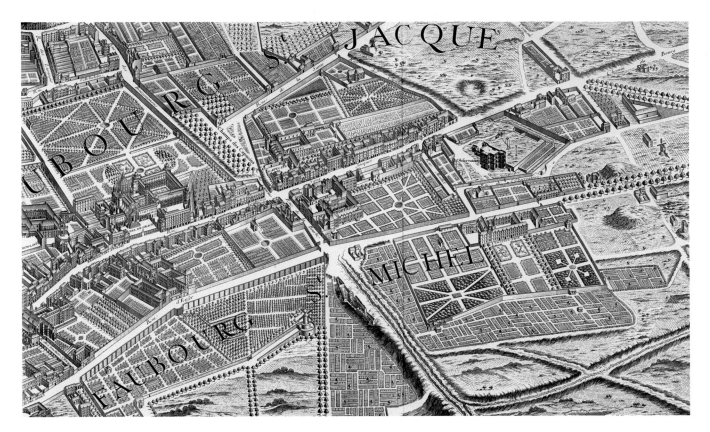

populous than the City, they became better locations for barbers, butchers, doctors, and retailers; and growth began to feed on itself. None of these people had any economic reason to belong to the London guilds, or to live in the City.

The market for land had a role to play. In fact, the workings of the land-market around the two cities were so different that they might have accounted for the difference between the two cities in the absence of other factors. Put simply, the outskirts of London had a free market in land, while the outskirts of Paris did not.

A major reason was religion. Catholic Paris was hemmed in by the holdings of parishes, monasteries, and convents, a situation that grew far worse in the first half of the seventeenth century, at the flood-tide of piety in the Catholic Reformation. In addition to the dozens of convents and monasteries that Paris already possessed in 1600, Parisians created and endowed the almost incredible total of seventy new ones between 1600 and 1650. Each of these monastic establishments was a self-sustaining world, with acres of gardens, orchards, and vineyards. Each took up a lot of space. Collectively, they blockaded much of the growing city, particularly along its southern borders.

Parisian Convents from the Plan Turgot. There are more than a dozen convents in this picture, each with its own geometrical array of gardens and walks. Together, they made spreading development impossible.

And they were very hard to move. Unlike families, ecclesiastical bodies never died out or needed cash for dowries, and they hardly ever spent beyond their means. Thus they never needed to sell land against their will, and their abbots and abbesses held onto every square foot with almost invincible tenacity. The exception that proves the rule is the development of the Ile-St. Louis, perhaps the loveliest neighborhood in the most beautiful of great cities. At the beginning of the seventeenth century, the island was owned by the Canons of Notre Dame, who pastured cattle on it. When a developer with royal support tried to buy and develop it, the Canons proved so obstinate that the King himself had to intervene; and even that was not enough to prevent almost forty years of lawsuits. As for the hapless developer, he went bankrupt decades before the Canons finally lost to his successor. The only unusual elements in this story are the persistence of the developers and the eventual happy ending.

None of this was happening in or around Protestant London. By the time of Elizabeth's 1580 proclamation, England's monasteries had been closed for more than forty years, long enough for the initial purchasers of church land to die off and their heirs to need money. London builders thus encountered a suburban landscape whose owners could often be induced to turn their acres into cash. London was not hemmed in.

Just as the Church blocked Paris on the south, the king and his courtiers blocked it on the north. With land around Paris so hard to get, only people with powerful court connections could buy it in any quantity, and such people were not interested in slogging through generations of lawsuits in hopes of a trickle of profit from a houses or lots. They had their eyes on the great prizes of the early modern state, the revenues and powers that flowed in a swelling stream to the favored few who could please their monarch and his ministers. They would live in whatever way seemed most likely to favor their advancement at court; and their monarch, and ministers like Cardinal de Richelieu, encouraged them to build palatial hotels. They obliged by building hundreds of them.

The result was a city of splendors and miseries. While the rich and the courtly called forth new streets and quarters of palaces, each a private world of order and refinement, the poor and the middling jammed themselves more and more tightly into the old city. As the city's population increased, there was a marked and growing movement to demolish rickety old *colombage* houses and replace them with stone houses that offered more rooms for more people on the same acreage. Paris got denser and denser.

It is interesting to speculate whether Paris might have spread out like London if the French Revolution, which confiscated Church lands and sold them to private owners as the English Reformation had done, had occurred in 1539 rather than 1789 – by which time the elegance of Parisian palaces had created a dream world for the people, and the constriction of the Parisian land-market had formed habits of high-density living.

The Birth of London Classicism

This was all well and good, but the actual results on the ground around London, an explosive shantytown sprawl, could never have made London a great city, much less the shining model for cities throughout the North Atlantic world. London had to achieve the three requisites of Renaissance urbanity: classical architecture, straight streets, and dignified public places.

This was not going to be easy. London had nothing remotely like the strong governments that shaped Dutch cities. The London suburbs, governed by a patchwork quilt of amateurish parish vestries and manorial courts, could not hope to come up with anything resembling decent plans or diligent enforcement. Even the solidly-built core of Shakespeare's London, the City, was still a medieval mess, without a single building that would have pleased an ancient Roman or a Renaissance Italian.

But the preconditions for large-scale classical development – wealth and taste, as Sir John Summerson says – were there, or were at least developing. After a century of peace and good government, England was becoming prosperous, and was about to become rich through overseas trade. Moreover, the Tudor monarchs had done much to improve taste by de-fanging the semi-literate warlords of the nobility and gentry and turning them into an order of judges and administrators with university training. England in 1600 had the best-educated upper classes north of the Alps, a fact that Shakespeare exploited masterfully.

Pre-conditions, however, are not actions. London needed a man, or a small group of men, to spark its urban revolution.

As if on cue, London produced one of the greatest classical architects in history. Born in the City in 1573, Inigo Jones combined artistic mastery with stylistic conviction and the ability to get and keep positions of power and responsibility. Like so many designers of calm buildings, he seems to have been quirky, irascible, and bursting with energy. Though he may have had no architectural training, he was appointed Surveyor-General of the King's Works, the man in charge of all government buildings, in 1613; and he traveled to Italy, apparently at public expense, to study Italian architecture before taking up his post. He returned in 1615 as a confirmed partisan of the hyper-classical architecture of Andrea Palladio, and he promptly set out to bring Palladian classicism to England.

Jones was lucky that a project of the highest profile dropped into his lap early in his tenure, when the old Banqueting House at Whitehall Palace burned down in 1619. With the King's firm backing, Jones seized the opportunity to make a statement that no one could miss or ignore. His new Banqueting House was an Italian palace in pale stone, with a simplicity and clarity that even the greatest Italians had rarely achieved. A two-

Inigo Jones.

Banqueting House, Whitehall, London.

story façade, with columns and proper proportions at both levels, encased a single two-story room, luminous and perfectly proportioned. This relatively small building, effortless and magical, is England's equivalent of de Keyser's West Church.

It is not easy for us to imagine how the Banqueting House looked to contemporaries. No one could ever have seen anything even remotely like it in England. Although English designers had been inserting bits of classical detail into their buildings for half a century, their use of the Roman inheritance had been casual rather than systematic, like writers who drop Latin words and phrases into English paragraphs. Jones was the English Alberti, the first English architect to understand classicism as a complete architectural language, and the Banqueting House was the first truly classical building in English history.

Did contemporaries like it? Not immediately, it would seem. Ambitious builders in the 1620s made no effort to copy it, or even to show that they wanted to appear to be copying it. Considering that the Banqueting House was the biggest and most visible building built under royal patronage in living memory, its failure to stimulate emulation among courtiers is surprising.

Queen's House, Greenwich, the south façade.

But it pleased the King, and Jones was kept busy. Though James I was not one of history's great builders, he was freer with his money than the parsimonious Elizabeth had been. Jones built him a series of small buildings that collectively pointed the way to a classical revolution in England. Two are worth noting.

The Queen's House at Greenwich is the purer, the more revolutionary, and altogether the less influential of the two. Cool and pristine, it must have seemed as ethereal in the 1620s and 30s as LeCorbusier's villas appeared three centuries later. It is hard to look at the south facade without mentally adding things – perhaps a pediment (Jones originally planned one,) perhaps a dome, almost certainly a visible roof. The test of the building's equivocal influence came a generation later, when Sir Christopher Wren and Sir John Vanbrugh paid it the compliment of making it the focal point of their immense Royal Hospital; but they did not continue the compliment by working in Jones's idiom. Their Greenwich buildings, massive and busy and gloriously complicated, come from a different world.

Much more influential is the Chapel that Jones built for Queen Henrietta Maria in 1630. Here, behind an austere stuccoed exterior, Jones showed that a small classical

Queen's Chapel, St. James's Palace London.

church could be a beautiful and satisfying place. Although the interior has a good deal of classical ornament, its effect is of simplicity and calm. The element that is most beautiful, most original, and most prophetic is the large Palladian window above the altar, the first and best of thousands of such windows in English architecture.

Jones did most of his royal building in stone, which was expensive, or stucco, which was poorly suited to a damp climate and to coal-burning London's caustic atmosphere. But London builders were already turning to brick, probably under the influence of the Dutch, who were devising cheaper techniques of brick-making in Jones's decades. By the middle of the 1630s, brick was cheap enough to be used for the suburban villas of London merchants, and a kind of robust "artisan" classicism was already appearing in the buildings of middle-class people.

Jones may have had more to do with the development of London housing than would at first appear. He was not, after all, merely an architect. He was a high civil servant, with a large number of professionals working under him; and it was to him, in 1630, that Charles I gave the responsibility for enforcing the proclamations and statutes that regulated London's suburban development. Since London had long since outgrown the boundaries of the medieval City, and all new London building was suburban, this meant that Jones – a man with a mission to bring classical architecture and masonry construction to England – had authority over building throughout the entire metropolis.

But suburban development was still illegal, and Jones's new appointment meant that he had to implement the same wrong-headed prohibitions that Elizabeth had proclaimed in 1580. This was neither an easy nor an elegant assignment, and it seemed to promise that a creative talent would bog down in grubby police work. But it did not. Jones and the King had seen to it that the laws and proclamations would have enough loopholes to make construction possible and regulation important. Although Charles' proclamation of 1630 began by forbidding new construction in the suburbs of London, it ended by laying down a new set of detailed specifications and design standards for new suburban buildings. What this meant, in its convoluted way, was more or less what modern building codes mean: there were standards, and anyone who would build to those standards – and pay a fee – could get permission to build. The King must have wanted Jones to set the standards. He certainly wanted Jones to enforce them. And Jones jumped at the chance.

Jones's standards were exemplary. In clear, brief statements that any builder could understand, they required orderly design and solid, relatively fireproof construction in brick or stone. There were careful specifications for the thickness of walls and timbers. House fronts were to be flat in the classical manner, without the projections that medieval Londoners called "jutties," and windows were to be rectangular, and set one above the other in even vertical bays, as in Italy. There were even requirements that all new buildings be aligned with the street so as to produce smooth and uniform street-walls.

Each of these requirements was a departure from London's common practice. Taken together, they required of Londoners a new architecture and a new approach to street design. Never again would Londoners darken their streets with oppressive overhangs. Gone would be irregular windows in skimpy walls of wood or plaster. Instead, the new houses of suburban London – at least its prosperous parts – would rise in neat brick rows, framing the streets without intruding on them. The new system of 1630, the system of Charles I and Inigo Jones, aimed to bring about precisely the results that the city fathers of Amsterdam were achieving in their carefully-planned canal belt. It is not hard to see why Charles wanted Jones for the job, or why Jones was willing to take it on.

The new system soon had a chance to prove its merit. The fourth Earl of Bedford, whose ancestors had acquired a great deal of Church property during the Reformation,

Covent Garden, by
Wenceslaus Hollar.

decided to develop a former convent garden at the western edge of London's built-up area. As a visible man in a visible location, he could not hope to evade the King's notice. Instead, he entered into negotiations that would take six years and cost him four thousand pounds in fees.

The result was Covent Garden. To the millions of people who know Covent Garden in its current incarnation as a shopping mall, or remember it as the boisterous Victorian vegetable market where Henry Higgins discovers Eliza Doolittle in *Pygmalion* and *My Fair Lady*, it may seem strange that Covent Garden should have begun its life as a quiet and elegant residential square. When it was new – it seems to have been complete by the time of the Earl's death in 1641- it was a rectangular open space framed by straight rows of brick houses. There was a remarkable church in the middle of the west side, and the Earl's own residence, Bedford House, took up the entire south side of the square. Although the years have been unkind to Covent Garden – the straight rows of houses have disappeared, and the square itself has been disfigured beyond recognition – it was a good address for a century, and it turned out to be the prototype for more than two centuries of London building.

No English city had ever had a square before. There had been courtyards within large complexes, but there had never been a planned, geometrically regular public space.

There was not even an English word for it. As the concept was Italian (probably filtered through Paris,) Bedford used an Italian word to describe it, Covent Garden *Piazza*. The architecture was half Italian and half Dutch, as if someone had set rows of brick Dutch houses on stone Italian arcades. The houses had everything the new building regulations required: smooth, flat fronts, identical windows, and the first straight, classical cornices in English urban architecture.

Considered as architecture, the Covent Garden houses were far from perfect. Their upper stories looked small and thin above the mighty piers and arches that supported them; and the covered walks behind the arches, which would have been useful in commercial buildings or in the heat of an Italian summer, served merely to darken the first two stories of Bedford's houses, a serious problem in rainy, smoky London. These mistakes would not be repeated. But the square itself, and the rows of classical brick houses, succeeded in every sense and were endlessly copied – unlike the very similar 1610 Place Royale in Paris, now the Place des Vosges, which failed to find imitators. For all its flaws of detail, Covent Garden showed Londoners how to get the three essentials of seventeenth-century city design – classical architecture, aligned streets, and dignified public places – in one fell swoop. As London grew, it would become known as much for its squares as for its wealth or its shopping.

While Covent Garden was still under construction, a speculative developer named William Newton undertook a much larger and even more classical project just a few hundred yards to the east. Along the south side of Great Queen Street, a new straight street fifty feet wide, Newton built the longest continuous row of houses ever built in London, before or since. Taking his architectural vocabulary from Covent Garden, Newton extended a three-story range of brick classical houses for an astonishing 628 feet. In the process, he corrected most of the Covent Garden mistakes. He banished the light-eating arcades, not to be seen again in London until John Nash brought them back for the convenience of shoppers on Regent Street 175 years later; and he made his decorative pilasters robust enough to give his very long row an effective monumentality. Together with Jones, Charles I, and the Earl of Bedford, he deserves to be known as a founder of the English school of city design.

Newton's houses in Great Queen Street, now destroyed, were very large, averaging forty feet wide. They made an interesting contrast with houses of the same size that were being built at the same time along the Quai de Bethune on the Ile Saint Louis in Paris. The Parisian houses were conceived as small hotels, with courtyards and carriage entrances for the reception of noble visitors. Newton's houses, though large, were simply houses, upmarket brick versions of the common type. There were no courtyards or carriage entrances. Anyone approaching one of these houses in a carriage had to get down onto the street and enter the front door like a Dutchman. The ordinary London

Lincoln's Inn Fields.

house had achieved classical grandeur without becoming a palace; and people of high rank, with titles and carriages, were happy to call such a house their home.

By 1640, having proven his ability to execute grand conceptions, Newton was ready for an even grander project. King Charles, advised by Jones, smoothed his way by granting him permission to build on Lincoln's Inn Fields, a large parcel of open Crown land at the end of Great Queen Street. Here Newton created a second residential square, considerably larger than Covent Garden, and set about bordering it with three long rows of houses. Despite the strenuous objections of the lawyers of Lincoln's Inn – it must have been fun to watch the mob of lawyers and law students that once attacked Newton's workmen – the King stood firm, and Newton kept moving ahead, with none of the delays that were hobbling developers in Paris.

Most of the west row of this immense square was complete within three years. That the result was an artistic triumph is evident from Lindsey House, a proud survivor of Newton's original group. Finished in 1640 or 1641, and long attributed to Jones himself, this beautiful five-bay house is the English Palazzo Rucellai, the first successful marriage of Roman classicism with a practical and local way of building. Nothing is too small or too large, nothing clumsy or crude. It is almost as fine as the houses of similar size that Philips Vingboons was building at the same time in Amsterdam.

Civil Wars

By 1642, the new district of brick houses and open squares was already attracting noblemen and gentlemen in large numbers, and it would soon acquire such prestige that modern Londoners still call it by its seventeenth-century name, the West End, even though London's actual western edge has by now moved twenty or thirty miles farther out. A visitor strolling along Great Queen Street from Covent Garden to Lincoln's Inn Fields would have seen so many new houses and new spaces that he or she would have thought of it all as a distinct environment, separate from everything around it, and would have said that it met the best seventeenth-century standards of architecture and city design. Buildings were classical, streets broad and straight, and the rectangular open spaces of Covent Garden Piazza and Lincoln's Inn Fields were exceedingly dignified public places – as sunny, breezy, leafy, and striking as the great canals of Amsterdam.

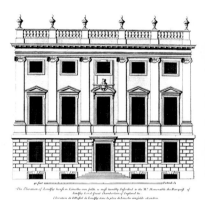

Lindsey House, Lincoln's Inn Fields.

The strengths of this new London way of building were obvious and important. London's fashionable architects and builders had found a way to build classically in economical local materials, and to produce satisfying urban landscapes that met market demand. But there were weaknesses. The West End was strictly a luxury product, confined to a few streets and two squares in a part of town whose residents were rich enough to pay for classicism, masonry, spaciousness, and the steep fees that made it all legal. There is little evidence that less fashionable areas received anything like the same treatment. Most suburban building was still catch-as-catch-can, a cheap mixture of wood and plaster, with gables and primitive windows looking out on dark, dirty, crooked streets. London was not becoming pleasant as Amsterdam and the other Dutch cities were becoming pleasant. Nor was there any reason to suppose, in 1642, that the West End model would ever spread through the entire inchoate metropolis.

It was also a weakness that the movement for good design in London appeared to depend on the commitment of the King, a mortal man. How would Londoners build if something were to happen to him?

They were about to find out. In 1642, the political tensions of forty years exploded in a Civil War that pitted the King against Parliament, with heavy casualties on both sides and the many special horrors of warfare among friends and neighbors. When the battles were finally done, in 1649, Charles lost his head on a scaffold erected in front of Jones's Banqueting House; and the House of Commons, backed by Oliver Cromwell and the New Model Army, abolished both the monarchy and the House of Lords. England became a republic.

We began this chapter by asking why seventeenth-century London, the capital of a monarchy like France, chose to build like republican Amsterdam rather than like Paris.

The Execution of Charles I of England, by John Weesop.

The English Revolution provides much of the answer. England was not as monarchical as it had seemed in 1600, and was not monarchical at all by 1649. The Commons of England, organized in their House in Westminster, governed the country. In 1651, Oliver Cromwell seriously proposed a political union between the English republic and the Dutch.

Who were the Commons? They were in no sense "the poor". They were, for the most part, the gentry, the squires, the rich but untitled people who owned most of the English countryside. Individually, each of them was about as rich as a Dutch merchant. Collectively, historians estimate, they had seven times more landed income than either the king or the 121 members of the House of Lords. Although England's thousands of gentry families were scattered throughout the land, the House of Commons gave them a strong sense of corporate identity and provided them with time-tested ways of working together.

It also mattered that the gentry no longer depended on the nobility, the result of a century of Tudor effort to prevent a recurrence of the Wars of the Roses by dissolving the medieval ties that bound a gentleman to follow his lord in war. Now, in the 1640s, the Tudor policy of liberating and strengthening the gentry recoiled upon their successors.

It is of course true that England was not ready to be a republic in 1649. Passion could not take the place of habit, and the people of England were unable to recognize, in their new Commonwealth, an effective principle of legitimacy. The sovereign House of Commons bickered pointlessly year after year, usually about religion, until an

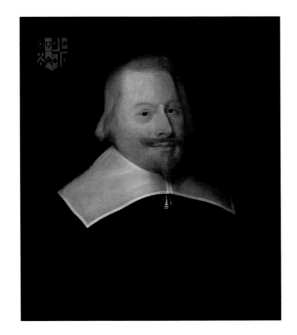

exasperated Cromwell decreed a military dictatorship. This unpopular innovation survived its innovator by a good deal less than a year, and the political nation was only too glad to restore both King and Lords in 1660. That said, the genie was out of the bottle. The gentry was henceforth to be the dominant body in the English state. Though kings would quarrel with the Commons, they would never again try to rule without it. Ministers and peers would use vast resources of money and influence to control the Commons, not to evade it or suppress it.

It is usual for the ambitious many to emulate the powerful few. Just as the courtiers of Louis XIV imitated him, so the aspirants to power in England – even noblemen and kings – soon learned to imitate the Commons. And members of the House of Commons, most of them unable to afford sumptuous dwellings in both town and country, spent little money on London houses. Their power, after all, depended on the electors in their constituencies rather than the favor of the sovereign; so they spent their political money – sometimes vast amounts of it – on the needs and desires of voters in "the country." Members of Parliament courted their constituents in many ways, from plying them with free food and drink to building them new town halls to buying their votes with cash. Rich MPs, and aspiring MPs, built great country houses and turned them into centers for politics and society. Whatever they did, they did it outside London.

It is one of the minor glories of English history that London architecture played so small a role in the political strategies of most successful politicians. Parliamentary

The two houses of Prime Minister Sir Robert Walpole. A simple house in St. James Street, London and a splendid country palace, Houghton Hall, in his constituency in Norfolk.

leaders made it their business to know who could speak well, who was trustworthy, who was stupid, or who could hold a divided constituency at the next election – and who, away from the House, was good company, sober or drunk, and a friend to one's friends. But London architecture had little if anything to do with it. Few MPs in the seventeenth and eighteenth centuries owned houses in London, or even rented them. Members who had families often left them in the country, joining bachelor colleagues in inns or renting rooms in private houses, and doubtless doing their bit to maintain the capital's enormous *demi-monde*. For the sometimes more innocent pleasures of conversation, drinking, music, and gambling, they invented that characteristic London institution, the club.

Architecturally, in the years after 1649, the gentry took up where King Charles left off, and fears that the end of the monarchy would cause a regression into non-classical chaos proved to be groundless. Gentlemen and their ladies wanted to be stylish without ruinous expense, and the Dutch-style buildings of the West End suited them well. Despite the harsh treatment meted out to Inigo Jones in the Revolution – he was captured at the end of a siege, imprisoned for a time, and stripped of his offices – he achieved his mission of bringing classical architecture to England.

Architects in the West End may even have pulled ahead of the Dutch in the Commonwealth Years, at least stylistically. A contemporary engraving of the north and south sides of Lincoln's Inn Fields shows rows without pilasters or columns. Their anonymous designer – certainly not Jones, who was disgraced and may already have been dead – may have invented what the Dutch call the Flat Style, which did not become common in Holland until a few years later.

The Return of the King

Above. St. James's Square.
Left. Clarendon House.

The Restoration of Charles II in 1660 had the potential to change the course of London's development. The new king had spent much of his exile at the court of his first cousin, Louis XIV, and his return brought French fashions in dress, music, and poetry. It seemed, for a moment, as if London might also get a courtly architecture on the French model, with courtiers building city palaces on the model of French hotels. Charles's first minister, the Earl of Clarendon, built a sprawling 10-acre residence near St. James's Palace, and two other courtiers imitated him.

But it was not to be. Another nobleman, the Earl of St. Albans, equally close to the throne, used his influence to obtain forty acres of Crown land, as close to the Palace as Clarendon's house was, and developed it into St. James's Square, the first place in London to which the word "square" was applied. It filled up rapidly with large brick Anglo-Dutch houses of the West End type.

Fashionable London had passed judgment. From that time forward, for more than two hundred years, noblemen and gentlemen would build row after row and square after square. Most new squares were commemorated in engravings, a sign that people would pay money merely to have pictures of them.

To speak of "fashionable London," however, is to pre-suppose the existence of a united upper class. This did not yet exist in the 1660s. Though titled noblemen were beginning to live next to commoners in similar brick houses, many social barriers still divided a nobleman from a gentleman. Now that members of the House of Commons were full participants in ruling the state, it was necessary to find ways for people in the different layers of England's elite to mingle comfortably with each other and speak to

Thomas Gainsborough, St. James's Park, 1783 London's fashionable parade at its height, on the grounds of St. James's Palace. St. James's Park is still a very pleasant place for a stroll.

each other more or less as equals. There was a need for new social rituals, and new places in which to perform them.

Charles II, famous today mainly for mistresses and carelessness, does not get enough credit for recognizing this problem and taking the first step towards solving it. He had seen how Parisians turned their city's abandoned fortifications – boulevards in French, sharing an etymological ancestry with the English "bulwarks" – into public promenades, and he had seen how social walking, as this activity is now known, brought a new kind of polite pleasure to Parisian life. He opened a piece of the park around St. James's Palace to be a promenade for well-dressed people of all ranks, and he set an example by walking in the open with his people. Soon lords and ladies were promenading with squires and gentlewomen, all in a lovely part of the King's own palace garden.

The best way to understand the importance of social walking is to consider the name of the area that Charles II set aside for it, a former ball field for an Italian game called Palla Maglia (mallet ball) quickly Anglicized to The Mall. One of the royal mallet ball fields became a fashionable street, Pall Mall, while the other, known simply as The Mall, became England's first and greatest promenade. The English-speaking peoples have used the word "mall" ever since to describe a linear space designed and managed for polite, informal promenading – as do today's developers of shopping centers.

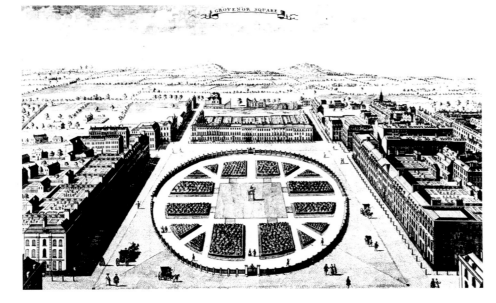

Golden Square.

Since England's ruling class was mainly based in the country, and was forever leaving town and returning to it, social walking served the practical purpose of allowing people of fashion, noble and gentle, to show that they had arrived in town, to see who else was there, and to be seen to good advantage, in their best clothes and in a good outdoor light. Friends would meet, daughters would be introduced to sons, and visits would be arranged. Because families from all over England came to London for government and society, social walking also played a role in creating a national identity.

Rows of houses, garden squares, parks and promenades – these are the signature elements of London as we know it today, and they were all in place by about 1675. Joan de Jean, in a brilliant recent book, has shown that "Paris became Paris" during the middle decades of the seventeenth century. London became London at the same time. Both cities developed large urban districts of order and beauty and created opportunities for upper-class people to move about freely and form social networks based on common interests and shared pleasures.

In the race to become a center of civilized leisure, Paris, the capital of a much bigger country, with a richer court and larger upper class, got off to a brisker start. But the race was on, and the lead would change frequently. Through it all, the patterns established in the middle of the seventeenth century would prove to be durable. To the extent that today's Parisians can afford to, they live in stone buildings that resemble the hotels of baroque courtiers, and they stroll on boulevards. To the extent that today's Londoners can afford to, they live in row houses that overlook squares, and they stroll through landscaped parks.

The Great Fire of London, 1666.

The New City

Meanwhile, two miles to the east of Parliament and the Court, the mercantile City of London was still what it had been in Shakespeare's day, a stinking mess of ramshackle houses and twisting alleys. Every square foot of it had been built over by the time of Elizabeth's 1580 proclamation against suburban building, and hardly anything had changed thereafter. Business was booming for City merchants in the 1660s, as they began to outdistance Amsterdam in the heavily-armed race to control global trade, but the growing intensity of business meant only more crowding, more noise, and a foul atmosphere compounded of smoke and fog – "smog", as the gentleman polymath John Evelyn first called it in 1661.

The fact that the City was primarily made of wood suddenly became important in the middle of the night on Sunday, September 2, 1666, when a fire broke out in a bakery. The weather had been oddly dry for months, and the wind was strong. London was no stranger to fires and fire-fighting, but this time the Lord Mayor dithered as flames spread to nearby buildings, and the blaze got out of control. By afternoon, the conflagration had formed firestorms and was devouring whole streets. By evening, the diarist Samuel Pepys saw "onely one arch of flames … a mile long." By the end of three days, the City lay in ruins. The Great Fire destroyed 13,000 houses, 87 churches, most of the guild halls and public buildings, and St. Paul's Cathedral. Steel bars melted on the docks, and molten lead from the Cathedral roof coursed down the streets. A few days later, Pepys and Evelyn found eighty thousand homeless people encamped in the fields around the built-up area.

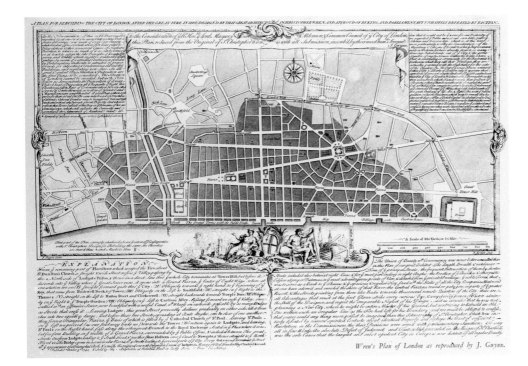

Wren's Plan of London as reproduced by J. Gwynn.

Wren's Plan for rebuilding London. Dark shading represents the burnt district.

The City of London now had its opportunity to make a decision like the one the West End was making. Would it return to its old ways, its gables and jutties and plastered wood? Would it emulate the baroque models of Paris and Rome? Or would it follow the Dutch pattern set by the West End?

The first rebuilding proposals were baroque. Within days, two courtly intellectuals, Evelyn and a mathematician-turned-architect named Christopher Wren, submitted two different plans to rebuild the City as a baroque capital, with broad, straight avenues converging on spacious plazas and showcasing the major buildings of church and state. Either of their plans would have given London the kind of magnificence we now see in Paris and Rome.

There was a moment in which a baroque rebuilding received serious consideration, but it was measured in hours. Though generally admired, the plans of Wren and Evelyn would have led to insoluble difficulties and fatal delays, and there was little appetite to reframe London's business district as a giant billboard for absolute monarchy. Wren and Evelyn took their defeat with good grace. When the King and Parliament adopted a regime of Dutch-style brick houses on an incrementally reformed street plan, Wren was invited to serve on the committee formed to oversee the rebuilding, and he accepted immediately.

The rebuilding of London after the Great Fire moved forward with a speed and a sure-footed confidence that would be enviable in any age and were astonishing in seventeenth-century England, beset as it was with inefficiency and corruption. King and Parliament, frequently at odds, for once worked together smoothly. A royal Proclamation of September 13, less than a week after the Fire, required that all new buildings be built of brick or stone, and that all main streets be widened, all bottlenecks removed from streets, and an exact survey made of all streets and pieces of property. Within seven weeks, Parliament had before it a Rebuilding Act that included detailed standards for all new buildings.

This quick work was possible only because the drafters of Proclamations and Acts knew what they wanted and had a set of field-tested regulations at their disposal. They wanted the rebuilt City to look like the new West End, and their Rebuilding Act required all new buildings to meet standards very like the ones that Inigo Jones and his successors had been enforcing in the West End for 35 years.

The King and the members of Parliament were not aesthetes. They did not seek architectural uniformity only as an artistic end in itself, but also for the down-to-earth reason that it would speed their work. The Rebuilding Act states:

> *And to the end that all Builders may the better know how to provide and fitt their materialls for their severall Buildings Be it enacted That there shall be onely fower sortes of Buildings and noe more...*

Having established four sorts of buildings, the Act stated where each sort of building was to be built. Houses fronting on "high and principal streets" were to be four stories tall. Three-story houses were specified for "streets and lanes of note, and the River Thames," while two-story houses were required for properties "fronting by-streets and lanes." The Act ended with an admirably brief building code in easy-to-follow table form. For each sort of building, the Act stated exactly how tall each story was to be, how thick [in bricks] the walls were to be, and how thick the pieces of lumber were to be in various parts of the house.

All of this made the life of a London builder very simple. As T.H. Reddaway, the historian of the rebuilding, says: "In many important respects the Act designed his [the builder's] house for him." This made for short contracts – one surviving agreement merely requires the builder to erect two houses "of the second sort ... mentioned in the late Act of Parliament" – and a high degree of standardization in the production of bricks and the sawing of lumber.

All in all, the Act was a tremendous success. It saved money, worry, and precious time. It also produced houses and streets that were as modern as anything in the West

End. Gone were the twisting alleys and sagging gables of the old City. Gone too, finally and forever, were the "jutties" that had darkened the streets of London for centuries. Streets were now tolerably straight, houses were properly aligned, and travelers no longer needed to swerve to avoid buildings and cellars in their path. Everything was orderly and smooth. The Rebuilding Act made gables inefficient, and almost all new houses rose with stylish classical cornices. It all looked like the Flat Style in Amsterdam. When the last house was finished, seven years after the conflagration, London was the cleanest, neatest, most modern city in the world. Ninety years later, young James Boswell would walk from the West End to the heart of the City every Sunday without noticing an architectural difference.

All this work took more builders than London had on hand. The City had been built-out for so long that the building guilds had too few members. Charles immediately solved the problem by decreeing that any master builder from any part of England could come and build in London. Almost overnight, London swarmed with builders from all over the country. During the seven years of the rebuilding, thousands of "foreigners" (so Londoners called them) came to London and learned how to construct brick row houses in conformity with the Rebuilding Acts. London became, in effect, a university of house-building.

Next came churches and public buildings. These were too expensive to be financed by ordinary means, but Parliament and the King again rose to the occasion. Their solution, a tax on coal, was as simple and innovative as the Rebuilding Act and worked equally well. Public buildings came first, and work was soon under way on markets,

St. James, Piccadilly by Sir Christopher Wren.

The City and St. Paul's.

quays, and jails. Christopher Wren, who became Surveyor-General in 1669, designed a splendid Custom House, a necessary building for collecting the taxes on which the King's government depended. In a magnificent gesture of community pride, the City erected, to designs by Wren and Robert Hooke, a giant Roman column, called simply The Monument, to commemorate the destruction wrought by the fire and the resolve of the people of London to rebuild.

Churches took longer. A number of small parishes had to be consolidated (itself a time-consuming process,) but even so there was a need for 51 new churches, and they were so expensive that the coal tax had to be doubled in 1670 to meet the cost of church-building. And no one was sure what a church should look like; Protestant England had built hardly any churches since the Reformation. Someone would have to do the kind of pioneering work that Hendrik de Keyser had done in Amsterdam at the beginning of the century, and would have to do it dozens of times over, on sites of every size and shape, managing the personalities of bishops, ministers, and the lay members of dozens of parish committees. The task called for a man with an inventive mind, a knowledge of design in foreign countries, impressive social skills, and a considerable fund of self-confidence. Such a man, fortunately, was the new Surveyor-General, Christopher Wren, who began work on the City churches as soon as the new 1670 coal tax provided the funds.

Wren's 51 City Churches form a long sequence of small masterpieces, like Shakespeare's Sonnets or Haydn's String Quartets. No two are alike. Each responds to a different site, to different solar orientation, and, doubtless, to the passions and fears of different churchmen and parishioners. Some of Wren's churches are better than others, but even the worst are good, and, taken together, they suggest the possibilities of their form without exhausting them. Each is content to be small, and to give pleasure with well-proportioned effects. Even now, after the destruction of about half of them by the governments of Victorian London and Nazi Germany, their disciplined variety is astonishing. Wren's ingenuity breaks forth in most of them, as does his knowledge of architecture ancient and modern, Dutch and Italian and occasionally French. His classicism is lively, not rule-bound. He even built a couple of churches in Gothic, prompting today's architectural historians to ask (inconclusively, so far) whether Gothic was still a living architectural tradition in Wren's generation.

Like de Keyser, Wren solved the problem of making great sacred art out of the preaching halls that suited word-centered, non-sacramental Protestant worship. Moreover, he invested small buildings with a sometimes almost overwhelming classical grandeur. His churches, and those of his immediate followers like Nicholas Hawksmoor and James Gibbs, would shape church building on both sides of the North Atlantic for a century and a half.

Wren crowned his work on the rebuilding with a new St. Paul's Cathedral. This is the building that would later symbolize London's indomitable spirit during the Blitz, the building that now forms the background for Wren's portrait on a £50 note. If his City Churches are like sonnets or string quartets, St. Paul's is like an epic poem or an oratorio.

As the first new cathedral built from the ground up in England for more than 500 years, it was conceived as a national statement on the largest possible scale, and money was no object. Wren's mission was two-fold: to show that England was the leading power of Protestant Europe, uniquely able to look papal Rome and Catholic France in the eye, and to proclaim that the English people had repented of their folly in abolishing the Church of England during the Civil Wars. As the son of a distinguished Anglican clergyman, Wren was fully in harmony with his assignment. Sixty years in the building, grand in mass and fine in each detail, St. Paul's dominated the City's skyline for 300 years and remains a landmark today, even as eccentric skyscrapers begin to overtop it.

When the rebuilding of the City was complete, every house in the City and the West End, from tiny two-roomed cottages in narrow courts to the mansions of the great in spacious squares, followed the same general architectural approach, the brick, Dutch-style classicism that Inigo Jones and his king had created for the West End in the 1630s. London had proven that the Dutch-style row house, evolved in small canal-side cities, could meet the needs and uphold the honor of a lusty young imperial capital, the biggest and richest city in the known world.

By then, after almost a century of revolution in politics and architecture, London had made its big choices. England's government would henceforth have a strong republican element, and the people of England's capital would live in brick row houses enlivened by the greenery of squares and parks. London had become London.

Chapter Three

THE BRITISH URBAN RENAISSANCE

By the autumn of 1674, the work of rebuilding London was done, and England's capital was the freshest, cleanest, most modern city in the world. The only people who were unhappy were the men who had built it, most of whom suddenly found themselves unemployed. As usually happens when work is scarce, things got nasty. Native-born Londoners turned against the "foreigners" who had come from provincial England and worked beside them in the rebuilding. Fights and riots broke out, and most of the foreigners returned to the places from which they had come. Wherever they went, they carried the ability to build in the new London style, the economical brick classicism that Parliament's bill-drafters had adapted from the gentry architecture of Jones, Bedford, and Newton.

Because so many builders had come to London, had learned the new London way of building, and then had then gone back into the English countryside, it is logical to assume that a revolution in English architecture would soon make itself visible in the provinces. But did it? And, if so, how soon? And how would the tiny towns and villages of seventeenth-century England mold and change a way of building developed in, and for, one of the biggest cities in the world?

We might have begun to learn the answers on the night of September 20, 1674. A fire broke out that night in Northampton, a town of some three thousand people, sixty-seven miles from London. A strong wind was blowing, and the center of town was destroyed within minutes. Northampton's leading citizens immediately pressed their MPs for a Rebuilding Act like London's, and Parliament obliged by creating a Fire Court on the London model, giving it the power to widen and straighten streets, and appointing certain men, listed by name, to serve on it. If the worthies of Northampton had taken pity on us, they would have copied the building regulations of the London Rebuilding Act, and we would be able to say with conviction that the new London way of building had penetrated sixty-seven miles into the provinces at the first possible moment. Such pity was not in them. Although the Northampton Act, obviously framed under the direct guidance of local people, gave Northampton's Fire Court specific power to widen streets and remove the foundations of buildings that encroached on the new thoroughfares, it did not speak clearly on the design and construction of buildings. Other than requiring fireproof materials for roofs, it left everything about the design and construction of buildings to the discretion of the court. It is probably fair to take this as evidence that

Warwick houses from before the Fire of 1694. Most small English towns looked more or less like this in the seventeenth century.

Warwick, post-Fire houses.
Note the fourteen-inch cornice
on the three-story house at left.

the new London way of building had not reached the squires, lawyers, and rich tradesmen who ran Northampton.

Northampton emerged nonetheless as a strikingly modern place. When the redoubtable traveler Celia Fiennes visited twenty-five years later, she wrote that Northampton was "a large town well built, ye streets as large as most in London Except Holborn and the Strand, the houses well built of brick and stone, some all stone, very regular buildings." The key word here is "regular." The word still meant "according to the rules," and the rules were those of Jones, Wren, and Ancient Rome. This suggests that Northampton's builders, the men who actually did the work, were more familiar with London practice than the laymen on the Fire Court – probably because some of them had worked in the rebuilding of London. It also suggests that the members of the court, who had not known enough about London building to specify it in advance, liked it when they saw it and were willing to pay for it.

We were luckier twenty years later, on September 5, 1694, when a fire destroyed the center of Warwick, another town of about three thousand people, forty miles from Northampton and ninety-six miles from London. Again, the local notables procured a Rebuilding Act (they paid a London lawyer £5 to write it,) and created a Fire Court with the power to widen streets; but this time the Act also contained detailed specifications, modeled on London, for the design and construction of buildings. Thanks to Warwick's Rebuilding Act, we can say with confidence that the new London way of building houses had penetrated into Warwickshire, the heart of England, Shakespeare's home county, by 1694.

We can even tell what the result was, because Warwick, unlike Northampton, has changed very little since the 1690s. It looks like a small Dutch town in a hilly landscape. The streets are broad and straight, and the two-story brick houses are properly aligned – something that was still revolutionary in the heart of England in the 1690s. Most of the houses survive and still carry the big wooden cornices and dormers that were the fashion in 1694. The worthies of Warwick wanted, and got, the new London way of building on a miniature scale, and it is still there. Fiennes wrote: "Ye streets are very handsome and ye buildings Regular and fine." Daniel Defoe, a few years later, praised Warwick's rebuilding "in so noble and beautiful a Manner that few Towns in England make so fine an Appearance."

None of this happened by accident. Thanks to the preservation of the Fire Court's records and their brilliant analysis by Michael Farr, we know that the Court met dozens of times over many years, and we know, in extraordinary detail, what it did. We know, for instance, that the members of the court wanted to create a square on the London model in front of the parish church. The records show us how much work this required, how many surveys, how many purchases of small corners of property, how many disputes. And we can walk outdoors and experience the square itself, as it was planned – though it is so small that few of us would notice it without knowing the story behind it. We know, too, that the Court wanted to mark the center of the town by requiring the owners of the three burnt buildings at the main intersection to build identical three-story houses – very noticeable in this two-story town – with big wooden cornices fourteen inches high. This was done, as the court ordered, and the three houses are still there, still a story taller than their neighbors, their fourteen-inch cornices as proud as when they were new.

We also know who made up the Warwick Fire Court, and what kind of men they were. They were not, as might be expected, the leading burgesses and merchants of the town of Warwick. Almost all of them were landed gentlemen from the Warwickshire countryside. In fact, the principal nobleman of the county, Lord Brooke, who dominated the town from his seat at Warwick Castle, attended more meetings of the Court than any other member and interested himself in the smallest details of design and construction. He played, in person, the role that Charles II had delegated to Wren in the rebuilding of London.

This is not to say that Lord Brooke was an intentional architectural innovator. He was not, and that is important; for his activity in the rebuilding of Warwick shows that the new "regular" London way of building had by 1694 become a kind of genteel common practice throughout the kingdom, the kind of building that any nobleman or gentleman would want and would be willing to work for– often in a daily grind against the wishes of less sophisticated neighbors.

The experience of Warwick would prove prophetic for the small towns of England for most of what British historians call "the Long Eighteenth Century," a period stretching from the Glorious Revolution of 1688 to the full impact of the Industrial Revolution in the 1830s. Throughout this period, rural nobles and country gentlemen invested a good deal of time and trouble to ensure that their towns would present a "regular" appearance. Such was the power of the nobility and gentry in the Long Eighteenth Century that, in matters of architecture and urban design, as in most other matters, the lawyers, craftsmen, and shopkeepers of England's towns tended to defer to them.

Gentry Values

Gentry dominance meant that England and English towns would get architectural classicism and a new system of manners that contemporaries called politeness. These two concepts, classicism and politeness, are the key to architecture, urban design, and most other things in this period.

Classicism was the more obvious and predictable of the two, given that education, in this period, meant a deep saturation in the literature of Greece and Rome, and the British gentry was the best-educated ruling class in Europe. Like Renaissance Italians, English gentlemen had an exaggerated notion of Roman greatness and attempted to equal the glory of the Romans by emulating their works. Addison put Cato on the stage, Burke modeled his orations on Cicero, and every nobleman with any pretensions to culture brought back at least one piece of ancient marble from the Grand Tour. Their greatest poems (in their own estimation) were Dryden's translation of Vergil and Pope's of Homer, and they seeded the English countryside with houses whose chief characteristic was a well-proportioned symmetry.

The second gentry value, politeness, was a vague but very powerful aspiration towards neatness, smoothness, and refinement in all aspects of art and life. Fully compatible with a love of classical architecture, the aspiration towards politeness was shared from one end of the country to the other, from ports on the coast to market towns deep inland, for more than a century, by millions of people. It informed most of their buildings, their paintings, their poems, their casual judgments. Many people today misunderstand this. They think that the politeness of eighteenth-century art is a portrait when it is really a prayer, and they take the period's endless praise of polite virtues for self-congratulation instead of exhortation. Shepherds do not write pastorals, and eighteenth-century Englishmen would not have sought politeness if their England had been a polite place. Englishmen feared to walk their streets at night. They drank too much and spoke too lightly of breaking each other's heads. The cult of politeness showed that they were tiring of violence and stupidity, not that they had banished them. Englishmen – and, even more, Englishwomen – were beginning to hope that they could make progress by increasing the amount of order and system in their doings; and they used the arts, including the arts of architecture and town planning, to give form to this hope.

Their master-art, the greatest invention of the age, was conversation, an easy give-and-take of talking and listening that flowed unaffectedly from the discussion of subjects to anecdotes about friends or remarks about the weather. Strange as it may seem to us, conversation was still a new skill in the eighteenth century, a French invention that had come to England with the Restoration. Before the coming of conversation, English ways of speaking had involved a good deal of commanding and flattering, as befitted a hierarchical society. Gatherings of equals, when they occurred, had featured story-telling and competitive wit, much of it obscene. Conversation was different. It struck a stylistic middle ground between the learned sermon and the dirty joke; and it made talking and listening into tools for learning and information. Thus, the Lunar Men of Birmingham, meeting on full-moon nights, used conversation to share and advance scientific knowledge, while almost all literate people participated in the less rigorous probing of individuals and individuality that began as tattle and flowered into the novel.

The middle-ground conventions of politeness and conversation had important political consequences, because they allowed a relatively large number of people to speak to each other more or less as equals. Johnson, a tradesman's son, and Boswell, the son of a lord, could converse with each other, and with a range of acquaintances from noblemen to shopkeepers. By the end of the period, the old forms of pride and subordination had become ridiculous, like the oily subservience of Austen's Mr. Collins or the dim-witted snobbery of his patroness. It is Austen too who lets us see that the great gainers in the age of conversation were women. Though there was plenty of deference and "humoring" in eighteenth-century conversation, and the law still governed women medievally, women controlled the tea table, and the old ways of bossing women or beating women could get a man ostracized from polite society.

Politeness avoided the extremes of exaltation and self-pity. It fitted an age of prosperous peace, a people tired of religious fanaticism and political revolution. It was, as you might expect of a gentry virtue, a gracious middle ground between high and low, appropriate to a country whose dominant institution was the House of Commons. Despite the sneers of Romantics in the nineteenth century, politeness was not a pallid straightjacket. It was, as Pope said of architectural regularity, "bold." It was an enthusiasm, a very long-lived social excitement. Though it ran its course, as enthusiasms do, its course was very long, and it left a great legacy. Social trust increased, and daily life became more peaceful, more pleasant, and more predictable. People learned to differ,

A polite small-town street Broad Street, Ludlow.

even about important things, without resort to violence. We still use the eighteenth-century phrase "civil society" to describe the private underpinnings of ordered liberty, and the enthusiasm for politeness did as much as any single thing to make the Long Eighteenth Century the first great age of responsible freedom. Englishmen in the age of politeness stabilized representative government at home and invented representative democracy in North America.

The excitement of politeness is what we should feel when we walk down a Georgian street in an English town. The street itself is made for our comfort and use. It is broad and unobstructed, clean and well-paved. The buildings that frame it, in their shapely and repetitive simplicity, assure us that their inhabitants, even if they are total strangers to us, will share our values and treat us politely. That we can take such things for granted today is a tribute to the men and women of the Long Eighteenth Century.

A Golden Age

A modern scholar has called the Long Eighteenth Century the golden age of the English town. It is easy to see why. Most towns achieved the urban ideal of growing richer without growing bigger. High crop yields enriched the gentry, creating thousands of landowning customers for craftsmen in country towns. For the first time, even small towns like Warwick blossomed forth with specialist craftsmen: clockmakers and gunsmiths, workers in brass and iron and silver, makers of carriages and sideboards. The number of different trades roughly doubled in the average town, and country gentlemen found that, unlike their fathers, they could meet quite civilized needs without going or sending to London. English towns became reservoirs of skill, as towns in France and Italy had been for centuries.

With a few dramatic exceptions, noble and gentle landowners shaped the small towns of the Long Eighteenth Century, as Lord Brooke had shaped Warwick. In addition to pride and electoral politics, they had three practical reasons to do so.

The first of these was that many gentlefolk lived in towns. Since gentle status applied to every clergyman, every officer in the army and navy, every graduate of a university, and every son of a nobleman or gentleman, there were lots of gentlemen, probably about 20,000 of them at the beginning of the eighteenth century. For every landed gentleman in a big country house there were perhaps a dozen gentlemen, or gentlewomen, who were significantly poorer. Some of these non-landed gentry acquired large incomes and influence through government service or the church, particularly the bishops and other well-paid clergymen in the cathedral cities. The rest needed to live relatively cheaply in places where they could find friends and, often, earn their livings.

Towns were an obvious resource for them. The son of an English gentleman could become a lawyer, a medical doctor, or even (though this was more difficult) a merchant without jeopardizing his social status, earning enough for silver and servants if not for country houses. Modern historians call these people "town gentry." A key component of the town gentry were the thousands of officers in the army and navy who needed to live on half-pay in intervals of peace, or on modest pensions after retirement or wounds. A surprisingly large number of gentle town-dwellers were independent women, many but not all of them widows. When, as often happens, Fiennes and other travelers describe a town as "full of gentry," it is town gentry that they mean.

The second reason for gentlemen to care about towns was that even the greatest of landowners had to spend a lot of time in them. The English gentry was not a leisure class. It was a ruling class of unpaid judges and administrators, and it governed the English countryside through institutions that met in the principal towns of each county

Chester's Roodee.

or administrative district, the "county" or "shire" towns. Each of these towns was a small capital, and the rulers of counties came to them as the rulers of the kingdom came to London. Most gentlemen went to their county town at least four times a year for the basic judicial and administrative meetings of their county, the Quarter Sessions. Many came more frequently for the meetings of grand juries and the ad hoc bodies – Fire Courts, for instance – that proliferated in the period. All of them came to their county towns twice a year for the Assizes, when a circuit-riding judge arrived from Westminster with his Marshal and his suite of barristers for a full week or two of serious trials.

The Assizes were not optional. The entire nobility and gentry of each county was required to form a procession and escort the King's judge to his lodgings in a ceremony of medieval pomp. They were then required to remain during the ensuing week or two of trials. With so many gentlemen in one place for so long, society came to form around the Assizes. Wives and children abandoned their rural splendor and enjoyed the only truly sociable days that many of them ever had. Matches were made, hearts were broken, and fashionable innkeepers grew rich, while prisoners trembled.

The third reason for rural gentlemen to care about towns was that landed families used them as resorts, particularly in winter when roads were bad and country life lonely. Those who could afford to go to London did so, as they had done for centuries. But now even the lesser gentry – the vast majority of landed families – were rich enough to spend their winters in regional centers that were closer and cheaper than London. Towns

Assembly Rooms, York.

understood the economic impact of attracting landed families, and they competed vigorously for their patronage, with perhaps a hundred towns succeeding to the extent of developing regular "seasons."

Architecture and city planning had a role to play here, and the county towns of England owe much of their classical regularity to the competition for seasonal residents. But stylish buildings and tidy streets were not enough. At least equally important were opportunities for entertainment and sociable meeting. Every town supported coffee houses, and a few towns were big enough to build theatres. Many towns created or improved courses for the suddenly-popular sport of horse racing. The best-preserved of these, the Roodee, in Chester, still lies like a fairy green beneath the snug little city's Roman walls. But it was dancing and social walking that did the most to bring genteel people together, and these social activities forced many towns to build their grandest buildings and lay out their loveliest outdoor spaces.

Genteel dancers needed rooms that suited their dances, all of which, except the minuet, were what are now called social dances. These were closely akin to Scottish dancing and American square dancing today, usually involving "sets" of five or six couples in two interweaving lines. Such dances needed long rooms, and the term "long room" arose to describe the dancing rooms built by ambitious innkeepers in competitive towns. Such rooms were still the standard for very small towns at the end of the eighteenth century, when Austen's Emma Woodhouse danced in one.

By that time, however, larger towns had long since done better. A town with a large Town Hall, or a County Court House, would usually open it for balls and assemblies. Many towns, in fact – Abingdon in Oxfordshire is the most famous example – courted gentry by building bigger and fancier public buildings than they needed for justice and administration. In other towns, entrepreneurs or syndicates of gentlemen built special Assembly Rooms or Assembly Halls, often as large and magnificent as major public buildings. The York Assembly Rooms, designed by the Earl of Burlington in 1731, ranks among the greatest works of English architecture.

By contrast with dancing, which required elaborate buildings of a special design, social walking was a simple-seeming amusement, a mere stroll in a pleasant public or semi-public place. Charles II, after all, had created the first social promenade at almost no expense by setting aside The Mall in the park around St. James's Palace. Most English towns, however, lacked palaces, or any pleasant outdoor places, so the vogue for social walking stimulated important developments and changed the form of English towns in ways that were large, visible, and frequently long-lasting. Malls had to be created, like buildings. They were the first polite public places that most English towns had ever had. Music and refreshments were often provided, and entrepreneurs sometimes seized on the opportunity to charge admission to private places of pleasure and beauty, provincial versions of London's Vauxhall and Ranelagh. Though social walking went out of fashion in the nineteenth century, any street with the words "Mall" or "Parade" in its name was a place for social walking at some time in the Long Eighteenth Century.

Eighteenth-century writers were accurate in describing the gentry as "people of fashion." There was no harrumphing old-money reticence about them. They made it their business to be up-to-date, and any town that wanted to attract them had to remake itself, or part of itself, on the new London model. Since fires were few, progress in most towns was necessarily slower than it had been in Northampton and Warwick, but most towns moved along the same lines and sought to create regularity in streets and buildings. This was not as easy as it sounds.

Consider street widening and maintenance. This was a pressing practical need in a period of carriages for the gentry and booming long-distance traffic for trade, but it required public action; and English town governments lacked the power to take private property or to levy taxes for streets. Only Parliament could grant such power. Thus it was that the leading citizens of hundreds of towns went to the Commons and the Lords for special Acts, turning Parliament into a kind of national town council (and guaranteeing close relations between town gentlemen, relatively poor, and the country house grandees who alone could afford unpaid Parliamentary service in London.) While street-building, street-paving, and the recent invention of street-lighting were the most common subjects of local Acts of Parliament, there were many others, and any English town worth its salt eventually acquired one or two special-purpose commissions, each with its own members, its own grant of powers, and, usually, the power to tax some or all of the citizens. Together with the myriad other unpaid bodies that managed everything from poor relief to the maintenance of roads and bridges, these boards and commissions – often called Improvement Commissions – were the very lifeblood of local politics, and they created countless opportunities for prosperous townsmen to work with landed gentlemen. In time, the top tier of town society, particularly the members of the learned professions – doctors, lawyers, and clergymen, often gentlemen themselves or the cousins of gentlemen – became something of a mediating class between the squires in the countryside and the artisans and small dealers in the towns. They reduced friction in a very unequal society and tended to be the moving spirits in most schemes of town improvement.

Improvements in architecture were easier but even less systematic. Everything depended on the taste of individual owners. Although the tastes of the time were clear and quite coherent, building was sporadic in most places, and rebuilding was always a matter of whim or unpredictable necessity. In the absence of fires and Rebuilding Acts, classical architecture gained ground unevenly. Since most towns were growing richer without adding population, there was more pressure to update old houses than to build new ones, and many a classical brick façade conceals medieval structure. As usually happens when buildings are renovated one at a time, this process produced few uniform streets. The modernization of earlier buildings was, moreover, less complete in England than in the Netherlands; and the juxtaposition of classical houses in brick or stone with half-timbered "black-and-white" houses of an earlier age is one of the charms of the typical English town.

Another charm of old English streets is the diversity of size among houses. It is hard for us to realize how new are the class-segregated neighborhoods that we take for granted. Among English cities and towns in 1700, only London had a big enough housing market to allow a builder or developer to fill up any large piece of land with houses of only one size and price. Smaller towns were almost always what modern planners would call "mixed-income communities". The biggest house in the shire town of Chichester, built in 1696 and as elegant as a country mansion, shares its section of the high street with houses of many different sizes. Rich people and poor passed each other on the street every day, in town as in the country, the rich enforcing a system of deference that made proximity palatable to them.

There was enough growth, however, for most towns of any size to create at least a few new streets, or new extensions to old streets. Here all houses were new and could resemble each other closely in size and design. The architecture of houses in prosperous streets could be very regular indeed, and became steadily more so as designers and clients got the hang of the new London style. Regularity, however, was rarely uniformity. Because houses were usually built one or two at a time – housebuilding did not become a big business until the very end of the period, and then only in the biggest cities – subtle differences enlivened most rows and terraces, albeit at some cost in monumental grandeur. Sometimes a landowner with land adjacent to an improving town would lay out a new street and establish architectural guidelines as rigid as any in a Rebuilding Act. A solid gentry estate, or a charitable foundation like a church or a college, well capitalized and well staffed by agents and solicitors, worked hard to maintain and enhance the value of its property; and private development regulations, backed by a landowner with the means to sue for their enforcement, gave builders and residents as much protection against offensive neighbors as was possible before modern zoning ordinances. Everyone could be sure, at least, that the people in their own street would not build smaller or less stylish houses, or conduct noxious trades, or otherwise diminish the value of surrounding property.

A few big towns grew fast enough to justify the kind of large-scale planned development that noblemen like Bedford and entrepreneurs like Newton had pioneered in the West End of London. Not surprisingly, Bristol, the second port of the country in 1700 and one of the two second-biggest towns, took an early lead. The city government laid out six acres for Queen Square on an undeveloped site in 1699, and the merchants of Bristol, rich with the new American trade, joined with gentry of various ranks to frame it quickly with big Dutch-style houses. By the 1790s, with the aid of medicinal springs that made it a gentry resort, Bristol became an exceptionally big market for fashionable urban housing, and the city's builders responded to the opportunity with England's second-biggest array of squares – not to mention splendid Assembly Rooms, new churches and bridges, a palatial Exchange for merchants, and an assortment of Malls and Parades.

Palladio and a National Classicism

Though many of the successors of Jones and Wren were as skillful as they, few are as famous. There were too few opportunities to build the kinds of buildings that make an architect immortal. Parliament kept the Crown on short architectural rations, and London failed to burn again. Turning their eyes from the court to the country, architects served the nobility and gentry, the actual rulers of the state, as Jones and Wren had served the king. Thus it was that an earl, not a sovereign, shaped English Palladianism, England's first-ever innovative national movement in architecture.

Richard Boyle, third Earl of Burlington, seems to have fallen in love with the architecture of Inigo Jones when he was a very young man. By 1714, when Burlington was twenty, peace allowed him to travel to Italy, and he followed Jones' footsteps to

Bristol, Queen Square.

Palladio's hometown of Vicenza, annotating his copy of Palladio's *Four Books* as he inspected the author's buildings. When he returned home, he set out to create a British national classicism in all the arts, using his large landed income to commission Epistles from Pope and operas from Handel. But it was architecture that mattered most to Burlington, and architecture, for him, meant Palladio. He commissioned two English editions of Palladio's book and gathered a circle of young architects with the express intention of founding a British school of Palladian architecture. His own first design, built when he was twenty-three, was a small pavilion behind his family's old red brick Chiswick House outside London. Modeled more or less faithfully on the Rocca Pisana, a country villa by Palladio's pupil Scamozzi, it was as shocking a piece of cool geometry as Jones' Queen's House had been eighty years before.

Chiswick House, London.

Burlington chose his model well, for Palladio, whose clients were provincial gentlemen of modest wealth with a boundless admiration for ancient Rome, was the ideal architectural patron saint for England's gentry in the so-called Augustan Age of the eighteenth century. As the first architect ever to build small, cheap buildings of convincing grandeur, Palladio offered England's squires, a hundred and fifty years after his death, exactly what they wanted and needed. If Burlington had developed a passion for Michelangelo or Bernini, intensely personal architects whose effects required immense budgets, he would be remembered, if at all, merely as another of England's many noble eccentrics. But the gentlemen of England could afford the simple geometry, plain masonry, and moderate scale of Palladio and Palladianism, and Burlington's effort to found a national school succeeded to such an extent that, by 1735, English prestige was stimulating a Palladian revival in Vicenza itself.

Of the many kinds of Roman classicism, Palladianism is the simplest and the most robust. There are few curves, and expensive ornament is strictly optional. It is very masculine. It is, moreover, very Protestant, in that it can succeed without elaborate carvings, mysterious light, or ubiquitous fresco. As England fought one long war after another against the Catholic absolutism of France, Palladianism became the architecture of English patriotism.

Books spread the new classicism with unusual speed. Colen Campbell's majestic and expensive *Vitruvius Britannicus or The British Architect* – first published in 1715, while the young Burlington was still poking around Vicenza – celebrates the work of Jones and Wren and documents that noblemen were already building Palladian houses. Burlington's two editions of Palladio swelled the stream, and the innate simplicity of Palladian classicism made it a good subject for cheap books aimed at builders without architectural training. William Salmon's *Palladio Londinensis*, published in 1734 and subtitled *The London Art of Building*, made it clear to provincial artisans that Vicentine classicism was also London fashion. Further down-market, Batty Langley and William Halfpenny cranked out practical manuals that builders could carry in their pockets and consult on construction sites. A country craftsman with one of these books could execute classical designs in the approved London manner, with no hint of provinciality, even if he had never worked in London. Every English town has beautiful door cases built from these books. Without the likes of Langley and Halfpenny, and the big publishing industry of the eighteenth century, it would have been hard for England's small towns to look as polite as they were in fact becoming.

Collective Grandeur

Politeness, however, is not quite grandeur. The noblemen and gentlemen of England were rulers, and successful rule requires the projection of greatness. The essence of England's situation was that its nobility and gentry were devising ways of equaling royal grandeur by working together through oligarchical institutions – vestries, quarter sessions, improvement commissions, Parliament itself. This was hard, messy work. Not surprisingly, efforts to represent England's quasi-republic in architecture and city design were also messy and halting. Noblemen and gentlemen wanted to express their collective grandeur through urban development, but they did not know how, and experiments were prohibitively expensive.

Experiments were cheaper in the countryside, where hills could be moved and walks laid out at less expense than in a town, and where one proprietor and one team could try what they wanted without endless committee meetings. English landowners hit on a completely new concept of landscape, and it was landscape architects who shaped their approach to organizing space.

They organized it very informally. When one of their great landscape designers – Lancelot "Capability" Brown, for instance – redesigned the landscape around a country

Prior Park, outside Bath. Designed by John Wood the Elder for Ralph Allen. Palladian symmetry in a landscape of studied informality.

house, the new landscape looked as if it had always been there. Unlike Le Notre and the other great French landscape architects, who sought to show that civilization gave man power over nature, the English designers aspired to show that civilization was natural – with the implication that milord's domination, like the rise of hills and the clumping of trees, was part of God's plan. And they did it at an unprecedented scale. Even the great Elizabethans, Burleigh and Sackville and the rest, had set their enormous houses in tightly walled gardens, carving out little islands of ordered beauty in a land of ugliness and chaos that they felt powerless to ameliorate. Their eighteenth-century successors took down the walls, called in armies of pick-and-shovel men, and made England a green and pleasant land.

But what would happen if people tried to build a town, or a city, that would combine classical architecture with the ordered informality of a landscape by Capability Brown? The answer is Bath, still probably the loveliest city ever built by speakers of the English language.

As its name implies, Bath was a health resort, centered on a group of hot mineral springs. It was the first city since Baiae in the days of Cicero whose only function was to allow people to get away from the stresses of running a country; and it was the first

Bath from the Air.

in the long line of fashion-setting resorts that runs to Newport and Miami. Hundreds of families came there for the Season every year, at considerable expense, merely for the pleasure of good company, whether or not they had an invalid member who needed to take the waters. Bath's draw was national, like London's, and it attracted prosperous people of all ranks, from the haughtiest of the titled to the daughters of country clergymen like Austen's Catherine Morland and her creator. This social breadth presented problems for conversation in the early eighteenth century, when social distinctions were obstructive, and the richest of commoners was still expected to bow to any peer and await his request to speak. But Bath had a kind of magic, and it was far away from London and the pressures of real power. People felt free to try things there, as they do at resorts today. And Bath had four men, strong characters all, who worked together for decades to create a wonderful social and physical place.

The first of these was an odd character named Richard Nash, invariably called "Beau" Nash, though he was no beauty. After failing at three or four things, including the army, Nash came to Bath in 1708 and gained success as a flamboyant social drill-

Men of Bath: Beau Nash, Ralph Allen, George Wade and John Wood the Elder.

sergeant. For fifty-three years, he had the official title of Master of Ceremonies, with duties that would be familiar to the Activities Director on a modern cruise ship, imposing his will on three generations of his social betters and forming England's first polite society. He banned swearing, dueling, and high-stakes gambling; he enforced the kind of conversational and social equality that Addison and Steele were modeling in *The Spectator*; and the most powerful people in England accepted his authority. It took decades for Nash to achieve his goal, but he had decades, and he got it done.

The second and third men, Ralph Allen and General George Wade, formed a team. Allen, known to contemporaries and posterity as "the Man of Bath," rose from poverty by reforming the regional postal system and earned the alliance of Wade, a Member of Parliament and the military commander of southwest England, by uncovering a treasonable plot in the mails. With his native ability and Wade's patronage, Allen rose quickly and soon controlled the national postal system, bringing him as much income as a nobleman. He bought the limestone quarries outside Bath and looked about for ways to make the physical Bath as splendid as Nash's social Bath. Wade brought parliamentary power and national connections. He also brought a firm commitment to Palladianism, to such a point that he built his London house to Burlington's design, on Burlington's land, next to Burlington House itself.

Finally, in 1727, by one of those English coincidences like the one that brought forth Inigo Jones, the fourth man arrived, the man who could translate Nash's politeness and the power of Allen and Wade into great architecture on a large scale. John Wood was a Bath native who had gone to work for a builder in the West End of London. He returned with West End tastes, a good deal of business acumen, and a bizarre but unshakeable belief in the greatness of his native town. He and Allen bonded immediately, and Wood set out to build beautifully in the stone from Allen's quarries. For Allen himself he built both an astonishing little city house in the heart of the city and Prior Park, the most satisfying of Palladian country houses.

With the support of Allen and Wade, and others, Wood brought the whole process of urban development – design, construction, and finance – under his control. Though humbly born and without formal training, he was the greatest English architect of his period, and he brought to the task a profound, if somewhat ridiculous, passion, based on a home-cooked mythology of Bath's greatness that involved Romans, Greeks, Druids, and King Solomon the Wise. Wood was the urban equivalent of Capability Brown. He could see whole landscapes yet lavish attention on tiny details. It was at Bath, under his guidance, that the gentry values of classicism and politeness first achieved grandeur through a marriage with the new English vision of ordered informality on a manorial scale.

Bath is the oddest place, a classical wonderland in a romantic landscape, a palace for five thousand families without a sovereign. It evolved over a period of a hundred years without any sacrifice of coherence, because its designers and developers, like all Englishmen in the long eighteenth century, remained true to the same general approaches in architecture and planning. This consistency, together with not infrequent flashes of genius, makes Bath a place, like Paris, that combines complete coherence with delightful surprises. Much of Bath is steep enough to make you wonder how invalids without modern footwear ever managed to get home – or to make you pity the burly men who carried sedan chairs and pushed "Bath Chairs" up and down the hills. And Bath benefited from the very eccentricity of its first great architect. You really do not want to know why John Wood wanted to build a huge Roman Circus at Bath – Druids were involved, and an ancient British king named Bladud – but you *do* want to walk around the Circus and marvel at it. It is the crowning work of an odd genius, a big clear window into an entire period of history, and a reminder that cranky people have often done the best job of creating smooth, balanced, classical art.

The Circus was modeled on the Theatre of Marcellus in Rome – a contemporary said that Wood had turned the Theatre of Marcellus inside-out – and it has the grandeur of a palace or an important public building; but it is not a public building. It is a ring of terraced houses, each modest in scale but forming, collectively, a creation of imperial grandeur. There are no visible lines between one house and the next, so that the whole composition looks like one great structure, three stories of engaged columns, garlands, and ram's skulls, all in perfect Palladian proportions. Unlike much English Palladianism, the Circus is warm and domestic as well as grand, and it glows with the honey-colored Bath Stone that Allen supplied and Wood was the first to cut finely. It would be nice to know if Wood had seen or heard of the circular Place des Victoires in Paris, which he surpassed.

By the time Wood designed the Circus – he did not live to complete it – he had already invented the central architectural symbol of England in his age. He took this revolutionary step at Queen Square, just down the hill from the Circus, a development project that occupied him from 1727 to 1736. Anyone who walks up the hill from the center of town and approaches the square beholds a palace in Palladian style, three

The Circus, Bath.

hundred feet long, with giant pilasters, a broad central pediment, and pavilions at either end. But no monarch ever had his seat at Bath, and Wood's palace is not a palace at all, but a terrace of seven individual houses.

No one in any country had ever conceived of such a thing before. Even the rulers of Amsterdam, who picked fights with the kings of Spain and England, had contented themselves with individual houses of greater-than-average size. Even the great men of London's West End, who chased two Stuarts from their thrones and wrecked the ambitions of Louis the Great, had shied away from the pretentiousness of linking private houses into the semblance of a royal palace. But magic Bath was a place for experiment. Here in this little resort, far from the pressures of power and statecraft, John Wood, self-taught and brilliantly half-crazy, found the right formula for representing his society's political realities through the art of architecture. He showed the noblemen and gentlemen of England how, by working together, they could be the equals of their king and the terror of his enemies.

From then on, for the rest of the Long Eighteenth Century, most terraces in Bath were palatial. Wood's son, John Wood the Younger, built the most spectacular terrace of all time, the Royal Crescent, a hundred yards or so from his father's Circus. It sits atop a green hillside like a giant Palladian country house. Those who think of it as a rival to Versailles are only doing what they are supposed to do.

With the completion of the Royal Crescent in 1774, Bath had an entire civic precinct of classical grandeur and meticulously-planned informality. It is all still there, in beautiful condition, and we can experience the symphonic progression of spaces and buildings that the Woods created. Like Capability Brown and the great landscape designers, they knew how to vary scale and elaboration as a composer varies tempo and texture. As you climb the hill on Barton Street, plain limestone terraces make a calm approach to Queen Square, which opens to your left like a trumpet call. Climbing farther, you walk past another quiet stretch of limestone fronts, by now called Gay Street, and then come to the great event of the Circus. Walking west on Brock Street, you are

The Royal Crescent, Bath.

surrounded by houses that are smaller than the Bath average and quite austere, such as you might find at the edge of a town, and you are not surprised to see green fields ahead. But the climax awaits, for the green fields are not open country and the end of town. They are the lawn of the Royal Crescent.

Just as resort fashions today eventually find their way into everyday life, so the innovations of Bath – the palace terraces, the elaborate classicism, even the facades of stone rather than brick – gradually filtered into British common-practice building, most visibly in the endless stucco terraces of London, whose stucco was originally painted and scored in imitation of Bath stone. But the first and greatest development in the school of Bath occurred in Edinburgh, the capital of Scotland.

Though the Act of Union in 1707 had abolished Scotland's Parliament, with a consequent flight of a few dozen ambitious people to London, the benefits of Union more than compensated for that loss. Scotland boomed to such an extent that tax receipts in 1800 were thirty times greater than they had been a century before. And Edinburgh was still the center of Scottish society, the seat of Scotland's national courts and its national church. It still had – still has – something of a capital's pride.

These things alone would have sufficed to make it a considerable place, a place "full of gentry". But Edinburgh added the yeast of culture to the flour of prosperity. The Long Eighteenth Century was its golden age in literature and scholarship. Edinburgh was the center of the Scottish Enlightenment, a place "crowded with genius." Its university gave the best teaching available in the British Isles, and literary lights from David Hume to Sir Walter Scott spent most of their lives there.

The New Town, Edinburgh, from the Air.

All the same, Edinburgh was an unlikely spot for English terraces of any kind, much less for palace-terraces in the manner of Bath. Its building traditions were utterly different from anything in England. Scotland was the only part of Great Britain in which townspeople dwelled in apartment buildings rather than single-family houses, and Edinburgh was by far the biggest, and the most overcrowded, of Scottish cities. As late as 1750, forty thousand people – Hume good-humoredly among them – clung to the city's vertiginous hillsides in tiny flats within seven-story buildings. The density of its population was Neapolitan, the state of its sanitation such that a generally uncomplaining age nicknamed it "Auld Reekie."

Fortunately, politics gave the city fathers a prod. They had not resisted Bonnie Prince Charlie's 1745 rebellion with adequate vigor, and his defeat left them with a sudden and pressing need to display their loyalty to the victorious House of Hanover in London. Everything in Scottish life became more English, including architecture and city design. It was to Edinburgh's advantage that Scottish city governments had much more power than their English counterparts. Edinburgh's city fathers were able to plan a large new extension of their territory, to buy land on their own authority, to hold a planning competition, and to specify an English pattern of development. The result,

Charlotte Square, Edinburgh.

Edinburgh's "New Town," arose in a thoroughly Bathonian style, with squares and long palatial terraces of single-family houses. The original street names celebrate the names and titles of the royal family, or the union of Scotland and England into one polity.

The New Town is a serious Bath, a sober Bath, a Calvinist Bath if you will, a Bath built for a learned town gentry of lawyers, doctors, professors, and Presbyterian divines. It is not informal. Its street plan is rigid and rectangular, with identical squares at each end of its main thoroughfare and public buildings to terminate important views. But no buildings could be more like those of Bath. Even Robert Adam, the London-based Scot whose hyper-refined buildings were the best British work of the late eighteenth century, paid John Wood the tribute of copying the seven houses of his palace terrace in Bath's Queen Square, then fifty years old.

Walk around the New Town with images of Bath in your mind. If Edinburgh's building stone were as warm as Bath's, you might mistake one place for the other. Generations of Edinburgh developers showed fidelity to Wood's style as they extended the New Town, in one section after another, deep into the nineteenth century. If anything, the resemblances to Bath increased through the years. Street plans became freer, and two great circuses varied the original grid. The first and greatest of all resorts inspired one of the finest urban districts in the world.

Ireland at Peace

Suppose every town in England had burnt down when Warwick did. It is not hard to imagine what would have happened. After much financial strain, and dozens of committee meetings, noblemen and gentlemen would have built an entire country full of towns with regular streets and regular houses. This, for different reasons, and with different mechanisms, is what actually happened in Ireland. When peace came to Ireland in 1660, after three quarters of a century of murderous warfare, a national rebuilding began which continued throughout the Long Eighteenth Century.

A good thing too. Ireland desperately needed towns in 1660. No part of Western Europe was so thoroughly rural. Even Dublin, the capital and by far the biggest city in the country, was only as big as Bristol, one-twentieth the size of London. Half a dozen smaller towns were on a par with Warwick, or only somewhat bigger, and that was more or less that. Most of the island was "beyond the Pale," where there had been no central government since the fourteenth century, and the incessant warfare of kings and chieftains had cut most of the island's trade routes and stifled the trading towns. It was not until the seventeenth century that Elizabeth, Cromwell, and William III, in their three frightful wars, created, however brutally, the preconditions for trade and trading towns; and new settlers, lured from England and Scotland, sketched a new urban network. When peace finally came, first in 1660, then finally in 1691, their grateful descendants began to color it in.

There were a lot of them to do it. Historians estimate that 300,000 settlers came to Ireland from England and Scotland in the century between 1600 and 1700. This is as many British settlers as came to the American colonies in the same period, a fact that should get the reconstitution of Ireland more notice than historians in Britain or America generally give it. In many ways, Ireland's new settlers found what their cousins were finding in North America: a fertile country with a native population that was poor, rural, tribal, and resentful; and, like their American cousins, they set about creating a new world without much reference to the traditions they were displacing. But there was a crucial difference. The Irish were Europeans, used to farming, hierarchy, and smallpox. They did not die or move away, as Native Americans did. They were always there, the English always a watchful minority.

Not since 1066 had English history offered so many bold men an opportunity to rise in the world. In fits and starts through the bloody seventeenth century, tens of thousands of them gained independent farmsteads, several thousand amassed large estates, and hundreds acquired hereditary titles. They made a second England. Ireland had its own nobility and gentry, its own Parliament, its own Houses of Commons and of Lords. Irish gentlemen and Irish peers administered Irish counties through the familiar mechanisms of Quarter Sessions and Grand Juries. They built hundreds of country houses, some of which stand comparison with any houses in England, and they shaped hundreds of landscapes in the English manner of ordered informality.

Ireland once more became a significant part of Europe during the Long Eighteenth Century. It sometimes seems that half of the great writers of the English language in the Augustan Age were Irish. Johnson's Club would have been a poor place without Edmund Burke and Richard Brinsley Sheridan – and that is not to mention Oliver Goldsmith, Maria Edgeworth, and Bishop Berkeley. To form their taste, Irishmen had Trinity College in Dublin, which grounded them in Cicero and Vergil. To pay their builders, they had what still counts as the longest period of peace and prosperity that Ireland has ever seen. Year after year, crops and cattle went to market, sheep were sheared, flax was harvested, wool and linen were spun and woven. Irish butter supplied Spain and Portugal, and Dublin ranked among the largest trading partners of Bordeaux. Arthur Young, the greatest agronomist of the age, thought that no country in the world had ever advanced as quickly as Ireland.

All this prosperity required far more buying and selling, shipping and investing, than Ireland's urban network could accommodate. The old towns – except for Dublin – were battered by a century of war, their merchant oligarchies broken, their trade at a standstill. Though new towns had been founded in the seventeenth century, they were little more than walled trading posts, altogether inadequate to the tasks of peace. After 1660, and more so after the final peace of 1691, the Irish set about rebuilding their old settlements and turning their new ones into real towns. They wanted what their contemporaries wanted in England, regular streets and buildings; and they could get those things with a good deal less trouble, inasmuch as the rights of conquest had given many Irish landlords more control than Lord Brooke enjoyed at Warwick. Under such circumstances, the rural gentry played an even greater role in town planning and development than was the case in England – as great a role, in fact, as barons and bishops had played in the creation of new towns during the Middle Ages. Irish historians like to say that every Irish town is a castle-and-a-town, and the castle usually controlled the town.

This is why Irish towns, even the smallest of them, are regular and classical. The simplest are double files of houses along a stretch of road, inland versions of the little Dike Towns in the Netherlands, which they resemble; and houses are almost always connected to form continuous street-walls. The Irish did not build row houses out of necessity. Land was virtually free in conquered Ireland, as it was in North America, and towns were small; town planners could easily have laid out building plots big enough for free-standing houses. But the planners and builders of the new urban Ireland were Britons of the Long Eighteenth Century. They wanted what other Britons wanted in England and Scotland, and they seized the opportunity to build street after street, town after town, of polite regularity. Other than churches and the occasional castle, there are no pre-classical buildings in Irish towns. These were swept ruthlessly aside, often because their owners had been on the losing side in one civil war or another. The fascinating Rothe House, one of several dozen big merchant houses in sixteenth-century Kilkenny, somehow survived the banishment of its builders and is apparently the only pre-1600 town house still standing in the whole country.

The Long Eighteenth Century still shapes the look of Irish towns and the daily lives of Irish townspeople. Its classical buildings and streetscapes are still mainly there, preserved by economic stagnation in the early nineteenth century and depopulation after the famines that began in 1846. Ireland has fewer medieval buildings than any country in Europe, and fewer Victorian buildings than any country on either coast of the North Atlantic.

Maurice Craig, the great historian of Dublin's architecture, says the Renaissance came to Ireland in 1660, when James Butler, Duke of Ormond in the Peerage of Ireland, returned to Dublin as Viceroy after sharing the exile of Charles II. Ormond was the right man for the job. He was firm and steady and patient, with wide experience and wide culture, and he exercised vice-regal authority for twenty-eight years. From his seat in Dublin Castle, he inspired Dublin's bankrupt city government to replenish its treasury by forming a fashionable square on the London model and selling building lots to noblemen and gentlemen. The result, Stephen's Green, is still the largest square in Europe and still the center of polite Dublin. In Kilkenny, the Butler family stronghold, he began by turning his old grey castle into a Renaissance palace, with French gardens

O'Connell Street, Birr,
County Offaly.

and an entrance worthy of baroque Rome. Beneath his walls, he created The Parade, a tiny Mall for social walking. Whether the scale was large or small, Ormond set the pattern, and all Irish towns would follow it. Each would have a polite end of town, usually close to a castle, with a mall or parade.

If you want to experience this kind of town at its best, you can hardly do better than Birr, formerly Parsonstown, in County Offaly, at the very center of the country. Here, generations of the Parsons family, English adventurers eventually ennobled as Earls of Rosse in the Peerage of Ireland, patiently turned a fortified camp into a useful market town and an oasis of well-designed politeness. They started with a castle, seized from the princely O'Carrolls, a practical piece of military architecture that withstood bombardment as late as 1691. What passed for the town was merely a little market space beside the castle gate,. By the end of the next century, the town had a proper street of regular three-story buildings, with a square at the top of the hill and a triumphal column celebrating the Duke of Cumberland's victory at Culloden, conceivably the grandest architectural monument ever raised in a town of five hundred people.

As the town grew in the early nineteenth century (perhaps to fifteen hundred people – the scale of Birr is always miniature) the square became its center, with the best inns and a couple of substantial houses; and a polite end of town developed beyond the square. This was largely the work of the second Earl of Rosse, who in 1810 moved the

Oxmantown Mall, Birr.

castle gate several hundred yards and connected it to the main street, at a point beyond the square, with a grassy promenade for social walking. This is the Oxmantown Mall, a rare and precious survival, unspoiled by traffic and new buildings, bordered by a row of large, neat, classical houses that are flawlessly maintained and hospitably inhabited today. The overall effect is of great dignity on an intimate scale. By 1828, that work done, the Earl created a second mall a block away, centered on a beautifully-proportioned little Greek temple and framed on all sides with charming houses. Birr now had its own dollhouse version of the West End. If modern Ireland's authorities managed car traffic today as well as the Dutch do, Birr would give as much pleasure, and attract as many visitors, as any small town in the Netherlands.

Ireland's few real cities were predictably more complicated than the small towns. No single landowner ever controlled an entire Irish city, and each city had a merchant oligarchy that was master in its own house. But in this very rural country, where the owners of the land had overwhelming political and economic power, city governments, even more than their English counterparts, made the attraction of gentry families a part of their economic development strategies. The result, in one Irish city after another, was a bifurcated structure like that in Birr (or London, for that matter), with merchants at one end of town and gentry at the other.

This is splendidly visible in Waterford, a port city of moderate size on the south

Trinity College, Dublin.

coast. As trade expanded in the years of peace, the city government built almost a mile of quays along the waterfront, and merchants responded by building almost a mile of handsome quayside warehouses. Meanwhile, a hundred yards back from the water, on the top of a little hill, a polite neighborhood arose around the Protestant Cathedral, where the Bishop's very classical palace took the place of a castle. From its high terrace, the Bishop could – and we still can – survey strollers on a Mall below and playgoers at a Theatre Royal. Every Irish city did similar things. Limerick built a new quarter of elegant four-story terraced houses on a grid of regular streets, all centered on a spacious square. In Cork, if you walk down the Grand Parade and turn left on the South Mall, you can still see enough gentry houses from the late eighteenth and early nineteenth centuries to understand why one of these streets is called Mall and the other Parade.

For all the interest and beauty in Ireland's towns and cities, nothing in Ireland prepares you for Dublin, one of the great cities of the world. It was, and is, nearly as big and nearly as beautiful as Amsterdam. It grew to be the second city of the British Empire in the eighteenth century, with a population of 180,000 when Cork had 30,000 and Bristol 70,000. And it was a capital. Ireland was almost a nation, its Parliament almost a national government. A Viceroy, seated in Dublin Castle, exercised quasi-royal

Mount Street Upper.

power and kept a court that was the center of national Society. Hundreds of rural grandees, titled and otherwise, had houses in Dublin. Most lived in long brick terraces, with here and there the swagger of a family palace.

Georgian Dublin is the only place in the world where you can see and feel what the great streets and quarters of eighteenth-century London were like. Dublin's builders worked at London scale and in the London style, and it is all, or almost all, still there, undisturbed by Nazi bombs or twentieth-century developers. If you walk from the top of O'Connell Street to the bottom of Harcourt Street – it will take you at least half an hour – you will be in a magnificent Georgian environment almost every step of the way. You will see continuous vistas of grand, uniform terraces. You will pass Trinity College, a splendid ensemble of classical buildings, far bigger than any college at Oxford or Cambridge. And, every block or so, you will meet squares, some of them small, three of them among the biggest ever planned, with heart-breaking greenery inside the trim iron fences. If you stand in the middle of Molesworth Street, closely enframed by four-story brick terraces of the eighteenth century, you will find yourself staring at Leinster House, a splendid Palladian

James Gandon. The Four Courts, Dublin.

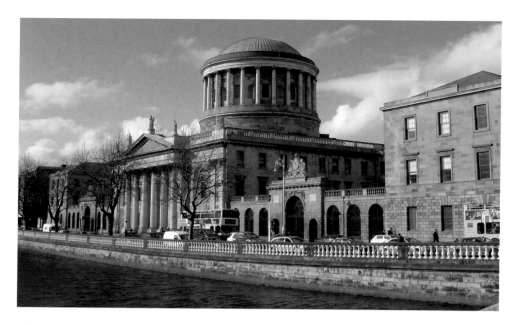

palace of 1745, now the Irish Parliament; and you will realize that Georgian Dublin was built to be the capital of a nation. This is the city where Jonathan Swift, the Dean of one of Dublin's two Protestant cathedrals, wrote *Gulliver's Travels* and *A Modest Proposal*. Here came George Frederick Handel, at the Viceroy's invitation, for the premiere of *Messiah* and a season of concerts that made him a rich man.

For much of the Long Eighteenth Century, Dublin was the only British city other than London that built enough, and grandly enough, to support architects. Dublin's architects had national – Irish – practices and built for the state as well as for the nobility and gentry. There was enough work of all kinds to attract and retain first-rate talents. Edward Lovett Pearce, an Irish gentleman with a seat in the Irish House of Commons, studied architecture with his cousin, Sir John Vanbrugh, the leading English architect of the early eighteenth century, and found his style in the buildings and books of Palladio. He designed the Parliament he sat in, a columned tour de force that is now the Bank of Ireland, and began a brilliant career that death ended too soon. But Dublin and Ireland were dynamic enough to keep going and draw talent from outside the country. Richard Cassel, the dominant figure at mid-century, came from Germany. He must have been able to work magic with builders. His buildings, like the Bishop's Palace at Waterford, are beautifully constructed and impeccably correct. James Gandon, trained in the office of Sir William Chambers in London, came to Ireland in the 1780s and built the buildings by which Dublin is best known today. His career began with the delicate splendor of the Custom House and ended, almost thirty years later, with the moody, powerful splendor of the Four Courts.

Dublin was not only a political and social center. It was also Ireland's largest port, its financial center, and its center of skilled craft work. Thousands of skilled artisans made luxuries and necessities, and Dublin's merchants exported more of Ireland's cattle, linen, and grain than the rest of Ireland's ports combined. In firm control of the city's government, they used their power to build roads and canals that extended their trade, and they embanked the River Liffey with a long series of commercial quays, lined with rows of four-story brick buildings that still give it the scale and feel of the larger canals of Leyden. But their ideas of grandeur were not grand enough for the noblemen and gentlemen who increasingly came to Dublin for Parliament and the Season. The builders of Ireland's country houses had worked with great landscape architects and learned their lessons. They could imagine vast spaces, improved and ordered by human skill. Thus, in 1757, the Lords and Commons of Ireland took the unprecedented step of seizing the power to plan and build much of their capital city.

For the next fifty years, the noblemen and gentlemen of Parliament's aptly-named Wide Streets Commission widened old streets, laid out new ones, and regulated the design and construction of buildings. Not since the four-canal plan of Amsterdam, almost a century and a half before, had any group of men possessed so broad a mandate to design and re-design a major European city. What the governments of London and Warwick had done in an emergency, the Irish Parliament did voluntarily, without necessity, for the open and avowed purpose of making Dublin grander and more beautiful.

If you go to Dublin today, you will see the work of the Wide Streets Commission without being conscious of it. It is regular, and it is bold. In the fashionable part of the city, which lies to the east of Dublin Castle and occupies a good deal of land on both sides of the river, streets are broad and straight. Impressive public buildings terminate vistas, and the streets are framed with terraces of big, plain, elegant houses. The architecture of these houses is so simple, so severe, that photographs make them look dull. They are not dull when you walk the streets of Dublin. They make their effect, not in short bursts of poetry, but in great coherent masses of prose, in the length of the terraces that they form, the warmth of their red brick walls, the broad and welcoming delicacy of their fanlit doors. It is all still here, preserved for two centuries in the amber of poverty, and recalled to life by the roar of the Celtic Tiger.

For a long time it was the fashion to ignore Irish towns. Foreigners came to Ireland for its enchanting countryside. The Irish themselves, after the end of British rule, tended to look on their British-model towns as symbols of oppression. Only in recent years, through the work of Patrick Shaffrey, of the Irish Georgian Society, of Anngret Simms and David Dickson and a remarkable community of urban historians have Irish towns begun to come into their own. It now makes sense to visit Ireland for the sake of its towns, almost as one would visit Holland.

Metropolitan Improvements

While the Scots, the Irish, and the small-town English were adopting London ways of building, London itself kept growing at a feverish rate. Its population roughly doubled between 1700 and 1800. This was the London of which Johnson said: "When a man is tired of London, he is tired of life." Joseph Haydn, arriving in the 1790s after a lifetime in imperial Vienna, was dumbfounded by London's size.

For all that, the most remarkable thing about London's physical development was its continuity. A London house of 1800 differed only subtly from a London house of 1700. Londoners followed and developed the fashions that Jones and Wren and the Rebuilding Act had set in the 1600s. Londoners walked on malls, practiced conversation, and praised each other's politeness. All the while, their builders were running up enough terraces of Dutch-style houses to accommodate an extra half- million people. Old squares like St. James' and Lincoln's Inn Fields remained first-rate addresses; and dozens of new squares – Hanover, Berkeley, and Grosvenor chief among them – followed their pattern. Streets adhered to the approach worked out in Great Queen Street and codified in the Rebuilding Act. The only significant change in domestic architecture was that facades grew plainer, as fire regulations in 1707 and 1767 banned wooden cornices and narrowed the wooden frames of windows. Most of Georgian London looked as its principal imitator, Georgian Dublin, still looks.

It was in the eighteenth century that Britain chased the French from America and India and built an empire on which the sun never set, and London became an imperial capital. It did not, however, acquire the trappings of one. No great boulevards terminated at palaces or churches. The only large public monument was the old column erected by Wren and Hooke in the 1670s to commemorate the Great Fire. Britain's imperial kings held court in a rambling old-fashioned palace without grandeur or grounds, and Earls and Marquesses returned from court to terraced brick houses like those of Dutch burghers. This was a good omen. It offered the hope that a free people could attain greatness without subjecting itself to the glamour of kings, priests, or generals.

All was not perfect, to be sure. The glittering London of Handel and Horace Walpole was also the desperate London of Hogarth and Jonathan Wild, gin-soaked, crime-ridden, and poxy. Except in the West End, and in prosperous new middle-class neighborhoods north of the City, most new development was cheap and unregulated. Peter Guillery is only now teaching us how much of unfashionable London was still being built of wood, and how many small houses were designed for renting out floor-by-floor as multi-family housing. But there was general progress, even in the poorest areas. The cheap wooden houses of eighteenth-century London were nothing like the medieval rookeries that had

burned in 1666. They had outlines and details like those of their brick cousins in Warwick – or Ireland, or Holland – and their facades were fitted snugly against the street. They differed only in size and material from the houses of richer people. High and low, then, London was architecturally coherent. It was also, by the standards of the day, healthy. Its people lived much longer than their contemporaries in Paris, where residential densities soared far beyond the London average.

All the same, it is hard to contemplate eighteenth-century London without a certain feeling of disappointment. A city is more than the sum of its buildings. It needs a general, binding order as an omelet needs eggs. Bath has such an order, intuitive and sinuous. Edinburgh has such an order, clear and rational. Dublin's order is a bit of both. London in the eighteenth century came perilously close to having no binding order at all.

This was not for want of competent architects: there was never a moment when the London building market could not, by a mere snapping of its fingers, summon to its service any architect in the three united kingdoms, and the eighteenth century was a good time for British architecture. The fault lay in the community as a whole. As has often happened, London had outgrown the imagination of its age. The men of the eighteenth century could not hold it all in their minds, could not see it through the tangle

Belgrave Square. Casual observers have trouble believing that this massive structure is actually a row of houses, each only three windows wide.

of personalities and institutions that obscured their vision. It was too big to be shaped by a small coterie, like the four men of Bath, and it lacked a unified city government, like Edinburgh's.

In the resulting vacuum, most London landowners developed their properties as if there were nothing else around them. Most eighteenth-century developments were too small for effective private planning, a few acres at most, and the tools for public planning had not been forged. Sloppiness and bewilderment resulted. Handsome streets dead-ended at property lines, and no one had the power to connect one developer's street to another's. Only Parliament had the power to make the vast metropolis usable and readable, and the nobility and gentry of England would have been grateful to them for doing it; but it is sad that the English Parliament seems never to have considered doing what the Irish Parliament actually did.

London muddled through, of course, as it always seems to do. The Fire Court had done its work well in the City, and three old roads (the Strand, Piccadilly, and the Oxford Road, now Oxford Street) gave the rapidly-swelling body of the West End a rudimentary skeleton. But great opportunities were missed. In the absence of a Wide Streets Commission, London's architects and developers built buildings, streets, and squares for a century and more, many of them handsome and some of them glorious, without creating cherished or memorable urban places. This left their work easy prey for developers in the 1920s and 30s, and most of the best houses in eighteenth-century London were gone before the Blitz.

Finally, in the last third of the eighteenth century, two noble families, the Russells and the Grosvenors, undertook to develop projects that had enough acreage for good planning. The Grosvenor Estate alone was as big as all of Georgian Dublin. The Russell

Russell Square in Bloomsbury.

Estate was almost as big as Georgian Bath. Both estates had competent management and pursued consistent strategies over multiple generations. In their service, James Burton and Thomas Cubitt – the first really big developers, it would seem, in history – built thousands of houses in harmony.

The results show what London could have achieved earlier if someone had created an agency or Commission to coordinate smaller developments. The Russells and Burton made Bloomsbury a beautiful and coherent network of terraces and squares. The Grosvenors and Cubitt, slightly later, called forth a hundred acres of order and grandeur in Belgravia and Pimlico. Though Pimlico was heavily bombed, Belgravia stands today as Cubitt built it, rank on rank of giant houses forming squares like Wellington's fusiliers at Waterloo. Cubitt's architects gave terraced houses an architecture of command and discipline, befitting the seat of a global empire. Belgravian addresses are still, in most cycles of the housing market, the most desirable on earth.

The finishing touch to London's transformation came from almost the last place that any observer of Georgian England would have expected, the Crown. After a drought in royal building lasting more than a century, George III went mad in 1811, and his extravagant son took over as Prince Regent, dreaming of an imperial capital. The Regent was slippery enough to get money, and he had at his disposal a man, John Nash, who could think and build at an imperial scale. To say that Nash was an architect is like saying that Walt Disney was a cartoonist. Nash was a producer of extraordinary environments. Though his buildings were often poorly built and crudely detailed – he sketched them on small pieces of paper and left the fine points to others – he could make a street twist and turn without losing its Roman dignity, and he stuccoed his buildings (the first London architect to do so as a general rule) to imitate the finely-cut blocks and warm golden browns of Bath stone.

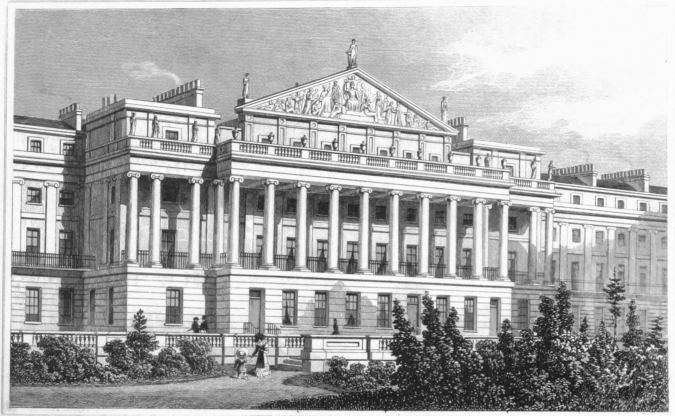

Drawn by Tho. H. Shepherd. Engraved by W. Wolf.

THE CENTRE OF CUMBERLAND TERRACE, REGENT'S PARK.

Cumberland Terrace, Regent's Park. From Metropolitan Improvements.

And luck was with him. No sooner had the Regent assumed his powers than the large Marylebone estate, hundreds of acres at the north end of fashionable London, reverted to the Crown. While the Regent courted Parliament and overspent his income, Nash turned part of Marylebone into a huge park, Regent's Park, and connected it to the Regent's palace on the Mall by threading a magnificent shopping street, Regent Street, through the seam between the West End and Soho. Suddenly, the vast blob of London was an organism with a spine. The whole thing was a triumph both of design and of business. In fifteen years of work, Nash created a high proportion of the places by which London is known today: Piccadilly Circus, Trafalgar Square, Regent Street itself, and Buckingham Palace, which Nash remodeled after his profligate patron bought it from the even more profligate Duke of Buckingham. Although Nash did not bring the palace-terrace to London, he created the most spectacular of them, almost a mile of them, to make a frame for Regent's Park. It is hard to believe that Nash's terraces are just rows of moderate-size houses rather than royal residences or government ministries.

Cumberland Terrace, Regent's Park, today.

A British Urban Renaissance

In 1827, Thomas Shepherd and James Elmes published a book called *Metropolitan Improvements*, celebrating the new classical London in page after page of beautiful engravings. Their London is mainly the London of noblemen and gentlemen, improved by taste and skill like a great country house landscape. Shepherd and Elmes are full of pride in what has risen around them in their own lifetime, and they look forward confidently to more and more of the same. The city depicted on their pages is the wonder of the world, the central city of western civilization. Her rivals in Paris, having wasted a generation in revolution and war, have fallen far behind, and will remain so for several decades.

It is easy to see why Britons like Shepherd and Elmes were proud of their country and its capital in 1827. The three kingdoms of the British Isles had put civil and religious war behind them and become The United Kingdom, the stable hub of a world empire. Byron, Shelley, and especially Scott were the central authors of the western world; Constable and especially Turner were the central painters; and London, without peer, was the central city. Britons had built the greatest city in the world, and they had formed a great national building culture based on the terraced house.

In 1827, a traveler could go from the southeastern corner of England to the northwestern corner of Ireland in the calm expectation of finding good inns, skilled craftsmen, graveled malls, coffee houses, and a schedule of Assemblies in purpose-built ballrooms. Best of all, he, – or she – could expect to find good conversation, whether in the lovely rooms within Georgian houses or in the equally lovely outdoor rooms – streets and squares, crescents and parades – formed by rows of regular buildings.

Like him – or her – we owe a great debt to the nobility and gentry of Britain's Long Eighteenth Century.

Chapter Four

NEW URBAN WORLDS

In 1607, when the first three little ships of London's Virginia Company dropped anchor at Jamestown and began what we think of as American history, the North Atlantic revolution of architecture and city design had not yet begun. Amsterdam was still wooden, London still indistinguishable from half-timbered Paris; and those first Virginia explorers, Captain John Smith and the rest, were carrying building traditions that were about to become obsolete at home. And home was far away. The ocean was two months wide at best, and often deadly. Over the next century, as England and Holland revolutionized the design of buildings and cities, how likely was it that later generations of Americans, born in the New World, would follow the lead of people three thousand miles away?

Consider how Britain's American colonists re-framed the institutions of British government. If they had simply copied the standard political arrangements of England in 1607 and followed England's lead through the political revolutions of the seventeenth century, America would have become Ireland. There would have been a nobility and a gentry, Quarter Sessions and Cathedrals, and a central government with a bi-cameral Parliament in a capital city. None of this happened. The constitution of each colony differed from England's in important ways, and most colonies differed politically from each other – theocratic republics in New England, Proprietary families in Maryland and Pennsylvania, Royal Governors in Virginia and the Carolinas, a philanthropic penal colony in Georgia. No part of North America reproduced anything like the full array of English political institutions. Instead, different groups of American settlers picked and chose among the elements of England's political tradition, and differences with the Mother Country grew larger over time rather than smaller.

For most of America's colonial period things were similar when it came to the building of houses, churches, and towns. There was no uniformity from one colony or region to another.

To some extent, how American settlers built houses and towns depended on where they had come from. Different counties and regions in England and Holland had distinct building cultures. More important, however, was *when* people emigrated. Did they leave before, during, or after the seventeenth-century revolution in architecture and city design?

The Atlantic Ocean. By John Thomson, 1814.

The first American colonists, landing in Virginia in 1607, came before the seventeenth-century urban revolution, but this would matter little, since neither the first Virginians nor their descendants built any towns worth the name for almost two hundred years. They planted tobacco, created representative government, and instituted racial slavery in a landscape of scattered wooden houses that owed nothing to Inigo Jones. Up to the Revolution and beyond, almost every Virginia planter could live on a deep Tidewater river and ship tobacco from his own dock, dealing with British merchants face-to-face in his house and trading hogsheads of tobacco for a floating department store of British goods. He had no need for local merchants or local craftsmen, thus no need for towns. Even Virginia's colonial capital, Williamsburg, was never more than a village of wooden houses with fewer than a thousand people – albeit with an ambitious street plan, four or five impressive public buildings, and enough charm to delight millions of modern tourists.

Nonetheless, towns or no towns, Virginians in the colonial period kept closely in touch with the mother country. The ships that brought shovels and damask to a planter's door brought books as well. Thomas Jefferson, born in Virginia in 1743, studied the works of living Scottish philosophers in his youth, and planters and builders alike could take their choice from among the builder's guides – Batty Langly, Thomas Halfpenny, and the like – that were helping to spread the London style throughout the English and Irish countryside.

The most valuable British merchandise that came to Virginia docks, however, was living British people. Every merchant on every ship was a profit-motivated missionary for the latest British fashions, full of news and advice about everything from plows to periwigs. Even more important were the thousands of Englishmen and Englishwomen who came to Virginia as indentured servants, paying their passage by promising to work for an American master. Many had marketable skills and wanted the opportunity that America offered to hard-working people without capital.

It is hard to find a better example than William Buckland, a trained London joiner who came to Virginia in 1755 under indentures to George Mason, the father of America's Bill of Rights, and carved the magnificent woodwork that still amazes visitors at Gunston Hall, his master's house on the Potomac. Once out of his indentures, Buckland became the best architect in the Chesapeake country of Virginia and Maryland. His two last masterpieces, the Chase-Lloyd House and Hammond-Harwood House, still face each other across a lucky street in Annapolis, Maryland's capital, and are open to the public. More than any books, people like Buckland kept this region in the main current of British architecture.

Buckland was lucky in his timing. The Chesapeake was home to a mature society by 1755, and its leading families were embarked on a building boom. Buckland found plenty of work, and he had plenty of competitors who were eager to make their fortunes by bringing the British Urban Renaissance to the notice of prosperous planters. By the

outbreak of the Revolution, in 1775, Virginians and Marylanders had built a hundred or more well-proportioned brick houses that resembled the best houses in polite English towns. Thanks to their work, anyone from the Chesapeake country today feels at home in a red-brick English town like Warwick or Holt or Chichester. Although it would be a very long time before Chesapeake planters needed to have ideas about building towns, their ideas would be North Atlantic ideas when the time came.

Very different were the next American settlers, and they arrived at a very different moment in the seventeenth-century architectural revolution. They were Dutch, representatives of the Dutch West India Company. Unlike the disorganized Londoners who founded Virginia, they knew that they wanted to build a permanent settlement and set about doing it promptly. Moreover, by the time they founded New Amsterdam, at the tip of Manhatton Island, the year was 1624, and old Amsterdam was already building revolutionary buildings. We do not have to guess that their settlement participated in the Dutch architectural revolution. Thanks to the visual culture of the Dutch Golden Age, there are more seventeenth-century views of New Amsterdam than of all the towns in English North America put together. We can see that the little settlement rapidly

William Buckland, the Hammond-Harwood House, Annapolis.

became a proper Dutch town, with a market place, a church, a fort, rows of gable-fronted houses, and a small canal coming in from the East River. Vermeer could have found little streets to immortalize.

Unfortunately, the streets of New Amsterdam, and the town itself, remained little for much longer than they needed to. Although the directors of the West India Company had a clear vision, their vision was selfish and myopic. Their New Amsterdam was to be a mere trading post in the fur trade. Company officials were to do all the real work, the buying and selling of furs, for the Company's sole benefit. The rest of the inhabitants could only load things, unload things, and give trappers and sailors and Indian traders a good time.

And so it was for decades. Though the people of the little town were a vigorous polyglot crew from the start, they were not citizens. They were just workers in a company town, firmly under the thumb of corporate managers. The effects of this were baleful. No one who wanted to be a merchant or a civic leader had any reason to come to New Amsterdam, and the West India Company was strong enough to frustrate the few people who tried to spread their wings. Although the Company relaxed its control in 1653, and English conquerors in 1664 gave their re-christened New York a regular English town charter, the little town suffered long from the political and commercial passivity forced on it by its corporate founder, and it missed out for decades on the trade that made other North American towns rich.

Gradually, however, it moved up-tempo. As new settlers filtered in after the English conquest, English and Dutch people worked together, intermarried, and built an Anglo-Dutch culture symbolized in the name of Franklin Roosevelt. The Dutch building culture merged gracefully with its cousin, the new London way of building.

Different yet again was the next town to be settled. Boston, founded in 1630, was the first large American town founded by English settlers and the first English town in America to grow to any size. It was the center of Puritan New England, the well-organized religious Utopia of English Calvinists persecuted by King Charles I and his Archbishop of Canterbury. From the point of view of architecture and city design, however, the theology of Boston's founders was less important than the timing of Boston's founding. Boston was born in the "Great Migration" of Puritans that began in 1630 and ended abruptly in 1642. After that date, English Puritans rebelled rather than emigrating, and hardly anyone came to New England from anywhere else until the Irish Potato Famine of the 1840s. There were few William Bucklands in Boston, if any.

What this meant for the building of Boston was that the new London way of building never reached it. Boston's founders left England before the building of Covent Garden and Great Queen Street. When a traveler named Josselyn wrote of Boston, in 1663, that "the houses were for the most part … close together on each side of the street as in London," he meant the jumbled London of 1663, the pre-fire London of narrow lanes and

NIEUW AMSTERDAM OFTE NUE NIEUW IORX OPT TEYLANT MAN

New Amsterdam.

frame buildings set higgledy-piggledy to the street. Two years later, a Royal Commission, probably including men who knew the West End, wrote more sharply of Boston: "Their houses are generally wooden, their streets crooked, with little decency and no uniformity".

Wooden Boston had great fires roughly every twenty years for its first century, each consuming hundreds of buildings, and Bostonians could have rectified their town's deficiencies as London and Warwick did. If they failed, it was not for want of good will, at least in the short run. They understood that close-packed wooden buildings were a fire hazard, and Boston's Town Meetings responded to every great fire by decreeing that all new buildings would henceforth be built of brick or stone. But Boston did not have a Lord Brooke to make sure that people did what they had promised to do, nor did Boston's labor force include men who had helped to rebuild the City of London. Time

Paul Revere's House, Boston.

and again, the inhabitants rebuilt in wood, the only way they knew. The Town Meeting renewed its fruitless decrees in every generation after every great fire, and Boston was still a town of wooden buildings when Paul Revere rode.

This is by no means to say that colonial Boston was a failure. For the whole of the seventeenth century, and some of the eighteenth, Boston was the biggest and the richest city in North America. It was Bostonians who pioneered the West Indian trade network that all urban Americans would follow until after the Revolution. Josselyn noticed this as it was happening and described Boston as "the mart town of the West Indies". Bostonians talk little today about their West Indian connections, but there would be no Boston without them.

It is not hard to understand why Bostonians are reticent about the West Indies. England's West Indian islands were nothing to be proud of. They were purgatories for enslaved Africans and vile monocultures that grew sugar for export and imported everything else. Founded at roughly the same time as the New England colonies, they devoted every possible acre and person-hour to the cultivation of their cash crop and imported everything else: tools, clothing, even food. When the English Revolution of 1642 disrupted transatlantic shipping, they became fair game for Americans with seaworthy boats and something to sell. From then on, Bostonians and to a lesser extent Newporters loaded their little ships with grain, lumber, hardware, salt fish, and cattle on the hoof and sailed for the West Indies. This was the making of Boston as a mercantile town and the foundation of American trade. Sooner or later, every port on the North American coast would trade whatever its farmers could grow, whatever its fishermen could catch, whatever its craftsmen could make, for sugar and rum from the West Indies. Boston and New York today have neighborhoods named after Jamaica.

Still more different was the next American city, Philadelphia. It was not founded until 1682, sixteen years after the Great Fire of London, and it participated from its earliest days in the new London way of building. Plain brick houses did not offend its Quaker principles, and it had at its head an English gentleman, William Penn, with gentry tastes and the will to shape his town as Lord Brooke had shaped Warwick. Penn could also draw on his experience at managing family lands in Ireland, a useful thing in a *tabula rasa* colony, and he had a grant of powers from the Crown like those of an Irish planter.

Penn was a careful man. He planned his new town before crossing the ocean and brought a surveyor with him to ensure that his ideas would attain physical form – something that neither the Puritans nor the Dutch had bothered to do. His plan gave Philadelphia the clearest, most orderly urban structure in the North Atlantic world of 1682, a perfectly regular grid pattern of streets covering more than two square miles, with a square of ten acres at the center and an eight-acre square at each of the town's four corners.

Penn hoped that Philadelphia would be "a greene country town," and his plan defined blocks big enough for market gardening. This was not to be, as Quakers proved to be good merchants and soon wrested much of the West Indian trade from their Puritan rivals in Boston and Newport. Fortunately, Philadelphians found ways to adapt Penn's plan to the needs of a trading city. By 1700, smaller streets and alleys were subdividing Penn's big blocks, each new street lined with brick row houses of various sizes and floor plans.

Penn did not concern himself with regulating architecture, but he did not need to. His colonists wanted the new London way of building as much as he did. By 1682, when Philadelphia was first settled, the rebuilding of London had been complete for eight years. Many of the first settlers were familiar with post-fire London; some, probably, were builders who had worked there. Philadelphia soon began to emerge as a town of regular brick houses with proper alignment on broad streets. It is significant that the biggest brick house built in Philadelphia in the 1680s was known, not as "the brick house," but as "the slate roof house". This tells us that slate was unusual; brick could be taken for granted. By 1700, Philadelphia must have looked like a big riverfront Warwick, and the old streets of this great city, shaped by rows of houses in a warm Dutch red, still recall Delft and Leiden.

Elfreth's Alley, Philadelphia.

The last of the big colonial cities was founded late, in 1729, with no thought that it would ever become populous or dense. This was Baltimore, on a tributary of Chesapeake Bay in the Proprietary colony of Maryland. Unlike the other large colonial cities, Baltimore was not the capital of its province. It was a private land speculation, promoted by landowners in a newly-settled county who needed a village from which they could ship tobacco to England. The new town almost failed when it turned out the surrounding countryside was bad for tobacco; but a perceptive Irish visitor saved the day in 1754 by initiating a trade of Baltimore County wheat, which grew abundantly, for Ulster linen. In short order, Baltimore blossomed under the tutelage of Ulster linen merchants.

Because Baltimore was founded so late, it is the best-documented place to trace the process of maturing from a small settlement of frame buildings to a proper brick North Atlantic city, a process that occurred in most North American cities. A group of wooden row houses, now brightly painted and maintained like racing yachts, still stands in the waterfront neighborhood of Fells Point; and, by something approaching a miricle, three tiny wooden shanties survive nearby. Baltimore, however, matured fast. Brick became standard in the 1780s, and Baltimore has been a part of the North Atlantic urban world ever since.

*Wooden Row Houses,
Fells Point, Baltimore.*

If you had visited these four cities from some part of Britain in about 1790, you would have known what to make of them. Boston would have struck you as a strange fossil, a century and a half behind the latest fashions of the British Urban Renaissance. New York would have seemed more up-to-date, and Philadelphia would have impressed you as thoroughly modern. You would probably have marveled that a place so small, so middle-class, and so far from London could be neater and more orderly than any town in England. In Baltimore, you would have seen new rows of brick houses rising amidst cottages and shacks, and you would have inferred a future on the North Atlantic model.

In each of these new cities you would have noticed, probably with displeasure, the absence of noblemen and gentlemen. Americans would have assured you that this was a good thing, and hindsight suggests that they may have been right. At the time, however, the absence of gentlefolk in American towns would have struck you as a serious weakness, and it actually was so. There were, for instance, few skilled craftsmen, because there were few demanding customers. There were few artists or non-theological writers. And there were – a glaring weakness in the eighteenth century – few people capable of conversation. And how could it have been otherwise? There were few university graduates in any town, few urbane clergymen with scholarly hobbies and time on their hands, no actors or musicians on tour, no people who regularly experienced the great worlds of London, Dublin, or Edinburgh. An unduly high percentage of America's great men in 1790 were squires from the rural South.

Because America subsequently became a great nation, it is tempting to think that these early American towns were bigger and grander than they were. They were very small. Philadelphia had fewer than 29,000 people in 1790, when Dublin had 180,000 and London almost a million. Boston and New York hovered around 20,000, as they had for decades, and Baltimore, early in its growth curve, was still a town of about 13,000. Their ships and cargoes were small, their merchants middling, their buildings unspectacular.

And there was slavery. Each and every one of the early American cities, north and south, depended for its livelihood upon this darkest aspect of the North Atlantic world. Bostonians built their economy by feeding West Indian slaves, supplying them with tools, and buying the sugar they grew. Bostonians also bought and sold slaves, and kept plenty for themselves. Twenty percent of Bostonians were black in 1700, most of them unfree. Other New England ports were no different. A slave named Tituba was scapegoated in the Salem witch craze of 1692, and the pretty town of Newport dominated the American slave trade for a century. Farther south, New York had a permanent slave market at the foot of Broadway, and New York authorities suppressed a suspected slave revolt in 1741 by burning dozens of people at the stake. In Quaker Philadelphia, where the benevolent William Penn was a slaveowner, slaves were auctioned on the main streets. Baltimore remained a slave city and had big slave markets right up to the Civil War.

Commercial Cities in Britain

While middle-class Britons in North America were building four new cities based on commerce, manufacturing, and slavery, their cousins in England and Scotland were doing the same thing on a larger scale. They too built four new cities based on the same three pillars. Whichever side of the ocean these new commercial cities were on, they had more in common with each other than with cities dominated by the nobility and gentry. They were new urban worlds.

None of this would have happened unless Britannia had ruled the waves. Once she did, by 1700 or so, her merchants brought the whole world into their commercial orbit, and her craftsmen sold the whole world their wares. West Indian sugar and Chesapeake tobacco were part of the new global trading system, but so were Chinese tea, Russian furs, Irish linens, and Indian silks and calicos. All flowed into the ports of Great Britain, and most flowed back out again, along with woolens from Yorkshire, cottons from

Lancashire, hardware from Birmingham and Sheffield. A ship that came in with one cargo – sugar, for instance, or tobacco – would go out again with twenty or a hundred different items, ready to stock Virginia plantations and other places.

London, as usual, had the cream of this trade, and Bristol, England's traditional second port, grabbed enough to double its population between 1700 and 1770. But London and Bristol were in the south of England, and the centers of export manufacturing were in the north. Britain needed new cities in new locations, and it got them – more or less as America was getting cities – through the efforts of merchants and manufacturers, without much help from the nobility and gentry. Although these cities were not new as the American cities were new – each had a medieval church or two and a long if undistinguished history – the Commercial Revolution of the eighteenth century gave them a second birth. By 1790, each of the four new British cities was as big as Bristol, though not one of them had a cathedral or a schedule of assizes.

Liverpool was the first of the four new cities to establish itself dramatically. It was a port, and almost nothing but a port. There was little or no manufacturing, and it was most emphatically not a center for noblemen and gentlemen: its cathedral was twenty miles to the south, in Chester; its assizes were fifty miles to the north, in Lancaster. Although Liverpool was an old town, chartered in 1207, its location had worked against it for centuries: it was too far from Europe for foreign trade and too far from London for domestic. What first energized Liverpool's economy was the revival of Ireland, a short voyage away. Liverpool also benefited from its location during the French wars that broke out in 1688 and lasted for 62 of the next 125 years. Liverpool was a long way from France, and French privateers, which harried shipping near London and Bristol, had trouble getting around England and Wales to cruise the Mersey. Finally, Liverpool gained from the re-orientation of English trade away from Europe and towards the wide world. Although Liverpool and its hinterland had fewer consumers than London, that mattered little at a time when England was primarily engaged in re-packaging and re-exporting its imports. If anything, Liverpool's lower cost of land and labor gave it an advantage in this kind of trade. By 1700, the ugly duckling of English ports was becoming a swan.

Liverpool still had one major drawback; the tides of the Mersey were enormous. Low tide was never less than fifteen feet below high, and a maximum difference of thirty feet was reached in every lunar cycle. Ships that could load or unload at high tide found themselves keeled over in the mud when the tide went out, and work was impossible for half of every day. No one had ever found a way of building a great port under such conditions, and there was no successful strategy or technology ready to be copied. Nonetheless, in 1713, with a French war coming to a profitable end, Liverpool's merchant rulers set about it. They had gumption, and they were lucky that their city

The Old Dock, Liverpool.

government was almost uniquely rich, owning and charging rent on most of the city's land. With the freedom to plan and the resources to build, Liverpool backed an engineer who had a revolutionary scheme to build what he called a "wet dock," an artificial lake with sturdy gates to keep the water level constant while the tides rose and fell. When the dock opened, in 1715, it halved the hours required for loading and unloading and counted as England's first engineering marvel. By 1800, there were five wet docks in the port of Liverpool, sixty acres of calm water in man-made basins with walls of massive granite; and Liverpool, second only to London in volume of shipping, had a skyline of masts.

Forty miles inland from Liverpool, and largely symbiotic with it, was Manchester, the second of Britain's new cities. Again, Manchester was not new as Philadelphia was new. It had existed for centuries and had served as the central market for thousands of rural and small-town weavers. But weaving went from a small business to a big one in the eighteenth century, and Manchester grew with its trade. In the symbiosis of the two cities, Liverpool merchants brought raw cotton from India and Egypt and sold or consigned it to Manchester merchants, who put it out to spinners and weavers. When cloth was ready for export, Manchester merchants sold it or consigned it to Liverpool merchants, who shipped it to global markets – all to the economic advantage of both cities. Manchester was primarily a merchant town, not a manufacturing town, throughout the eighteenth century. Only the dyeing and pattern-printing of cloth took place there.

Unlike Liverpool, Manchester did not have a rich city government. It had, in fact, no city government of any kind. It was legally a village, its affairs overseen by the private court of the lord of the manor. But this apparent deficiency does not seem to have inhibited its growth; and the diligence of Manchester's manorial lords, the Mosleys, with much to gain from the success of the town, led to several examples of unusually good urban design, including a square and a long park, named in imitation of London's Piccadilly, that is still the central green space in the center of the city.

The third of Britain's commercial and industrial cities, Birmingham, lay halfway between Manchester and London and did business with both. Its business was primarily metalwork: "Birmingham toys" they were called, everything from jewelry to nails, from brass buttons to clockwork to guns. Forges made Birmingham smoky from an early date, but the small scale of eighteenth-century smithies also made Birmingham uniquely democratic. It was a place of independent craftsmen working in small and relatively equal groups, the greatest of the reservoirs of skill that grew up outside London in the long eighteenth century.

Metallurgy is a science, and Birmingham became a center of technical innovation. When Benjamin Franklin wanted to meet the best scientific minds in England, he forsook London for Birmingham and joined the circle of those who met on full-moon nights and called themselves The Lunar Society. He found James Watt and Matthew Boulton as they were perfecting the steam engine, caught Josiah Wedgewood in the act of creating English porcelain, and traded both natural and political philosophy with Joseph Priestley, who discovered oxygen when he wasn't agitating against the established order in church and state. All these men, and a handful of others, gathered under the genial and opinionated aegis of Erasmus Darwin, a doctor and poet whose speculations on the evolution of animals resembled those that his grandson, Charles, would later work out in greater detail.

Birmingham was a thrilling place, if a gritty one. Industry and invention, like smoke, were in the air. A young man named William Hutton, moving there from Derby, recorded that the people of Birmingham were so active and energetic as to be "a different order of creation". When Boswell observed to Johnson that the people of Birmingham were more industrious than those of Johnson's hometown of Lichfield, the genteel Cathedral city whose diocese included Birmingham, Johnson replied with one of his best pieces of wit: "Sir, we are a city of philosophers, we work with our heads, and make the boobies of Birmingham work for us with their hands". And work they did. They built the broadest-based prosperity in England and laid the groundwork for political innovations that would flower late in the nineteenth century.

The fourth and last of Britain's great new cities was an amalgam of the other three, at once a port, a clothmaking center, and a hub of metalworkers. This was Glasgow, on the west coast of Scotland. Although each of the other three cities did more of its own specialty than Glasgow did, Glasgow was second-best at all three. It was also the seat of a major university, the only large merchant city in the new North Atlantic world that was; and it was a stroke of luck that the University of Glasgow should have enjoyed one of its several golden ages in the eighteenth century. Here Francis Hutcheson taught the philosophy that Thomas Jefferson studied in the backwoods of Virginia. Here Hutcheson's successor, Adam Smith, became the first man to see the new global economy clearly. Like Liverpool, Glasgow traded extensively with Ireland, particularly the Presbyterian settlements of Ulster in the north. By the middle of the century, Glasgow merchants had stolen half of the Chesapeake tobacco trade from Bristol and London and were hawking Irish linens, Scottish woolens, and Virginia and Maryland tobacco around the world.

As a Scottish city, Glasgow had laws, institutions, and habits quite different from those in any part of England. Its Calvinist clergymen, like their counterparts in Boston, worked harder and spent less time on learned hobbies than did Anglican divines. Its laws against theatres were stricter, and more strictly enforced, than those against bawdy houses. And Glasgow's people did not live in single-family dwellings on the English model. Like Hume and his neighbors in Edinburgh, Glaswegians had flats within large multi-family buildings called tenements, with population densities that would have been inconceivable in England. This began to change round about 1775, as Glasgow created its first square and began to build its own New Town, in imitation of Edinburgh, to the west of the old city, but change would come slowly.

If you had visited these four new British merchant cities in 1790 with a view to comparing them to their American cousins, the first thing you would have noticed was that they were much bigger. Each of the new British cities had roughly 70,000 people, meaning that each of them was roughly as big as the four biggest American cities combined. They were also busier and denser. On further acquaintance, however, you would have seen that they were making and spending their money in ways that Americans would have found familiar. Each of them, like their sister cities across the North Atlantic, had a few elegant churches, each a few dozen leading families with carriages and suburban villas. Each, too, had its crimes, its low haunts, its occasional riots. The riots were not incidental things: in one Liverpool riot in 1785, three thousand striking seamen bombarded the Town Hall with a cannon, and it was Boston riots in the 1760s and 1770s that paved the way for the American Revolution.

You would have noticed, next, that all of Britain's merchant cities except Glasgow housed their people in brick row houses and were part of England's post-fire building culture. You would not have said, however, that these cities were very well built. At their best, they had the look and feel of small towns like Warwick, not big cities like Dublin. And they were not always at their best. Too much of their architecture was drab and spiritless; too many of their streets were cramped, crooked, and filthy; too many of their people lived in too little space, in damp cellars or small crowded houses that gave onto dark and stinking courtyards. Even Dr. William Moss, Liverpool's warmest eighteenth-century booster, who had good things to say about the slave trade and thought it was healthy for poor families to live in cellars, had to admit, in 1797, that "the streets and squares (of Liverpool) do not possess all the regularity and elegance that might be expected". He assigned blame for this to "the Builders, who were mostly born upon the spot, (and) had no opportunities of improving their style, which was very limited". He even blamed the builders for something that was clearly the fault of the city fathers, the poor planning by which "the streets, even the more modern, were laid out in the confined, parsimonious way that may be perceived". And this was Liverpool, the only British merchant city whose government had enough land and money to do better. The other British cities had better excuses for equally poor performance. The merchant rulers of the new British cities cared more about the docks and warehouses that made them rich than about the streets and houses in which they and their workers lived, moved, and – often too young – died.

It is usual to use the word "frontier" when writing of American towns in this period. The word should be used on both sides of the ocean. All eight of these merchant cities – they were all "British" until 1776 – were essentially new creations, whether their people were starting out or starting over. And they did not have anything like enough money to do everything that needed doing. Their richest people were still poor by any gentry standard, and no merchant could predict his income as any squire could do. Readers of Jane Austen and the other gentry novelists of the period are used to hearing that some character "has" so many thousand pounds of income a year. That "has" is a gentry verb, backed by hundreds of acres of land with fixed rents and predictable crop yields. No merchant or manufacturer knew how many pounds would be coming in the next year, or the next month. Things beyond their control – big things like wars or little things like hailstorms – could ruin the richest merchants overnight. The builders of the merchant cities, on both sides of the ocean, lived closer to the economic edge than the builders of Bath and Dublin. They viewed their buildings and streets as tools, made for use rather than for elegance, and they were quite ready to discard them when better came along.

The Portico Library, Manchester.

Takeoff

The miracle is that better *did* come along, and came along at more or less the same time on both sides of the ocean. Beginning in about 1790, the new merchant cities of the North Atlantic world rather suddenly took off and began to acquire many of the characteristics of London, Dublin, and the other cities polished by noblemen and gentlemen. Rich merchants and their ladies formed assemblies and built Assembly Rooms, bought graceful mahogany sideboards and finely-wrought silver teapots, and supported portrait painters and scholarly teachers. There were, rather suddenly, subscription libraries, often in lovely buildings like the surviving Portico Library in Manchester, the Lyceum in Liverpool, and the somewhat later Athenaeums of Boston and Philadelphia. There were also some astonishing individuals, men who seemed to lift up the culture of entire cities with their own hands. The greatest of these, perhaps, was William Roscoe, a self-made Liverpool merchant who wrote the first important historical work on the Italian Renaissance while making and losing a fortune and sitting impatiently in Parliament. John H. B. Latrobe would play a similar role in Baltimore in the next generation. It is a mark of the genius of Benjamin Franklin that he had already played this role in Philadelphia.

The takeoff of the new North Atlantic cities after 1790 was a phenomenon as sudden, and as important, as the takeoff of the Dutch cities two centuries before. It is not easy to say why it happened when it did. If the British cities had experienced an artistic and social takeoff while the American cities did not, we could speculate that there must have been something magic about a population of 70,000 people or so. But the same kind of takeoff happened also in Boston, with only 18,000 people in the Census of 1790, and even in Baltimore, with only 13,000. Something larger was going on, some stretching of the aesthetic and civic muscles in men and women without titles or other hereditary privileges. Delft, after all, with a Golden Age population of only 20-25,000 souls, had built as beautifully as Leyden, with 70,000 or Amsterdam with 150,000.

The key was probably growth rather than mere size. The population of England doubled between 1700 and 1800, from about four and a half million people to about nine million. Scotland kept pace with England, and Ireland, buoyed by peace and potatoes, grew faster. America grew faster still, from no Europeans or Africans in 1600 to about three hundred thousand in 1700, and four million in 1790. Nothing like this was happening in any other European state, or had happened anywhere in recorded history. The merchant cities got their share of this growth, and, after 1790, more than their share, so that even a small city like Baltimore could add more people in a year than Liverpool or Manchester had been able to do for most of the years in the eighteenth century.

Any increase in population will spur some degree of economic growth, simply by providing more mouths to feed and more bodies to clothe and shelter. But the growing populations of the North Atlantic world did more than consume: they became more productive, with the result that their economies accelerated faster than their populations. On the American side of the ocean, the takeoff came from a boom in agriculture. American farmers doubled the amount of land in cultivation and increased their crop yield per acre, mainly by settling new land that was more fertile than the old; and they produced steadily-increasing surpluses that city merchants could sell overseas. On the British side, the great gains came through the introduction of machine production and the beginning of the Industrial Revolution. Businessmen like Richard Arkwright financed and managed craftsmen like John Kay, who invented machines that could make things at drastically increased speed with drastically less human labor and drastically less cost. With more to buy at lower prices, merchants sold more, manufacturers made more, farmers grew more, and the foundations were laid of a high-volume transatlantic trade.

Federal Hall and Broad Street, New York.

A VIEW OF THE FEDERAL HALL OF THE CITY OF NEW YORK, *as appeared in the year 1797, with the adjacent buildings thereto.*

In amazingly short order, the expansion of American agriculture and English manufacturing began to complement each other, creating a firestorm of supply and demand across the ocean, much to the benefit of farmers, merchants, manufacturers, and the North Atlantic cities.

America's cheap land and expensive labor made it efficient for Americans to farm, while England's expensive land and cheap labor made it efficient for Englishmen, and hundreds of thousands of Englishwomen, to make things. Pioneers in Ohio felled trees with British axes and yoked their oxen to British plows, while factory workers in Manchester and Glasgow baked American wheat to make their bread. The process accelerated during the generation of warfare that followed the French Revolution, when European agriculture was constantly disrupted by marauding armies. American farmers supported millions of Europeans, and English manufacturers paid for imported food with shiploads of cloth and hardware. It all added up to an unprecedented volume of trade.

The takeoff that began around 1790 was as dramatic in the fields of architecture and city design as in the increase in trade or the sudden efflorescence of fine silversmithing and cabinetmaking. The demand for gentry-quality houses suddenly formed a market large enough to stimulate large-scale production. Builders no longer needed to wait for

Rodney Street, Liverpool.

commissions or bend their taste to the whims of a single person. They could build elegant houses on speculation. And the results were as happy in architecture as in silver and furniture. Prosperous merchants wanted what the gentry already had, and builders seeking their custom put up whole streets, whole neighborhoods, in accordance with the rules of classical regularity and well-proportioned politeness.

No single image captures the architectural impact of the late eighteenth-century takeoff better than a famous view of Broad and Wall Streets in New York in the 1790s. The buildings in foreground are pretty ordinary stuff, a mix of small Dutch houses with crude gables and small English houses with indifferent proportions. And then, at the end of the street, looking like a spaceship from a remote galaxy, is Federal Hall, the first Capitol of the United States. It would have been stylish in Dublin, and only a decade or so out of fashion in London.

The same thing was happening more grandly in Liverpool. When the Town Hall burned in 1795, the city fathers hired a high-profile London architect, James Wyatt, to rebuild and embellish it. His massive cupola rose, and rises still, above the cluttered and cacophonous town like a bigger, grander version of Federal Hall. At the rear of the

Custom House, Liverpool.

structure Wyatt added one of the most magnificent Assembly Rooms in England. The creation of Wyatt's Assembly Room did not mean that the nobility and gentry of Lancashire had transferred their affections and assizes from pretty Lancaster to Liverpool. It meant that the merchants and shipbuilders of Liverpool now aspired to gentry politeness and knew what it looked like.

Not surprisingly, it was in the same decade that Liverpool builders and financiers – the great Roscoe among them – set about building houses and streets to a gentry standard. Walk down Rodney Street, where Gladstone was born in 1809, or Hope Street, or the other streets and squares that are now called Georgian Liverpool. You will find them as fine as anything in a gentry town like York, and your thoughts may stray to Georgian Dublin, a city that the merchants of Liverpool knew well. Liverpool's takeoff houses are three stories tall, built of a pleasant red brick, with plenty of white stone trim and wide, welcoming fanlights at their doors. No one had ever built houses of such quality in Liverpool before – and here, suddenly, was a whole neighborhood of them, complete with elegant churches and, in 1815, a second Assembly Room.

By this time, too, Liverpool had an architect, John Foster, on the municipal payroll, the first English city other than London to do so. Though Foster's most important duties had to do with the expansion of Liverpool's docks (always the first concern of Liverpool's merchant rulers,) he designed buildings as well; and his son, John Foster, Jr., may have become the first architect in English history to carry on a great practice from a base in a merchant city. Young Foster studied architecture with leading London masters, and accompanied one of them on one of the first architectural study tours of Greece, returning in 1824 as a herald of the Greek Revival in architecture. In any earlier period, he would have settled in London and looked about for noblemen and gentlemen with a hankering to build. Instead, he guessed, correctly, that Liverpool could give him scope for his substantial talents. From then on, Liverpool had its own master and would produce its own masterworks. Foster's Oratory, a chapel in Liverpool's principal cemetery, is one of the best Greek temples in the English-speaking world, and his splendid Custom House, which reared its proud dome above the Old Dock for more than a century, became a symbol of the city.

Foster's career would have been unusual before the takeoff of the merchant cities, but it became quite typical afterwards. Each of the merchant cities, on both sides of the Atlantic, had at least one excellent architect and experienced the quickening of architectural pulse that great designers can bring to a city's building culture.

The best-studied example of this phenomenon is Benjamin Henry Latrobe, an experienced English architect who emigrated to the United States in 1796 and became the first full-time professional architect in American history. Latrobe could write and converse engagingly in a number of languages, and his skills included enough mechanical and civil engineering to get him contracts to design steam-powered municipal water systems. He found his way almost immediately to Philadelphia, still the political and the commercial capital of the United States, and soon designed the Bank of Pennsylvania, the first imposing business building in America and the first American structure informed by the architecture of ancient Greece. But Latrobe's

Cathedral, Baltimore.

competence was not limited to the adaptation of classical antiquity. He had traveled widely in Europe and had a much greater experience of contemporary European architecture than was usual among English architects. His other great Philadelphia building, the Central Square Water Works, now lost, showed his familiarity with the revolutionary French classicism of Boullée and Ledoux. While working on these projects, he trained a young man named William Strickland, who would become a great Philadelphia architect in his own right and would spread Latrobe's gospel of romantic classicism as far west as Tennessee.

But Latrobe was not destined to become the John Foster of Philadelphia. President Thomas Jefferson, no mean judge of architecture, made him the architect of the Capitol, and Washington was his base of operations for most of his American years. As the Capitol demanded less than all of his time, he had the opportunity to work more widely, partiularly in booming Baltimore, forty miles away. For Baltimore's Catholic Archbishop, John Carroll, Latrobe designed America's first cathedral, still one of America's greatest buildings, now beautifully restored. For the city's merchants, he

A Professional Architect Influences a Builder-Designer, Waterloo Row, Baltimore, 1815. Hamilton Street, Baltimore, 1817.

designed the greatest of America's early Exchanges, an immense granite pile with a central Pantheonic dome ninety feet above the floor.

Like each of the great merchant-city architects, Latrobe had a good influence on lesser people. As he had trained Strickland in Philadelphia, he trained Robert Mills in Baltimore, who launched his brilliant career by winning the competition for Baltimore's monument to George Washington and was soon building elegant rows of houses. He in turn influenced a local builder-architect named Robert Cary Long, who adapted the expensive classicism of Latrobe and Mills to projects with smaller budgets. To see how the work of a high-style architect could influence the taste of an entire community in this takeoff period, compare Mills's elaborate Waterloo Row of 1815, demolished but well-documented, with the surviving row of smaller and simpler houses that Long built two years later in Hamilton Street, a narrow street a few blocks away. Long turned the exotic classicism of a professional architect – many people today assume that the big three-part windows were added in the 1950s – into an affordable vernacular of considerable charm. Each of the merchant cities, on both sides of the ocean, had its Latrobe or its Mills, each its Long.

It is a pity that Latrobe never worked in New York. He would have had more opportunity there than anywhere else. The city had shaken off its lethargy by 1790, and its takeoff was the fastest of the eight merchant cities. New York's secret was navigable water. It sat at the meeting point of three great waterbodies: the Hudson River, Long Island Sound, and the Raritan River system of New Jersey, any one of them as big as the bays that supported Boston and Baltimore. Since water transportation cost only a tenth as much as oxcart transportation on land, this gave New York a unique advantage. A high percentage of all Americans gradually found that they could get their best values by buying, and selling, in New York. As the city grew, it built well, even without Latrobe. By 1800, the lower stretches of Broadway were worthy of any polite town in England, Ireland, or Holland; and the Battery, with its spectacular view of New York Bay, was the world's most beautiful spot for social walking.

New York's two greatest buildings of this period, Pierre Charles L'Enfant's Federal Hall of 1788 and Joseph-Francois Mangin's City Hall of 1802, illustrate an influence that was felt more strongly in America's merchant cities than in their English partners: France. There were some good architects among the thousands of educated Frenchmen who fled one stage or another of the French Revolution. They found much less competition in America than in England, and they contributed disproportionately to the architectural takeoff of American cities. In all of the United States, only Latrobe could have designed as sophisticated a building in 1802 as Mangin's City Hall.

By 1800, then, the new merchant cities were learning to build elegantly within the traditions of the British Urban Renaissance. Each city, moreover, was developing its own hallmarks of style and plan: broad fanlights in Liverpool, high front steps in New York (still called "stoops," with Dutch pronunciation,) long back wings in Philadelphia and Baltimore. It would be nice to know how these local variations evolved.

Of the eight new merchant cities, six had the opportunity to develop their styles organically within the system of habits and practices that came out of the rebuilding of London. The other two, Glasgow and Boston, had to make a conscious change in their traditions.

Glasgow continued to build tenements at higher and higher densities until the 1780s. Then, as the takeoff came, rich Glaswegians abruptly built their own New Town, like Edinburgh's, beginning with a square and continuing with a grid pattern of streets and rows of stone houses. By the early years of the nineteenth century, Glasgow was following the North Atlantic pattern and bidding fair to rank as high among commercial cities as Edinburgh did among the haunts of the nobility and gentry.

That left Boston. As late as 1790, Boston was still an old-fashioned city of wooden buildings on an irregular street plan. Since Bostonians had never picked up the new London way of building, they could not evolve their own variants organically, as New York and Philadelphia were doing. They could not even build a row of ordinary brick houses. Or, at least, they had never done so. Boston needed a man with a mission, an Inigo Jones or a Lord Brooke.

His name was Charles Bulfinch. The son of a comfortable Boston family, he toured Europe after his 1784 Harvard graduation and returned with a young man's zeal to bring

City Hall, New York.

modern British architecture to his hometown. He may, at first, have had more zeal than skill, if it is true that he was responsible for the painfully provincial copy of the Liverpool Town Hall that the State of Connecticut celebrates as its Old State House. If so, he learned quickly, and he had a natural sense of proportion that was well suited to the delicate simplicity of British architecture in his generation. By 1798, when he was chosen to build the State House for his native Massachusetts, he had made himself a master.

He had also gained the respect of his fellow citizens. Although he was feckless in business, and once suffered the indignity of being imprisoned for debt in a building of his own design, the people of Boston elected him to be their chief magistrate for eighteen consecutive years, from 1799 to 1817. That was an honor; but the honor was unpaid, and Bulfinch was chronically short of money. Worse, the job saddled him with grinding, time-consuming duties of law enforcement that had nothing to do with his personal mission. Why did he accept such a burdensome honor? For the same reason Jones had accepted a similar honor in 1630: because it gave him control over the design, construction, and maintenance of streets and buildings. Any building project in Boston needed his approval, and not every project received it.

It was a stroke of luck that his term of office coincided with Boston's China Trade takeoff and a consequent building boom. The city's population, long stagnant at 20-25,000, grew to 43,000 by 1820, and Boston's merchants created an economy that gave their city the highest per-capita income in the world. By the time Bulfinch took office, he had built enough excellent buildings to make Bostonians see what was

Charles Bulfinch.

Right. Park Circus, Glasgow.

possible, and to train workmen who could build what he wanted. Now he would ensure that they did.

Bulfinch was a very skillful architect. A number of his houses survive on Beacon Hill, a neighborhood whose street plan he probably laid out. There are free-standing mansions and groups of row houses. But his own designs are not the best measure of his achievement. If you walk around Beacon Hill, you will have trouble telling his houses from the rest. That architectural coherence is his best monument. He created, from scratch, a way of building that allowed other architects and house builders, less famous than he and conceivably less talented, to build almost as well as he did. The whole beautiful neighborhood of Beacon Hill, built by dozens of different people over a period of half a century, is as much his work as any single building. By the time he left Boston in 1818, to succeed Latrobe as architect of the Capitol in Washington, large parts of his city looked as Beacon Hill looks today.

Once the merchant cities had mastered the art of gentry building, they were ready to take the next step. They built squares that are still, in many cases, the best pieces of urban design in their respective cities. Although Manchester had built a small square as early as 1704, squares did not become general in the merchant cities until the 1820s.

Beacon Hill.

Then, quite suddenly, they emerged everywhere. Philadelphia may have led the way; it already had the four eight-acre parks of Penn's 1682 plan, and it set about developing two of them, named for Franklin and Washington, in 1825. New York followed suit immediately. Its Washington Square, laid out in 1826, almost as big as Lincoln's Inn Fields in London or St. Stephen's Green in Dublin, was the focus of fashionable development in the 1830s and remains a great central place in the ever-changing neighborhood of Greenwich Village. Union Square, now a bustling business district, and Gramercy Park, still quiet and heavily-forested, open only to adjacent property-owners, followed in the early 1830s. Liverpool's two squares of the 1830s, Abercromby and Falkner, are still the finest urban precincts in the city.

In two cities, Boston and Baltimore, squares of the 1830s have taken on a kind of mystic significance among locals. Boston's Louisburg Square, on Beacon Hill, is small, but no one has ever wished it larger than it is. Its original red brick houses from the

Above. Washington Square, New York.

Right. Abercromby Square, Liverpool.

Opposite left. Louisburg Square, Boston.

Opposite right. Mount Vernon Place, Baltimore, in 1852.

1830s and 1840s still gather round its little green rectangle like happy guests at a well-set table, and its name is still a Boston by-word for old-money elegance. Baltimore's Mount Vernon Place is as grand and public as Louisburg Square is small and private. Some brilliant designer – probably Robert Mills – had the idea of laying out four rectangular parks in a cruciform pattern around Mills's remarkable Washington Monument. The ensemble was and is a unique mixture of public grandeur and domestic comfort. America's greatest urban critic, Louis Mumford, called it the best urban space in America, and, after many house alterations in various Victorian styles, it is the best single place in the North Atlantic world to understand, and delight in, the various architectural approaches of the nineteenth century.

A Firm American Core

Bostonians like to say that the winding streets of their downtown were "designed by cows". Actually, Boston's lack of concern for street clarity was typical of the merchant cities on both sides of the ocean before the takeoff that began around 1790. If anything, poor planning – or an absolute lack of planning – was an even bigger problem in the British merchant cities, inasmuch as they were larger than their American cousins and had sharper class divisions. It was rare to find entire elegant neighborhoods in Manchester and Birmingham, and the poor huddled miserably in dark and insanitary alleys. The maze of

streets in English cities was such that only the web of old country roads, usually named for the cities to which they ran, provided a measure of intelligibility to people who did not already know where they were. Every English city seems to have a street called London Road, and every stranger with a small map is glad to stumble upon it.

Penn's grid plan for Philadelphia offered a refreshing and democratic alternative. Many Philadelphians, perhaps most, at almost all social levels, lived on well-formed streets that were wide enough for light and air. As Philadelphia became the central city for America's middle colonies (attracting Boston-born Benjamin Franklin among others), the founders of eighteenth-century towns from New Jersey down to Virginia imitated its orthogonal plan. The Virginia town of Fredericksburg, planned in 1747, had a clear grid set beside a river, ready to receive the regular buildings that eventually arose there; and twenty-year-old George Washington helped to survey an almost identical gridiron of streets for the nearby town of Alexandria five years later. Philadelphia's influence increased in the years around the Revolution, when it was usually the nation's capital. The Founding Fathers enjoyed their long stays in the trim little city and brought back good reports of it when they returned to their home states.

It was in the planning of streets that Americans made their first original contribution to the design and building of cities. The broad, straight streets that all Europeans had desired since the Renaissance were an everyday reality in Philadelphia. New York and Baltimore adopted grid plans in the first quarter of the nineteenth century, and small

The Cannonball House, St. Michaels, Maryland. A row house without a row, built in 1803 in a town of 300 people.

towns throughout the middle states and the south joined the parade. The most dramatic of American plans, for the new national capital of Washington, was created by the Frenchman Pierre Charles L'Enfant in 1791. He overlaid a Philadelphia grid with a pattern of broad avenues modeled on the design of French baroque gardens. The city was designed both to facilitate the daily life of its people (the grid) and to proclaim the power of the new nation (the avenues). By the beginning of the nineteenth century, all new American towns of any size were planned before they were built. Most plans were simple grids, often with a public square for the county court house at or near the center.

The spread of the grid plan was part of the knitting together of a new American region of architecture and city design, the result of which was to bring a large part of the young republic firmly into the building world of the North Atlantic. By about 1830, you could find North Atlantic houses in small towns as well as in big cities. This meant what it had meant in the Netherlands since the 1600s and the British Isles since the

1700s: people could move from one town to another, or from a small town to a big city, and feel at home, while ambitious country builders could take their skills to big cities, and big-city architects and craftsmen could extend their practices by bringing the latest metropolitan refinements to ambitious clients in smaller places. Urban Americans used their post-1790 takeoff period to create a regional common practice of architecture and city design, as the Dutch and the British had done before them.

You can see the results of this everywhere in the eastern half of the Middle Atlantic States. The pre-takeoff houses in any small town, if they survive, will be built of wood or stone, and will be irregular in style. But a change will become visible after about 1790, and most houses will have the characteristics that Dutch and British towns have taught you to expect. They will be houses, for one thing, not multi-family buildings; they will be made of brick; they will be architecturally regular; and they will be properly aligned to streets that are straight, airy, and tree-lined (unless vandalized by highway departments or ignored by absentee landlords). Many of these houses will stand in rows, and brick rows will form the image that you carry away. Though the houses in these rows will be similar to each other, there will be little uniformity – partly because the peculiarly British delight in uniform terraces does not seem to have crossed the ocean, but mainly because there were few large-scale developers in early America. Most American row houses of the takeoff period were built alone, or at most in groups of three, and many went through some period of standing alone, often for decades, before being connected into rows. Under those circumstances, it is not surprising that even free-standing houses have floor plans and façade designs like row houses. It may be accidental that they were never incorporated into a larger composition.

Today's Americans, accustomed as they are to automotive suburbia, think of row houses as a high-density housing type, and America's old towns strike them as oddly, often undesirably, crowded. When Americans are asked why there are so many row houses in their country's older cities and towns, they tend to say that people back then needed to live close together because it took them a long time to go anywhere, or that settlers needed to live close together for protection against the Indians. Neither explanation holds any water. Dozens, perhaps hundreds, of American communities began to build row houses while they were still small villages and could be traversed on foot in a few minutes. As for the Indians, they were long gone by the time people began to build row houses. Masonry row houses were much more expensive than log cabins or frame dwellings; they rarely appeared before the second, third, or fourth generation of a town's life, long after the threat of Indian attack had subsided.

Why, then, did Americans in small towns want to build like Philadelphians? For the same reason that Englishmen wanted to build like Londoners, Irishmen like Dubliners, and Scotsmen like Edinburghers. Great cities have the power to set fashion. Small-town people follow big-city fashions in architecture and city design as middle-class people follow the fashions of the rich. The row house was the sign that a place was a city, or aspired to become one, in the long eighteenth century. It was what the skyscraper became in the twentieth century.

If you like to drive, and have the willpower to ignore twentieth-century sprawl, you can go from town to town in large parts of several contiguous American states and feel that you are in a region of the Low Countries or the British Isles. New Castle in Delaware, Alexandria in Virginia, Carlisle and Lancaster and Gettysburg in Pennsylvania, Frederick and Annapolis in Maryland – these are among the loveliest creations of the North Atlantic urban world, and there are hundreds of others, as consistent as the small towns of Ireland or the Netherlands. Even farmers commonly built farmhouses that were identical in form and plan to row houses in towns, something practically unknown on the European side of the ocean. It is quite usual to see a deep, narrow, side-hall house in the middle of plowed fields. Larger farmhouses are three windows wide with side halls, and some, particularly in eastern Pennsylvania, are four windows wide with two separate doors, so that each farmhouse looks like a pair of semi-detached houses in a town.

America's North Atlantic region had its center in the Middle Atlantic states, where the influence of Philadelphia, New York, and Baltimore was determinative. Pennsylvania is full of proper cities in the North Atlantic tradition. Albany, the capital of New York State, and Troy, its sister-city just across the Hudson, built marvelously in this period. And the city that reminds this author the most of The Hague, one of his favorite places, is Richmond, the capital of Virginia.

Manifest Destiny

Meanwhile, millions of Americans were moving west. Most of them were native-born Americans, not immigrants from foreign countries, and they carried American building traditions with them as they crossed the Appalachians. Each of the new Midwestern cities had a frontier period in which houses were built of wood and streets were notional, but they were all maturing by 1820 and adopting the North Atlantic pattern of row houses and gridded streets. If you walk the neighborhoods on the North Side of Pittsburgh, almost three hundred miles from the ocean, you could easily imagine yourself in an eastern Pennsylvania town like York or Lancaster. Nothing about the buildings and streets around you will suggest that they were built by people for whom Philadelphia was two weeks away by ox-drawn wagon, on the far side of arduous mountains.

The story was similar in Cincinnati, two hundred miles down the Ohio River from Pittsburgh. An engraving of Cincinnati's Broadway in 1841 is indistinguishable from any good street in New York at the same time. Though everything in that picture has

Row Houses in the North Side of Pittsburgh.

been swept away for skyscrapers, there is a lot of good work left beyond the boundaries of Cincinnati's downtown, and Cincinnatians today are proud to proclaim that their city has more row houses than any city in the Midwest.

If this is true, it must be because the people of St. Louis have demolished too many of their row houses in the last fifty years. St. Louis grew in tight business relations with Philadelphia and Baltimore, and the influence of these cities was visible in the creation of elegant terraces by the 1840s.

The North Atlantic world was growing fast, and the North Atlantic way of building was extending even into parts of the United States that had different and well-established building cultures. Portland, Maine, a hundred miles north of Boston, felt the influence of Bulfinch with a time lag of a generation and built beautiful Boston-like rows on State and Park Streets in the 1840s. More dramatically, at the other end of America's east coast, a thousand miles south of Boston, Savannah became the American Bath, the place par excellence where severe classical architecture meets a romantic landscape. Like Philadelphia, Savannah had a remarkable street plan as the legacy of a benevolent founder, James Oglethorpe, but it was Savannahians of the takeoff period who decided to continue Oglethorpe's system of squares beyond the four that he had planned in 1732. By the time they were finished, in the late

New York from Union Square, 1849.

1850s, they had formed twenty-four squares, each a full block in size. If you visit the twenty-one that survive, you will find yourself walking through gardens of tropical luxuriance in the squares and looking out at hundreds of severe London-like houses. As in Bath, the juxtaposition of art and nature can be overwhelming.

Even in New Orleans, founded by the French and enlarged by the Spanish, with a unique culture that had nothing to do with the manners and morals of the Dutch or the British, people began to build in the North Atlantic way after the Louisiana Purchase of 1803. A couple of New York architects brought the latest fashions from the northeast, and the city's new American Quarter filled up rapidly with brick rows whose long back wings betray the influence of Philadelphia and Baltimore – the two cities from which New Orleans appears to have bought its famous ironwork. Nor was it only American interlopers who built in the North Atlantic manner. If you look closely as you stroll in the French Quarter, you will find, behind pastel paint and lacy iron porches, solid side-hall houses that might have been built in any American, or British, city.

A Trans-Oceanic Region

The early nineteenth century, the takeoff period of the North Atlantic merchant cities, was the first time when people crossed the Atlantic for tourism, and many wrote about what they found on the other side (whichever side that was.) Charles Dickens wrote about the farmhouses of New England, and Washington Irving wrote about the country houses of the English gentry, things that were new to them and would attract the attention of their readers. But Dickens said nothing about the brick row houses of Bulfinch's Boston; and Irving, who devoted an entire essay to the praises of Liverpool's William Roscoe, said nothing about the architecture of Roscoe's city. This was not because these writers took no interest in urban

Good small houses, Queen Village, Philadelphia.

architecture. It was because, when they looked at cities across the ocean, they found the kinds of buildings they and their readers were used to seeing at home and saw no reason to write about them. Their silence is evidence that the United States had become part of the North Atlantic region of architecture and city design – as is the disappointment of Melville's fictional seaman Redburn on finding that Liverpool looked like New York.

There is plenty of additional evidence in the form of mass-produced city views. Lithographers in New York, Boston, and Baltimore created glorious bird's-eye panoramas that celebrated the ordered elegance of terraces and squares stretching out as far as the eye could see. A square was generally the central element in the foreground, as a skyline of skyscrapers is central to a typical city view today. These views resemble nothing so much as the engravings of squares in the West End of London a century and a half earlier.

As the new urban worlds of America and Britain came together, American cities were acknowledged to have surpassed the British merchant cities in two ways. The first and most obvious was clarity of plan. The second was an architectural analogue to American democracy: small houses in America were better than houses at the same social level in the big new British cities. They had finer proportions and better brickwork. Some had miniature fanlights or classical pilasters at their doorways. The triumph of the North Atlantic way of building in America was not confined to the squares and terraces of opulent merchants. Rather, the broad-based society of the American republic accomplished feats of middle-class and artisan elegance like those achieved by the similar society of the Dutch in their Golden Age. Take a walk through Bay Village in Boston, or Otterbein and Seton Hill in Baltimore, or Georgetown and parts of Capitol Hill in Washington, or Society Hill and Queen Village in Philadelphia. You will find yourself in small-scale environments that are as charming – as democratically charming – as most old urban districts in the Netherlands.

Chapter Five

HIGH VOLUME

We have seen how, during a takeoff period that began in about 1790, the merchants of Britain and America quite suddenly began to refine their taste, and the merchant cities on both sides of the ocean remade themselves in the image of cities that catered to the nobility and gentry. Middle-class citizens laid out and paved orderly streets and equipped their cities with the libraries, theatres, assembly rooms, and rows of elegant houses that were the marks of politeness. After their takeoff, the North Atlantic cities gained altitude pretty steadily for a long time. Between the coming of peace at Waterloo in 1815 and the outbreak of war in Sarajevo ninety-nine years later, these cities made themselves the most important places in the world. But they did so by submitting themselves the squalors and disciplines of a new industrial world that threatened to make them dark and satanic. While the gains of the Long Eighteenth Century were not lost, they seemed often to be overwhelmed.

Start with Britain, and with demographics. British cities began to grow beyond anything they had ever experienced before. From a population of about 70,000 in 1790, Manchester mushroomed to 250,000 people by 1850, and metropolitan Manchester had two million people by 1900. Liverpool and Birmingham grew at similar rates and reached similar totals, while Glasgow, which boasted of being "the Second City of the Empire," grew faster and topped out higher. Between them, the four British merchant cities had more than eight million people in 1900, almost as many as England's entire national population in 1800. London too grew explosively, but its rise from a million people to five million seemed sluggish by comparison with the merchant cities.

Where did all these people come from? Basically, from their mothers. The population of England maintained its unprecedented growth, from nine million in 1800 to more than eighteen million in 1851 and forty-six million in the summer of 1914. Scotland grew equally fast, and Ireland, before the Potato Famine of the late 1840s, outpaced them both. There was no room for all these people in the countryside. They were, as Malthus and Scrooge called them, a "surplus population". Many emigrated, but British cities put millions to work in foundries, factories, dockyards, and shipyards. England's Census of 1851 showed that more than half of the English people lived in urban areas, making England the first country to pass the fifty percent mark since the Netherlands two hundred years earlier.

Iron and Coal, William Bell Scott, 1861.

*Industrial Miasma,
Manchester from Kersal
Moor, by William Wyld.*

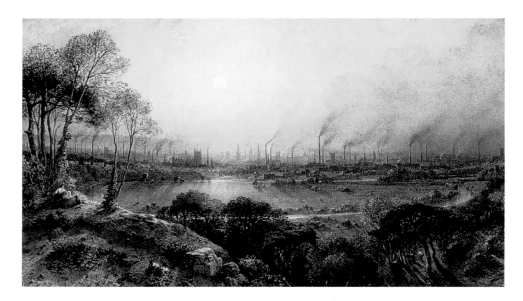

For none of this were British cities prepared. To start with the most basic things, no city had anything like enough water. Only London had reservoirs and distribution systems of any kind, and they were inadequate for the two million Londoners of Dickens's day. Manchester was worse, and more typical: in the 1840s its various wells provided only two gallons of water per person per day. Sewers were, to say the least, another pressing need. Except in parts of London, by far the world's cleanest and healthiest big city in the early nineteenth century, underground sanitary lines were generally unknown. Almost all human waste went into backyard privies, from which it often leaked into wells. When prosperous people began to install flush toilets, towards the middle of the century, things got worse before they got better. Since there were no sewers for the new toilets to connect to, much more water flowed into the same old leaky backyard privies, contaminating more wells and flooding the cellars in which the poorest people lived.

As the instance of toilets suggests, the people of these cities had an almost inconceivable absence of basic hygienic knowledge. They got richer every year, but they did not live longer. They could send ships around the world and harness the power of steam to make cloth; but they did not know that surgeons needed to wash their hands. They knew that it was healthier to live at the top of an urban hill than at the bottom, but they did not know that leaking privies at the top were contaminating wells at the bottom. They blamed water-borne diseases like typhus and cholera on bad air, which they called miasma. When London upgraded its sewer system in 1867, the Dean of Westminster, the very learned Arthur Penryn Stanley, protested because the well at Westminster School had run dry.

There was a political dimension to all this. Although the miasmatic theory of disease was incorrect, people were right to think that the tops of hills and the outskirts of towns were healthier than low-lying areas and city centers, and those who could afford houses on high ground bought them. This left the low ground and the congested town centers to the poor. Undernourished and cold in the best of times, the poor died of fevers and even starved during the frequent depressions that threw thousands out of work. Manchester factory workers and their families had a life expectancy of only seventeen years in 1842, while rich men in a suburb called Broughton could expect to reach forty-four. In case working-class Mancunians missed this, there were radical societies, radical newspapers, even radical preachers eager to remind them. Manchester's "Peterloo" massacre of 1819 became the founding sacrament of English labor history; and Friedrich Engels, a prosperous young German whose unhappy stay in Manchester from 1842 to 1844 changed his life, made Manchester statistics the stuff of Revolution.

There was also the matter of money. Even if people had known what to do, they could not have afforded to do it. Though the North Atlantic cities of the early Industrial Revolution were the richest cities in the world at that time, they were still desperately poor by modern standards. Labor was only beginning its productivity climb; capital was only beginning to form. And there were so many claims on what capital there was – canals, machines, ships, factories, railroads, all of them fabulously expensive. It was not easy to decide what percentage of a community's income should be withdrawn from wealth-increasing investments like docks and mills to fund public works like reservoirs and sewers, and harder still when it was a question of intangible services like teaching children or training teachers. Each of these cities was engaged in a race to see whether it could gain wealth and knowledge fast enough to save itself from public health catastrophe and social revolution.

This is not to say that horrible urban conditions were new. Pre-industrial cities had always been polluted deathtraps. The countryside had always been healthier than the town. Deaths had always exceeded births in big cities, and the growth of urban populations had always depended on immigration from the countryside. But the same old things were different this time.

The urbanization of the population was largely responsible for this. As the center of gravity of the literate classes moved from rural to urban areas, cities became the focus of attention as they had never been before. Articulate middle-class people watched their children die while country cousins lived; and the publishing industry, fueled by rising rates of literacy and falling prices for steam-powered printing, soon grew big enough to give voice to their fears and their hopes. Most of us think that Dickens's London, the London of the 1840s and 1850s, was poorer, dirtier, and markedly less fair than the chatty, roll-with-the-punches London of Johnson and Boswell a century earlier. This is completely untrue.

Cathedrals of Discontent.

Top left. University of Manchester, Manchester.

Top right. Johns Hopkins Hospital, Baltimore.

Left. Museum of Natural History, London.

Above. Massachusetts Institute of Technology, Boston.

Dickens's London was safer, cleaner, healthier, richer, more learned, and considerably fairer than any earlier London. The difference was not in London, but in Dickens, and in his readers. Their London may have been better than Johnson's, but they wanted it better still.

"The nineteenth century," said historian Herbert Heaton, "was the first time when stinks stank". Dickens and his readers were increasingly unwilling to put up with things that their ancestors had patiently endured. While we may wince at the sentimentality with which the Victorians treated the death of children, we should realize that it marked a real improvement over the stiff upper lip of all earlier centuries, when medicine had been an art and theology a science. By 1843, readers understood that the survival of Tiny Tim was not a matter for God alone. A bit of extra family income could make the difference between life and death for many a Christmas yet to come.

Slowly, steadily, the mental habits of the Enlightenment were sinking in. People were understanding that unprejudiced thought and diligent experiment could make life longer and easier. At first, there was little or no institutional support for the necessary research. Edward Jenner fought his vaccination battles alone, and Humphry Davy, the leading chemist of the early nineteenth century, lived by amusing fashionable amateurs with whizz-bang tricks. Things began to improve a bit in the 1820s, when investigators began to work together in organizations like the Manchester Statistical Society. But it was not until the middle of the century, the generation of Dickens, that the word "scientist" came into use, or that scientists founded institutions dedicated to the continual and systematic improvement of things. According to Donald Fleming, a great historian of science: "The institutionalization of discontent was the greatest contribution of the nineteenth century". Thenceforth, new scientific institutes and universities, often robed in the architecture of cathedrals, created in every city a culture that encouraged scientists to look for new problems, to solve them through experiment and teamwork, and to train the next generation of discontented experts.

Great as these problems were, they were not greater than the problems that faced other cities; but the courage and resourcefulness of the North Atlantic peoples were often greater and inspired both admiration and emulation throughout Europe and much of the world. Canadians merged their two traditions, British and French, to build Montreal, where a unique variant of the terraced house, with outdoor stairways, is still a cherished emblem of the city. In Toronto, new brick row houses are visible amongst frontier frame buildings in a remarkable set of photographs from 1856. Even in Germany, where city people lived and died at oppressively high densities, Hamburg commissioned an English architect to design its biggest church and an English engineer to build its water system; and Bremen, the leading German port in the American trade, passed building laws in the 1840s that turned it into a row house city on the American model, a stuccoed Brooklyn of row houses with high basements.

Row Houses in Bremen.

Everything Looks Different – Victorian Medievalism

It was not enough for the cities of the Industrial Revolution to be bigger, smokier, more productive, and more worried than cities in the Long Eighteenth Century. They also looked different. After two hundred years of laboring to adapt Roman imperial architecture to the needs and budgets of merchants and small gentry, the people of the North Atlantic abandoned classicism quite completely in the first Industrial generations. By 1851, Tennyson could look down a finely-proportioned Georgian street in Bloomsbury and dismiss it as "long, unlovely".

If the people of the North Atlantic world no longer wanted their cities to look like ancient Rome, what *did* they want them to look like? Tennyson's generation, the children who heard the joyous bells after Waterloo and came of age in the 1830s, had an answer. They wanted their cities to look medieval. The Gothic Revival, said Kenneth Clark, was "… perhaps the one purely English movement in the plastic arts".

Perhaps the oddest thing about the nineteenth century, from our point of view, is that intelligent people believed that the Middle Ages had been a Utopia. They did not come to this belief overnight, but they did come to it, and they remained in it for a couple of generations. Why did they abandon the imitation of ancient Rome, the Utopia that had inspired the best European minds since the days of Dante half a millennium before? And why did this tremendous change begin in England?

It is useful to remember that Renaissance Europeans had imitated the ancient Romans, not simply as a matter of aesthetic preference, but because they believed ancient Rome to have been bigger, better organized, and more powerful than any modern state. As seen from the paltry little countries of medieval and early modern Europe, Rome shimmered like a mirage of order and culture and, above all, power. By the first half of the nineteenth century, however, Britain had proved itself stronger, greater, and better-organized than Rome had ever been. Britain's ministers calmly dispatched fleets to all corners of the globe, and a private company, with offices in the City of London, exacted tribute from the princes of India.

When children outgrow the worship of their parents, they do not become self-directed adults overnight. The same rule seems to apply to nations. As the thinking people of Great Britain awakened to the fact that they had outgrown the ancient Romans, they looked about, as adolescents do, for someone else on whom they could model themselves, some society that had strengths or virtues or freedoms that they wanted to acquire. Like adolescents, they began with efforts that were to a great extent destructive: England's Romantic poets were the first people in history who tried to imagine ideal worlds that were less orderly, less predictable, less safe than the actual world in which they lived. But they soon found what they were looking for in various parts of the Middle Ages.

It is not hard to enter into their frame of mind, once you get over the initial strangeness of it. Walk into a great Gothic church or a great Gothic cathedral. Better yet, try to remember what it was like to walk into such a place when you were a child. Or stroll through a great university with medieval or medieval-revival buildings. If you happen to be near a large castle, go look at it, preferably with a raft of small and energetic boys. But you do not really need to go anywhere. You can get your fill of gallant knights and damsels in diaphanous gowns by reading hundreds of stories, downloading hundreds of movies, or playing weeks and weeks of computer games. Sir Walter Scott became the best-selling writer of the nineteenth century by modernizing the conventions of medieval romance, and those modernized conventions are still alive and well in the endless episodes of *Star Wars*.

The Middle Ages had another attraction for people, particularly men, in the North Atlantic world of the early nineteenth century. Medieval people were, or appeared to be, individualistic in a nineteenth-century way. In the real world of 1820 or 1840, huge fortunes awaited the man who worked hard, respected his elders, showed courage, and resisted temptation. But woe to the weakling! Any slip along the way, anything done or left undone, could plunge him into unspeakable horror. The Romans had not been individualists and could give no useful advice to the nineteenth century. In the Middle

Highclere Castle.

Ages, however – as depicted by eulogistic medieval poets and as understood by credulous British readers in the early nineteenth century – men had proved their mettle in single combat, on foot or in the lists, and high-born ladies had rewarded them with scarves and gloves to wear as talismans. Scott's *Ivanhoe*, published in 1820, for all its clanking of chain mail and people saying "Forsooth," is a standard rags-to-riches story of the nineteenth century. Its hero is a young man who rejects a stifling home life, works hard, plays by the rules, resists a formidable temptation, and ends with a knighthood, his father's blessing, and the hand of his own true love. The Middle Ages could meet the nineteenth century on its own ground.

In the anxious decades that followed the French Revolution, the Middle Ages offered comfort to people in every social group. To kings and noblemen, nervously feeling their way out from under the shadow of the guillotine, the Middle Ages gave visions of castles and chivalry. Scott's own house, Abbottsford, built near Edinburgh in the Scottish Baronial style, started a fashion for medieval country houses; and medieval-revival houses like Highclere, designed by Charles Barry in 1842 and televised as Downton Abbey, were soon rising in all parts of England, Scotland, and Ireland.

By the luck of London fires, this kind of fantasy chivalric palace became the symbol of the British Empire. When the Houses of Parliament burned down in 1834, all classes of Englishmen agreed that the new building, the center of their common life, should celebrate the authentic past of an institution and a nation whose roots were in the Middle

Houses of Parliament

Ages. Highclere's Charles Barry won a national competition with a design that proved, to discerning eyes, that the valorous England of Scott's twelfth century was one with the wise and wondrous England of Shakespeare's sixteenth. Fortunately, Barry was a great architect, not just an astute reader of cultural tea leaves. His Houses of Parliament, enormous in scale but refined in every part, rise from the river like an enchanted fortress; and Big Ben gives time to the world.

Then there was the Church. The French Revolution had killed thousands of priests and abolished Christianity, at least for a time, and the first half of the nineteenth century saw a determined religious counter-attack. English churchmen discovered an aspect of the Middle Ages that Scott had overlooked: the Age of Chivalry had also been the Age of Faith. Eager divines delighted to find that medieval piety had inspired charity at home and heroism on the Crusades, and they longed to restore the union of knowledge and reverence that the Enlightenment had endeavored to break. Gothic became the universal language of church architecture in England, and pointed arches and stained glass windows were made to carry a great weight of personal emotion and social concern. A.W.N. Pugin spoke for the age when he celebrated "The Present Revival of Christian Architecture" by showing thirty-nine Gothic churches of his own design as if they formed a single holy city.

A.W.N. Pugin, The Present Revival of Christian Architecture.

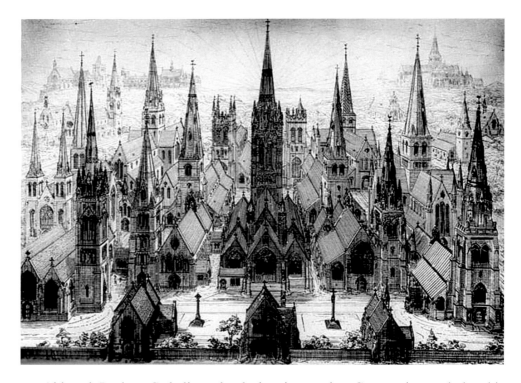

Although Pugin, a Catholic zealot, had no interest in a Communist revolution, his diagnosis of the problems of the industrial city was not vastly different from that of Engels. Both saw only impersonal cruelty and oppressive ugliness in their country's manufacturing towns. Pugin's 1841 *Contrasts* shows a town of 1440 as a beautiful grove of steeples, then shows the same town in its debased condition as of 1836. A stinking gasworks and a panopticon prison are the first sights a visitor sees, and faceless mills dwarf the broken spires of churches.

Early Victorian Christians heard a call in all this, and many heeded the call. Methodists and Unitarians took the lead, but even the Church of England, long a subordinate arm of the state, woke from its torpor. Clergymen led the fight that ended slavery and took on the enormous task of churching, comforting, and educating the laboring masses of the new industrial cities.

It is amazing how much passion and earnest longing went into the revival of medieval Christianity in Victorian England. You are meant to feel it, and may feel it, when you walk into a Gothic Revival church, for architects in the 1830s and 1840s felt the thrill of spiritual renewal as sharply as any other group of people. At first, they studied cathedrals and monasteries to learn the words and the grammar of Gothic. Then, after a generation spent in reproducing medieval buildings with increasing skill, they learned to think in Gothic, as classicist architects had learned to think in Latin, and they

A.W.N. Pugin, St. Giles RC
Church, Cheadle.

began to create work of an often startling originality. England built enough churches in
the second half of the nineteenth century to accommodate something like ten million
Sunday worshippers. As it did so, hundreds of architects threw themselves heart and
soul into the quest for church commissions, and Victorian Gothic churches, often the
worse for wear, still tower above thousands of British city streets.

It is easy to see why noblemen and churchmen found solace and strength in the
Middle Ages. Their position was rooted in the past and threatened by the present. But
what about the middle classes, the people who saw themselves as the vanguard of
progress? They noticed that merchants and manufacturers, people just like them, had
seized power in certain Northern Italian cities during the twelfth and thirteenth centuries,
and that these same cities had straightaway produced an unparalleled explosion of
creativity. Perhaps, they thought, such a thing could happen in England. Dante replaced
Vergil in the pantheon of poets during the 1830s; Florence replaced Rome as the object
of cultivated English pilgrimage. Finally, in 1840, a new word, "Renaissance," appeared
in print in English, and middle-class people suddenly had a ready-made story, illustrated
by acknowledged masterworks, to demonstrate that they could be trusted to rule
commonwealths and shape taste in the arts. By that time, several dozen British
merchants were as rich as noblemen, and thousands were as rich as town gentry. They
read books and went to lectures, and they were delighted to find in history, and advertise
in architecture, that merchants could be, and should be, merchant princes.

Palazzo Madama, Rome
Façade 1642

The Renaissance was less a discovery than an invention. It took a long time for scholars and critics to decide what it was and what it wasn't. By the time they were through, the Renaissance was revealed to have been a long period with regional and national variations and more than one architectural look. This made for cantankerous disputes in the middle of the nineteenth century, all of them based on the belief that modern Englishmen should imitate the art and architecture of whichever part of the Renaissance turned out to be the real right thing. John Ruskin spoke passionately, and at heavenly length, for the early Renaissance of Venice; and "Ruskin Gothic," with pointed arches and polychrome masonry, had a considerable vogue in most British cities, mainly for commercial and institutional buildings. At the same time, however, Charles Barry was building clubs in fashionable London that looked like late-Renaissance palaces in Florence and Rome, buildings two or even four hundred years newer than Ruskin's Venetian favorites. Ruskin hated everything about the late Renaissance, and attempts to revive it moved him to fury. Letters were published and podia pounded. In the end, Barry's version of the Renaissance received the Royal Assent, as it were, in 1844, when Prince Albert himself designed Osborne House, a villa for the Royal Family on the Isle of Wight, in Barry's Late Renaissance style. The builders of row houses soon followed his lead throughout the British Isles.

Throughout the British Isles – and throughout the North Atlantic world. For it is interesting, and significant, that Americans followed British fashions as closely as they could even though Americans faced none of the specific social and political issues that triggered the medieval revivals in England. Though the Great Republic had no feudal aristocracy, Americans read Scott avidly, and rich Americans began to build Gothic villas in the 1830s. And though no American churchmen had faced danger during the French Revolution, Americans in the first half of the nineteenth century had their own religious revival, the Second Great Awakening, full of strong emotion, and Gothic became the default style for churches in American cities during the 1840s and 1850s.

The Renaissance struck a very deep chord in America. Even more than in England, Americans thrilled to learn that middle-class people, people just like them, had achieved greatness in great cities, often in spite of selfish kings and wicked Popes. The new Athenaeums of Philadelphia and Baltimore, built in the late 1840s, looked like sixteenth-century Florentine palaces, while New York's Astor Library, opened in 1849, favored somewhat earlier models from Siena. In domestic architecture, Barry's version of the Renaissance, based mainly on the Italian seventeenth century, swept the field in America as it had in England. The typical New York "brownstone" is a row house embellished with the decorative details of a Renaissance palace in the Barry mode. Look at any complete row of brownstones, with their massive cornices and window moldings. The resemblance to the 1642 façade of Palazzo Madama and similar palaces is close enough. By building

A Row of New York Brownstones.

houses in rows of a Barryesque style, Yankee merchants could become merchant princes.

By 1850, then, the North Atlantic world was giving itself a new look. From London to New York, people could walk down new streets and see new buildings of medieval inspiration. Houses looked as much like Italian palaces as their owners and builders could afford, with heavy cornices at the top and, means permitting, heavy moldings around windows and doors. Churches – and there was at least one new church in any given vista – would be Gothic, or perhaps Romanesque, often lifting the sharp spire of the Church Militant above the street below.

The style of buildings changed more than the substance. Protestant churches, though covered with ribbed vaults and hammerbeam roofs, were still auditoriums for lessons and sermons. Houses, beneath their heavy Renaissance cornices, still followed the interior layouts formed in the seventeenth century. Rooms sometimes got a bit bigger as heating and lighting systems improved, stairs became a bit more dramatic, and families were more likely to furnish a single-purpose dining room; but that was about all. Changes in plumbing, heating, and interior decoration were much more dramatic than changes in plan. If a typical city-dweller of the eighteenth century – Ben Franklin, say, or Samuel Johnson – had visited London or New York in 1850, he would have delighted in newly-invented improvements like furnaces and toilets, and understood how to live and worship in the houses and churches of his hosts.

Inventing the Central Business District

But Franklin and Johnson would have been mystified and disoriented if they had walked around a city center in 1850. By that time, the heart of each North Atlantic city was on its way to becoming a new kind of place, a workplace pure and simple, with no residential population. Franklin and Johnson would not have known what to make of this. They were accustomed to cities where merchants and artisans lived above their shops, as merchants and artisans had done throughout the Middle Ages and, in fact, for all of recorded urban history. If Johnson wanted to buy a spoon, he walked to the house of a silversmith, whom he found either downstairs at his forge or upstairs with his family. If Franklin wanted to borrow a large sum of money, he walked to the house of a banker and arranged the transaction there, perhaps downstairs among the account books, perhaps upstairs over a bottle of claret. Even the richest merchants and financiers, men with country houses and seats in Parliament, lived above their counting rooms and stored goods in their houses.

This was fading fast by 1850. Most silversmiths were making their spoons in large workshops or factories. Most bankers had crowds of tellers and clerks. Most merchants had too much merchandise to store in their houses. Whatever their trade, however much money they were making, they left work at night and went home to a different place, usually in a different part of town. The people of the North Atlantic cities were inventing the Central Business District. They were not doing this because it sounded like a good idea. They were doing it because they needed to store too much merchandise and provide work space for too many employees. High-volume manufacturing and high-volume trade were forcing people to create high-volume city centers.

When did this change begin? The Battle of Waterloo, on June 17, 1815, is a good clear starting point. Wellington's victory ended a century and a quarter of global war between England and France and ushered in ninety-nine years of global peace. Suddenly the sea lanes were free, and merchants no longer needed to be blockade runners. A slow ship with a big hold was as safe as a speedy little Baltimore Clipper. For the next century, except in isolated instances – bringing tea from China or transporting miners to a newly-discovered gold field – capacity would matter more than speed. A new era of high-volume trade had begun.

And there was a high volume of goods to trade. It is convenient to speak of "the Industrial Revolution" as if, like a political revolution, it had begun and ended on fixable dates. But there is no simple beginning day or year for this mighty change in human affairs, only a nebula of years for the many little inventions and developments that eventually became a thing with a single name. It took generations, and anyone who cares

Watts Warehouse, Manchester.

can make an equally good case for any year in which some inspired tinkerer invented some useful device: 1733 for Kay's Flying Shuttle, 1769 for Arkwright's spinning frame, 1775 for Watt's final steam engine, 1793 for Whitney's cotton gin. Not to mention the decades of England's canal boom, from 1767 to 1815 and beyond, as navvies dug hundreds of miles of smooth inland waterways to move bulky goods at low cost – or the various years in which engineers connected the new machines to the power of water, whether flowing over mill wheels or vaporized into steam. Whichever dates one favors, these processes were well advanced by the morning after Waterloo.

They were advancing fastest in Manchester, the first city in which all the elements of the Industrial Revolution came together. With regular shipments of coal, Manchester mills could make cloth every day, and they rapidly displaced rural mills that depended on irregular and unpredictable streams. In the 1820s, Manchester's transformative decade, the city metamorphosed from a center of trade to a center of production, and the German architect Friederich Schinkel was shocked to find Manchester factories as big as the royal palace in Berlin.

Everyone, in fact, seems to have been shocked by Manchester in the second quarter of the nineteenth century. Some people thrilled to it and extolled the city for the raw power of its economy and the huge opportunities it offered to bold and ingenious men.

Others loathed it and damned it for the foulness of its air and water, the ugliness of its mills and neighborhoods, the misery of its toiling masses. Whatever people thought of it, they bought its cloth, and Manchester's merchants soon had much more merchandise to store than their houses could hold. If they had been Dutch merchants in the seventeenth century, or if their city had possessed a strong city government capable of harnessing their energy into collective action, they might have solved their storage problem by building large public warehouses. They were, however, English individualists in the nineteenth century, and their city was, in law, an unincorporated village, with almost no power to own or develop property; so they solved their storage problem individually, by moving out of the center of the city and giving their houses over to storage. John Bright, later a Manchester political leader, watched the best street in town go from houses to warehouses in two years, between 1832 and 1834. Manchester became the first British city to turn its center into a central business district.

Liverpool, the symbiotic port of Manchester, was not far behind. Everything that needed to be stored in Manchester – raw cotton in, finished cloth out – also needed to be stored in Liverpool. As people built more and bigger factories in Manchester, more ships and bigger ships sailed to Liverpool. On arrival, they met a competent city government, with a large annual income and a long tradition of dock-building, which made heroic efforts to accommodate both the ships and their cargoes. During the long and autocratic reign of Jesse Hartley, engineer and architect, the Liverpool Harbour Board built dock after dock until its network of artificial lakes lined the Mersey shore for seven and a half miles. Hartley also built the public warehouses that Manchester did not build, and built them on a more than Dutch scale. We can still walk around the massive complex of storage buildings with which he surrounded the Albert Dock in 1842, built for the ages, now a placid destination for tourists and museum-goers. But even Hartley's warehouses were not enough. The volume of goods was simply too great. One by one the merchants of Liverpool moved out of their once-proud houses near the Exchange and the Custom House. Bales of Manchester cloth piled up in the old bedrooms, and the city's central streets fell silent after dark.

If this was the experience of Liverpool, the only English-speaking city that had the traditions and the organization to cope with warehousing as Amsterdam had done, you can imagine what happened on the other side of the Atlantic. People were overwhelmed by goods. The first to feel the pressure was New York.

The first sign of New York's singular destiny came in 1817, when a group of New York merchants founded the Black Ball Line, the world's first shipping line, and announced that they would send a ship from New York to Liverpool on the same day of every week. It is hard for us to appreciate how bold this was. Before the Black Ball Line, ships had sailed only when their holds were full, and not before; it had often taken months, even in the big ports, to gather enough cargo to fill a hold. The owners of the Black Ball Line were the first shipowners in history to bet that they could fill a ship to the point of profitability every week. That they won their bet was a tribute to the Industrial Revolution in Manchester and the freedom of the seas after Waterloo, but it was also a tribute to the growing primacy of New York among the ports of North America. Seven years before the opening of the Erie Canal, New York was already the only one of the four big American ports whose hinterland was big enough to support the departure and arrival of a single sailing ship every week. But New Yorkers were about to get too much of a good thing.

Manhattan Island is long and narrow. Though its two rivers, the East and the Hudson, give it an almost infinite length of shoreline for piers and docks, there is very little land on which people can live and work. By a stroke of bad luck, the business district of New York was nowhere near the center of the island, but was in fact at the narrowest tip of it, where the Dutch had built their fort in 1624. This made for trouble when the post-Waterloo wave of cargo broke over the city. Goods replaced people in Lower Manhattan as fast as in central Manchester. It was in this period that New Yorkers coined the characteristic American word for a city center where one works but does not live: Downtown.

And this was only the beginning. In 1825, when the Erie Canal delivered the American Midwest into New York's hand, New York became the busiest port in the world, and the volume of goods – wheat and corn going out, plows and scythes coming in – outpaced the ability of New Yorkers even to conceive of it. The city's business district, stuffed with goods, exploded north past Wall Street; and Broadway, the city's main street, acted as a wick to draw businesses up from the island's tip. Rich New Yorkers moved steadily north, with commerce hot on their tails, gobbling elegant houses and turning them into store-rooms and display rooms. The life expectancy of a fashionable Broadway residence could be as little as a decade. And what was annoying to the rich, who complained in comfort and sold their houses at handsome profits, was a painful hardship for artisans and laborers, whose rented lodgings shrank steadily in space and grew steadily in cost.

The pressure of goods upon space was almost equally great in Boston, where land was almost as scarce as in Lower Manhattan. State Street became a double file of temple-fronted banks; and five-story buildings, both warehouses and offices, pressed up against Boston Common by 1860, replacing Bulfinch's first masterpiece, Tontine Crescent, in 1857. Housing grew expensive enough to justify the enormous cost of landfilling for new neighborhoods.

Philadelphia and Baltimore, surrounded by good building land, developed downtowns of the same type, but more gracefully. Their new neighborhoods stretched out in miles of unruffled rows – Baltimore's H.L. Mencken called them "placid" – that were spacious and

A Medicean palace in a commercial downtown. The Free Trade Hall Manchester.

Sculpted commercial allegories in a great Victorian downtown, the Eagle Insurance Buildings, Manchester.

Calling out loudly and grandly in Manchester,

relatively cheap. Philadelphia's waterfront area went commercial, and Market Street drew businesses away from the river as it had done in colonial times, or as Broadway was doing in New York. But the streets parallel to Market Street, which had been quiet and residential in colonial times, continued to be so, and that pattern persisted as the city grew inland. Walnut and Spruce Streets, which parallel Market Street to the south, remained residential for most of their length, and remain so to this day. Baltimore's main street, Baltimore Street, running parallel to the shoreline about a thousand feet inland, with the shop fronts and warehouses of hundreds of wholesale merchants, formed for half a century an almost impenetrable social border between the smelly dockside world of merchants and the polite Assembly-going world of their wives and families.

One of the reasons for the rapid expansion of central business districts was the small size and inefficient layout of their old merchant houses. Most of these were only three stories tall, and their interiors were cut up every twenty feet or so by structural brick walls. Nor could houses cover their entire lots, because, in the absence of good artificial light, every room needed to have a window. Thus the typical house, three or four stories tall above a basement and covering half its lot, was rarely more than twice as big as the plot of ground on which it sat; and a typical neighborhood had only two acres of interior space for every acre of land. This had never been a problem before, but now, with the volume of trade growing exponentially, the inefficiency of these old houses guaranteed that successful cities would convert housing into warehousing and workshops and drive out residents fast enough to threaten social cohesion. The fear that the physical space of the city was flying out of control was very present in Manchester by the 1840s and was becoming an issue in New York.

Help was on the way. Three new technologies – iron, steam, and gas – came together in the late 1840s and allowed the construction of much larger buildings. Cast iron became cheaper than wrought iron in the 1830s, and builders eventually discovered that a few cast iron columns could bear as much weight as a brick wall. At the same time, steam engines, formerly expensive monsters, became smaller, more efficient, and cheaper, like computers today; and builders soon found that they could afford to install freight elevators in relatively small buildings. Finally, after many fits and starts, gas lighting became a predictable piece of urban infrastructure, at least in the centers of large cities; and businessmen discovered that they could work or store goods by artificial light, far from any window. When these three innovations came together, it became possible to build business buildings that were five or six stories tall above a basement, with brightly-lit, unobstructed floors that ran from the front of the property clear through to the back. These new buildings offered at least twice as much usable space per acre as converted houses, and much more flexibility in moving goods or placing workbenches. Property owners felt a sudden and irresistible temptation to rebuild. Whole blocks, whole city centers, were cleared and transformed in the 1850s, absorbing enough goods and workers to slow the outward spread of business districts.

The new business districts were dynamic, sometimes cutthroat places, born in the glory days of unrestrained free-market competition. Every year seemed to bring a new British colony or a new American state, each of them a new world of buyers and sellers. New outposts of civilization sent new merchants to the North Atlantic cities every year; and, in each city, hundreds of wholesalers and manufacturers, risking their all in sole proprietorships or partnerships with unlimited liability, strove every day to capture new customers.

Architecture was soon pressed into the service of competition. The new business buildings of the 1850s were as big as palaces, towering above the street, and they had advertising value, both to show that a particular firm was solid and trustworthy and, more prosaically, to make it possible for country and foreign merchants, the bulk of customers in the new downtowns, to tell one firm from another. Business owners and speculative developers hired skillful architects and dynamic carvers to give distinctive, nay commanding, façades to their big iron-framed spaces.

Nowhere was the transformation more sweeping than in the City of London, the center of the world's economic web and the district where merchants were most princely. As City merchants moved out, and their little brick houses fell behind them, most rebuilders called in Barry and his imitators, and there arose a huge and florid rival to Medicean Florence – palace after stone-fronted palace, miles of pilasters, thousands of sculpted allegories, each building calling out loudly and grandly like a broker or an auctioneer. Most of London's great new buildings were offices rather than warehouses, hives for the armies of clerks whose calculations and fancy copper-plate hands

A New York Ironfront, the Haughwout Building, 1857.

coordinated the world's economy. The ornament was no less assertive for that.

Though the *Luftwaffe* destroyed most of the City's Renaissance splendors, you can get almost the full experience of a mighty mid-Victorian downtown in Manchester or Glasgow – or, on a somewhat smaller scale, in Leeds or Newcastle or Belfast. To walk through the downtowns of these cities is to experience thrill after thrill, until the thrills begin to pall.

America still had dramatically less capital than England; New York's Wall Street still borrowed from London's Lombard Street; and Medicean flamboyance was expensive. As a result, buildings in American business districts, though often as large as their opposite numbers in Britain, were less rhetorical in their design and a good deal less mighty in their materials and decoration. But American merchants also wanted to be merchant-princes in the Renaissance manner, and they took notice when an American inventor, James Bogardus, showed them how to achieve a high level of Renaissance elegance at a moderate price by using cast iron to imitate stone. The first iron-fronted building in the world, built in 1851 for a newspaper in Baltimore, proved that the new material could convey Renaissance grandeur with a delicacy that British stonework could not match – and with bigger, brighter windows than were possible in the heavy

Crescents and Squares for Middle-class People. Thornhill Crescent, Islington, London and Union Square, Baltimore.

stone walls of British buildings. In the long run, American ironfronts would give rise to steel-framed skyscrapers with curtain walls of glass. In the short run, American merchants were delighted with their new Italian elegance and used images of their ironfronts extensively in advertising. If you walk around New York's SoHo, where streets of iron-fronted palaces now shine again with fresh paint and expensive merchandise, you will see how iron allowed Americans, on limited budgets, to keep up with the business fashions of the North Atlantic's leading commercial nation.

Getting From Home to Work

All these mercantile buildings needed merchants and clerks, tens or hundreds of thousands of them. If they did not live on the premises, where did they live, and how did they get to work?

To say that almost all of them lived in single-family houses in residential neighborhoods is nowhere near as silly as it sounds. They were the first merchants and clerks in urban history who had ever lived away from the shop. When merchants and their clerks were freed to live as the gentry lived, they rapidly built gentry-style neighborhoods. In London, the world's richest merchant community built many of the places that tourists know today: the stuccoed Renaissance terraces of Bayswater and Ladbroke Grove and the massive terraced palaces of Queen's Gate and Prince's Gate, nervously disdained by Victorian noblemen. In Boston, when rich people ran out of land on the narrow peninsula of the colonial town, they filled half a square mile of tidal water and called forth the South End, a flat Beacon Hill of four-story brick terraces and charming, intimate garden squares, the high-water mark of the Bulfinch revolution.

Nor was it only the richest people who built in the London manner of rows and squares and parks. Middle-class people in London, Liverpool, and all of the American cities lined miles of streets with rows and terraces, crescents and squares, that differed only in size from the precincts of the rich. Much of their work survives in New York's Greenwich Village and Cobble Hill, in Butchers Hill and Union Square in Baltimore, in Brompton and Islington and myriad other parts of London.

Westbourne Terrace,
Paddington.

Living away from work was easy enough to do while cities were small, but there was and is a limit to the distance a person will walk to get from home to work. Beyond that limit, people must either cram themselves in at higher densities or find a way of moving faster. Paris and the other cities of continental Europe adopted the first of these strategies, building taller buildings with higher residential densities. The North Atlantic cities took the other path. They invented public transportation.

London predictably took the lead. Hackney coaches had carried Londoners around town like modern cabs since the 1650s. There were coach companies by 1800, calling their vehicles omnibuses or, for short, 'buses, carrying businessmen to the City from places like Paddington and Islington. Though small and expensive, and constrained by the poor quality of the streets and roads on which they had to run, horse-drawn buses could usually move twice as fast as a pedestrian. This meant that employed people with good incomes could live twice as far from work as they had ever done. Because the area of a circle increases as the square of its radius, the omnibus revolution quadrupled the acreage available for urban settlement, making it possible for the amount of development land to keep pace with a population boom.

London was almost ideally suited to the omnibus revolution. Its land was flat and congenial, its river narrow and frequently bridged, and City workers and Westminster functionaries had the full 360 degrees of development land at their disposal. Though London's population quintupled between 1800 and 1900, transit improvements kept the supply of land in balance with the demand for it, and the price of development land at London's urban fringe did not change from one end of the nineteenth century to the

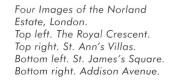

Four Images of the Norland Estate, London.
Top left. The Royal Crescent.
Top right. St. Ann's Villas.
Bottom left. St. James's Square.
Bottom right. Addison Avenue.

other. Omnibus-riding merchants and clerks found that they could live like gentlemen, in proper family houses without shops, and stroll through parks as gentry families had been doing since the seventeenth century. Londoners did a good job of preserving heaths and commons that adjoined or centered most of the new neighborhoods, and the gentry pattern of rows and parks became, in the omnibus era, the London pattern.

When middle-class Londoners arrived at the urban fringe, they found both large estates and old-established villages. These were very different kinds of environments, and two distinct kinds of development resulted.

The owners of large estates tended to create formal plans of an urban character. The Bishop of London's Paddington estate, the classic estate development of the omnibus era, was meant to be, and was, a seamless extension of the formal and aristocratic districts to the east. Its rows and squares were planned all at once and built according to plan, and the finished product resembled Belgravia to an extent that satisfied hundreds of opulent middle-class families like Galsworthy's Forsythes.

This kind of centrally-planned development was harder to pull off in the old-established villages, each of which had its parish church, its strong characters, its ways of doing things, and, in most cases, several dozen independent landowners with smallish parcels. As these villages came within commuting range of London, they proved to be an ideal habitat for small-scale developers. It took relatively little capital to expand an old village parcel by parcel, and no one owned enough land to impose a unified plan.

The result was a series of varied little worlds whose flavor often owed as much to the village as to the city.

For a delightful display of the urban and semi-urban options available to middle-class Londoners in the era of the horse-drawn 'bus, it is hard to beat the Norland Estate near Holland Park, a 52-acre parcel whose fidgety and under-capitalized developer kept bankruptcy at bay for a dozen years by trying virtually every kind of house available at the time. The face of the development is fully urban in the Georgian tradition, a large half-moon of four-story houses facing a semi-circle of tended greenery, begun in 1839 and endowed with the Bath-echoing name Royal Crescent. But head north, up St. Ann's Villas. Within two hundred feet, you will be in a different and much more informal world. You will think at first that you are walking between a double file of big free-standing Elizabethan mansions, built of red brick with diapering. But do not be deceived: each big villa is in reality two semi-detached houses, their doors cunningly placed to disguise the fact. Things change again when you turn right at the end of the block, on St. James's Gardens. You are abruptly in a small square with small Renaissance houses dated 1847, a stone Gothic church built in 1845, and a pair of Gothic cottages. One more right turn, onto Addison Avenue, and you are in an ideal village, a double row of stuccoed semi-detached houses, their large windows smiling out from shiny pastel faces. You can see it all in five minutes, though you may want to stay longer.

If London used the first mass transit innovation, the omnibus, to extend a corona of row house grandeur and village charm around the twin poles of the City and Westminster, Manchester used the second mass transit innovation, called the horse car in America and the tram in Britain, for village charm alone. Horse cars were an American invention, and a good one. They ran on practically frictionless rails instead of the bumpy roads that slowed buses, and a single horse could pull more passengers in more comfort at less expense.

The oddity is that Manchester should have adopted horse cars before London. On the face of it, Manchester did not appear to need horse-drawn mass transit at all. It was a good deal smaller than London, and there were no big rivers or hills to block the spread of the city. It had, moreover, a fine tradition of brick terraced building, and its leading families had established a fashionable area, with distinguished cultural institutions like the Portico Library, which bade fair to expand out gradually along two parallel streets, Piccadilly and the Oxford Road.

This would probably have happened if Manchester had been a city of office-workers like London, with a large middle class – or a port city like Liverpool or Philadelphia, with industry and working-class housing concentrated along the waterfront. But Manchester was a new kind of city, an industrial city, with a big proletariat and a relatively small class of white-collar workers. And its factories were not concentrated in any one area. They popped up everywhere beside the canals that were Manchester's trade routes, and Manchester's canals seemed to penetrate every part of the city. Wherever factories were built, workers needed to live nearby, and new slums mushroomed to house them. Inevitably, such a canal crossed both the Oxford Road and the London Road (the extension of Piccadilly) about half a mile out from the center of town. Vast clanking mills arose on the canal banks before middle-class development had got that far, with thousands of poor families packed into newly-built slums near their workplaces, and respectable people found their way blocked. It was the same in all directions. Manchester's downtown was surrounded by a sordid ring of canals, factories, and slums. It was impossible for Manchester to grow in the easy, urbane way of London, Philadelphia, or most other North Atlantic cities.

Thus, middle-class people in Manchester pioneered the use of horse cars because they needed to leapfrog the doughnut of slums that surrounded their city center. Once they had passed the doughnut, noticing little enough on their journey to excite Engels's wondering contempt, their horse cars brought them to unspoiled villages that had never before felt any pressure of urban development. It all seemed like paradise after the smoke and din and stink of what historian Asa Briggs called "the shock city" of the early Industrial Revolution.

Manchester's prosperous refugees forgot their urban traditions as fast as they could and embraced the new world to which the horse car had admitted them. The richest of them built free-standing villas, each in its own garden, with its own name carved on its own gate posts. Those a bit less rich built semi-detached houses that looked like free-standing villas, each with two pairs of names carved on two pairs of gate posts. Small developers made small fortunes as the world's first industrial city became the world's first suburban city.

The horse car had different effects in different cities. Many cities – Philadelphia, Baltimore, Liverpool, and London chief among them – were slow to adopt horse cars and saw few changes of urban texture when they did. The North Atlantic pattern of building had set down deep roots, not only within those cities, but also in the countryside around them. When residents of these cities rode horse cars into the nearby countryside, they found villages of brick row houses that looked like city neighborhoods and asked their builders to give them more of the same, creating seamless urban extensions instead of suburbs.

In those cities, in fact, the horse car era was the golden age of the London pattern of terraced houses and public parks. Thomas Swann, a brilliant railroad builder who became Mayor of Baltimore in 1859, made the linkage between horse cars and parks explicit by adding a penny tax to the four-cent fare of his city's horse car lines and using the money to build parks. Central Park in New York, the best-known and best-loved park in the United States, was started in 1857 as a horse car destination, long before houses were built around it. The North Atlantic pattern, the heritage of seventeenth-century London, was alive and well.

Dorchester, a horse car suburb of Boston.

Except in Boston. At first blush, it seems strange that Bostonians should have abandoned the North Atlantic pattern in the horse car era. Boston was not a degraded environment like much of Manchester, and Oliver Wendell Holmes's 1840s boast that Boston was "the Hub of the Universe" caught on so well that Boston headline-writers still refer to their city as "Hub". Bostonians loved their city and worked hard to embellish it. When they abandoned the Bulfinch tradition of brick row houses – as most of them did in the horse car era – they did so with pride, believing that they were embracing traditions that were older and better.

They were certainly older. Though Bulfinch's revolution had gained the city's upper classes, his brick row houses still seemed an exotic import to middle-class Bostonians, who retained a feeling for New England's traditions of wood construction and free-standing houses, a building culture rooted in the early seventeenth century, before Covent Garden and Great Queen Street. Thus the paradox that the richest Bostonians in the horse car era built two of the greatest row house districts in the North Atlantic world, the South End and the Back Bay, without inspiring emulation further down the social scale. This is a rare, perhaps unique, example of middle-class people failing to follow the lead of the rich in housing and neighborhood design.

As always in Boston, geography had something to do with it. Boston was a skimpy little peninsula, connected to the mainland by a narrow neck. That was why Bostonians took on the incredible expense of filling tidal water to build the new neighborhoods of the Back Bay and the South End. But only the rich could afford to buy building lots on the "new land," and the nearest old land was beyond walking distance from the city. There could be no gradual urban extension, as in London, no adding of street to street or row to row. There could only be leapfrogging, as in Manchester. When the first middle-class Bostonians rode their new horse cars out to Roxbury or Dorchester, they found typical

New England villages of free-standing clapboard houses, each on its own private lot, untouched by the Bulfinch revolution. Like their contemporaries in the very different countrysides around London and Baltimore, they liked what they found and asked for more, and old villages like Roxbury and Dorchester grew rapidly without changing their style. Those who could not afford single-family houses built houses that looked almost the same but had separate apartments on each floor. The result was something completely new in the North Atlantic world, an apparently endless village where many people lived in apartments within wooden buildings that looked like single-family houses.

The brick row house fared even worse in America's new Midwestern states. Many of their settlers were New Englanders, and many came from the rural South, both regions of free-standing wooden houses; and the new Midwestern cities were surrounded by virgin forests that made frame construction cheap. Unlike the cities of the East Coast, which had grown slowly in the age of sail, the new cities mushroomed at the speed of locomotives and reached big-city scale while their hinterlands were still being settled. And they had horse cars from their earliest days. Thus, Midwestern city-dwellers always had the freedom to live at village density, often the only kind of living they knew. They found plenty of frontier carpenters ready to build frame houses and few skilled masons ready to compete with them. Unless a Midwestern city had about twenty thousand people before the coming of the horse car, it built few row houses or none, and people came to disdain the few that they had. The novelist F. Scott Fitzgerald remembered his magnificent boyhood row house on the best street in St. Paul, Minnesota by saying: "I grew up in a second-rate house in a first-rate street".

The abandonment of North Atlantic tradition left most Midwestern cities with less density than they would eventually need and less grandeur than they would eventually want. New Orleans and Savannah dropped out of the North Atlantic world. Newer cities – Minneapolis, Omaha, Denver, Atlanta – never thought to join it. By the end of the horse-car era, in the 1890s, the American side of the North Atlantic region had been trimmed back to the area in which it had already set deep roots by 1800, a coastal strip running from New York on the north to Richmond on the south, and visibly weakening as one crossed the Appalachian Mountains. Pittsburgh, Cincinnati, and St. Louis were left somewhat in limbo. Neither as old as the eastern cities nor as new as the Midwestern cities, each of them had developed a North Atlantic building culture before the coming of the horse car. But their surrounding countrysides were still in their wooden-building phase. As these cities grew into their second and third generations, fewer and fewer of their people had memories of the coastal cities, and fewer felt instinctively that a great city needed to have rows of brick houses.

Then there was New York. To a casual eye, it was the American London, its long avenues carrying brick and brownstone rows up Manhattan Island as far as the eye could see. New Yorkers built their first horse car line as early as they could have, in 1832, the year of Manchester's first horse cars, but New York did not become a suburban city like Manchester. Manhattan Island was so long, and so narrow, that New Yorkers needed rapid transit simply to sustain row house development. The frontier of urban development was already more than three miles from Wall Street by 1850; and the next decade added a full two miles of continuous row house extension. New York in the horse car era became the urbane brownstone New York of Edith Wharton and Teddy Roosevelt. It built clubs to rival London and an opera house to rival La Scala.

Geography, however, was New York's implacable enemy. Manhattan was still an island, and it was still too narrow for anything like London's easy spreading. There were fewer than three square miles of land within walking distance of downtown, little more than a tenth of the total for London, and the laws of supply and demand operated with full vigor in a laissez-faire age. While the value of undeveloped land on the fringes of London was remaining unchanged – as it was for the full century from 1800 to 1900 – land values in New York were rising vertiginously. This meant durable wealth for landowning families like the Astors. Everyone else either paid more or fitted more people into less space, or – usually – both.

The Commissioners who created New York's gridiron of streets in 1811 believed that the problem would solve itself. They foresaw that the business center of the city would move north, creating a new downtown where Midtown is today, with docks and warehouses stretching out on both sides, giving the city a form like that of Liverpool or Philadelphia and putting most or all of the island within walking distance of the working waterfront. But this did not happen. Downtown stayed put at the tip of the island, adding jobs every year and forcing more people every year to live within the same walkable area.

A home-grown technology, Robert Fulton's steamboat, gave a measure of relief after 1814 by opening the rural town of Brooklyn to urban settlement. Immortalized by Walt Whitman, the Brooklyn ferries eventually carried a hundred thousand people a day, and Brooklyn very rapidly became a prosperous and elegant North Atlantic city in its own right, with miles of splendid rows in brick and brownstone. By the end of the horse car era, Brooklyn was the fourth-biggest city in the United States, and it too could claim to be the American London. If you walk the neighborhoods of Brooklyn Heights, Cobble Hill, Carroll Gardens, and Park Slope, your feet will be sore before you run out of distinguished North Atlantic streets.

If New York had been only the American version of Thackeray's London, the elegant home of a seemingly limitless town gentry, steamboats and horse cars might have been enough. But New York was also the American version of Dickens's London, the seat of an enormous proletariat, overcrowded and dangerous, the home of the Gangs of New York. The land shortage that forced prosperous people to ride on horse cars and steam ferries

New York Tenements.

had much grimmer consequences for the poor, who could not afford the five-cent fares. As the city grew, the number of poor people and poor families grew – and grew calamitously in the years around 1848, years of famine in Ireland and revolution in Germany. But there was never more land within walking distance of lower Manhattan. The overcrowding that began in the 1820s grew steadily worse. Old houses were divided and divided again. Thousands of large families lived in single rooms, and thousands of the poorest families lived in cellars. Densities, and death rates, climbed as high as in Paris.

When New York's first purpose-built tenements were built, in the 1840s, their builders had philanthropic motives, and the big new buildings were hailed as a solution to the problem of working-class housing. Tenements were the residential equivalent of the iron-framed, gas-lit buildings that were re-shaping downtowns. They were taller than the houses they replaced, and they covered a much higher percentage of their lots, with many more rooms per acre and many fewer windows per room. But living and working are not the same thing. Family life needed light and privacy, and the new tenements gave very little of either. "The Other Half," as reformer Jacob Riis called the New York poor, would live miserably until different forms of mass transit could get them cheaply to the Bronx and Queens.

Haussmann's Paris, Avenue de l'Opera by Camille Pissaro.

The Challenge of Paris

For all their faults, the North Atlantic cities were unquestionably the best urban environments in the world until the 1850s. In that decade, however, they got the first jolts of competition from an old high-density rival. Paris had been stagnant for a long time. Louis XIV had curtailed its growth almost two hundred years earlier by moving his court to Versailles, and the wars of the French Revolution had halted construction for a generation. By 1850, Balzac's Paris was a century and more behind Dickens's London, filthier, darker, more overcrowded, more dangerous; and the noses of nineteenth-century people noticed that it stank.

All that changed in the 1850s and 1860s. When Louis Napoleon created the Second Empire in 1852, he appointed an energetic and unscrupulous genius named Georges Haussmann to transform Paris, and Haussmann brought about the fastest and greatest urban transformation in history. He created the world's finest water system and made sewers that became tourist attractions. He built modern markets and railway stations. He landscaped parks that made the parks of London seem tired and prosaic. He rammed broad avenues through crowded quarters in every part of the city, tearing down one in five Parisian buildings and replacing them with elegant stone-fronted apartment buildings. A new Paris arose, splendid and coherent. People began to call it "the City of Light".

It was stunningly beautiful and amazingly uniform. Haussmann's regulations forced developers and their architects to build in a style based on the grandeur of French architecture in the seventeenth century. Avenues, parks, palatial apartment buildings – the new Paris proclaimed that middle-class Frenchmen could live like nobles in an empire that had embraced the Revolution. Tourists flocked, writers gushed, and Paris went from being an architectural backwater to the observed of all observers in less than a decade.

Suddenly the North Atlantic ideal had a persuasive competitor. The new Paris showed that a city of apartment houses could be beautiful, and that, with good design and good sewers, civilized people could live happy and healthy lives at densities higher than those of North Atlantic slums. This was not lost on the other capital cities of continental Europe. Even more than Paris, they were still what all Northern European cities had been in 1600, with noblemen in palaces and commoners in rented rooms.

Vienna was the first city to form itself on Haussmann's model of wide avenues and palatial apartment buildings. It was even more a court city than Paris, and its new middle classes wanted rather desperately to merge into the old imperial aristocracy. Vienna's enormous Ringstrasse project, started in the late 1850s, allowed middle-class people to live in huge and impressive structures – "rent palaces", the Viennese called them – and Viennese architects added the rambunctious ornament of the Austrian baroque to the Haussmann formula. Berlin and Rome, expanding fast as the capitals of big new national monarchies after 1870, improvised their own variations on the Haussmann theme. Commercial cities like Hamburg and Milan followed suit.

The people of the North Atlantic world felt the impact of Paris as fast as anyone else; but Haussmann's new city was so different from their own hard-won traditions that they picked and chose among Parisian innovations rather than swallowing them whole. Haussmann's wide avenues, built before the buildings that fronted on them, attracted imitators before anything else. Boston's Commonwealth Avenue, laid out in 1856 with a landscaped median strip running its full length, seems to have been the first of many avenues and boulevards on both sides of the ocean. French mansard roofs came next. They were appearing on hotels in England and America before the end of the 1850s and became standard on stylish houses throughout the North Atlantic world in the 1860s. The new city halls of Boston and Baltimore, both of them designed in 1862, followed French fashions as closely as their architects knew how.

Haussmann planted another seed that would eventually grow within the North Atlantic world, sometimes as a wholesome fruit, sometimes as a threatening blight. This was multi-family housing. It was not just that Haussmann's apartment houses looked grand from the street. They were also pleasant to live in. Earlier apartments, in Paris and other continental cities, had been cramped and makeshift; but Parisian architects had been improving room arrangements throughout the 1830s and 1840s, and they were ready for Haussmann's building boom. Although population densities in the new Paris were astonishingly high by London standards – four or five times higher in most cases – and Parisians had considerably less indoor space than Londoners of equivalent wealth, Parisian apartments

Glasgow Tenements.

were elegant and easy to live in, and Parisians did not feel that they were overcrowded. If their apartments were too small for entertaining – well, that is why Parisians perfected the café, invented the restaurant, and promenaded so enviably on their beautiful new avenues.

London took little notice of this – a few elaborate blocks of "Mansion" flats for rich bachelors and some cold-comfort charitable barracks for the poor – and most of the North Atlantic cities followed London. Glasgow and New York, however, leapt with joy. All but the very richest Glaswegians reverted almost instantly to the traditional Scottish pattern of building and living in multi-family buildings. The word "tenement" was no insult in Scotland, and row houses felt at least as foreign as they did in Boston. Many of the new Glasgow buildings, fronted in muscular stone, were well designed both inside and out, and the Second City of the Empire achieved a convincing grandeur in its own unique way.

New Yorkers did not have a high tradition of multi-family living, and the word "tenement" was reserved for the rookeries of the poor. But there was not enough land; something had to give; and Paris allowed New Yorkers to hail apartment buildings as heralds of progress and refinement. New York's first block of respectable flats was designed by a Society architect and built at a fashionable address in 1867. By the 1880s,

The Stuyvesant, 1869, designed by Richard Morris Hunt, New York's first fashionable apartment house.

respectable apartment houses, ranging in size from four-story buildings that looked like houses to the massive ten-story Dakota of 1884, were filling block after block in the new neighborhood west of Central Park. President U.S. Grant, the kind of neighbor one wanted to have, was living in an Upper West Side apartment at the time of his death in 1885.

It was easy for the monarchies of continental Europe to embrace the Parisian model in expanding their capital cities. This was more difficult in the capitals of the North Atlantic countries. These nations were not court societies, and cities of palaces would have offended their principles. Still, the question of capital cities had to be faced, because the North Atlantic countries needed to build three of them, more or less from scratch, in the nineteenth century.

First was The Hague. It was still a tiny place in 1815, the family seat of the Princes of Orange and little more, but it gained importance in that year when the Congress of Vienna made the Prince of Orange the King of the Netherlands. As the capital of a sizable country, including Belgium until 1830, The Hague became the first Dutch city since the seventeenth century to have an appreciable growth spurt. The great Dutch traditions were still, however, vital, and The Hague grew as only a Dutch city could. No royal capital could possibly be less like Paris. The new king stayed in his family's old house, a pleasant city mansion about as big as a second-tier country house in

England, and the courtiers and bureaucrats who gathered round him built sweet little terraces that looked exactly as middle-class London would have looked if London's bricks had been a warm red instead of a yellowy brown. Quietly, the little waterside capital added street to street, tried out the various forms of North Atlantic medievalism, and introduced little greens and parks of beguiling scale. One of them surrounds, quite appropriately, the Peace Palace.

The second new capital felt the pull of Paris much more strongly. Brussels had French as one of its two official languages. It had been the seat of a Hapsburg court for centuries, and courtliness had done as much as poverty to keep Brussels and its perennially war-torn provinces out of the main currents of the North Atlantic world. Prosperity returned after Waterloo, when the great Belgian port of Antwerp gained free access to the sea for the first time since 1648. In 1830, when Flemish and Walloon Catholics threw off the Protestant yoke of the Dutch, Brussels became the capital of a small but suddenly dynamic state. This led to explosive growth; Brussels grew exactly as fast as Philadelphia or Baltimore, from 66,000 people at the beginning of the century to almost half a million at the end. As it expanded, it evolved as an interesting mixture of continental and North Atlantic traditions. Like Paris, it built sweeping boulevards that terminated in monuments or palaces. Like London, it lined them with rows of brick houses.

In the third new capital, Washington, Americans had L'Enfant's French street plan, which in many ways prefigured Haussmann's work, as a foundation; but it took Americans a remarkably long time to realize that they could build an American Paris. The federal bureaucracy was rudimentary for most of the century, and the city was too small to need L'Enfant's enormous avenues. His giant mall, the central element of his design, with a broad, uncluttered vista west from the Capitol, was utterly undeveloped from one end of the century to the other. Much of it remained a marsh, and there was a railroad station in the middle of it, at the bottom of Capitol Hill. Architecturally, the government was content to project its modest grandeur with a handful of classical buildings that would have suited the scale of Dublin.

Washington's scale began to change after the end of the Civil War in 1865. The government began to grow, and a significant number of rich people moved to Washington, or maintained houses there, to enjoy life in political and, particularly, in diplomatic circles. Even so, Washington modeled itself for a long time on London rather than Paris. Government buildings favored dark brick over pale stone, and row houses were ubiquitous. When the city's administrators finally got around to paving the streets, in 1870, they found that L'Enfant's rights-of-way were too wide for their budget, and they saved money by paving only half of each street bed and planting the rest with grass and trees. This had the effect of setting houses twenty feet back from the sidewalks and turning the residential parts of the city into the kind of villagey row house suburbia that

Above. Official Washington, surrounded by Picturesque Row House Washington.

Above left. Residential Washington.

London had been building for twenty years. As Victorian architecture became more elaborate, Washington led the way, with an unequalled profusion of bay windows, turrets, and crenellations even on tiny two-story houses. Charm was almost unavoidable, and every front garden seemed to bloom in Washington's "depraved May" that Henry Adams rather guiltily loved. There was infinite picturesqueness, and no grandeur at all.

It was not until the beginning of the twentieth century that Washington finally set out to become grand in the Parisian way; but even then it got its Paris fashions second-hand, from the Chicago World's Fair of 1893. Chicago's "White City," a giant *papier maché* fantasia of columns and domes, put a sudden end to Victorian medievalism in America and awakened a reforming desire for clarity and light. Of the millions who went to the fair, most seem to have mistaken its French baroque architecture, rooted in Roman classicism, for the architectural classicism of the early American republic; and the fair awakened a desire to return to the ordered liberty of the Founding Fathers.

With this in mind, Washington was the obvious place to build a White City in permanent materials. The McMillan Plan of 1902 set out to realize L'Enfant's vision and legislated French classicism in architecture for the center of the city. The Mall was cleared, drained, and planted as a uniform promenade. New marble office buildings for the Senate and the House of Representatives, flanking the Capitol, were built to illustrate the new official style, and one government department after another got its own palace of limestone. By 1940, when Franklin Roosevelt opened John Russell Pope's National Gallery, the greatest work of American neo-classicism, Washington was an American Brussels, a mixture of continental and North Atlantic traditions: a super-sized American Paris surrounded by an easy-going American London.

The Golden City Years

All the while, the North Atlantic cities were winning their race against public health catastrophe and political revolution. They were building and constantly extending systems for water supply and sewage disposal, and parents no longer lost half of their children to water-borne diseases. They were organizing professional police departments, and people walked their streets in safety. And they were educating their children. Education was a huge political and religious struggle in all the North Atlantic nations, but the right side won. By 1914, almost every child, of every class or race or income group, could learn what Americans called The Three Rs – Reading, 'Riting, and 'Rithmetic – and many had the opportunity to learn more. There were free classical high schools for boys – and eventually girls – who aspired to college or university, and free commercial high schools, vocational high schools, and technical high schools for those who did not. Every city had colleges to train the next generation of teachers, and each city had at least one major university or technical college – some ancient, like Glasgow and Harvard, some new, like Johns Hopkins and the University of London – each bigger and more sophisticated than any institution in the world had been a century before.

If you think of cities as works of art – and this book has probably mystified you if you do not – you will also appreciate a triumph of an aesthetic kind in the North Atlantic cities at the end of the nineteenth century. Americans invented a kind of building that expressed, beautifully and clearly, the reality of a commercial city. Just as Dutch burghers in the seventeenth century had made family reality beautiful by turning the rattletrap medieval row house into capital-A architecture with durable materials, so American businessmen in the late nineteenth century made business reality grand by devising the skyscraper.

What does this mean? Think of ancient Athens. Anyone who approached Athens could see the Acropolis, a temple-crowned citadel, from far off and could surmise that Athens was a city whose central concerns were worship and warfare. Anyone who approached a medieval town, with a castle at the top and a church or cathedral nearby, could hear the same message in a different language. The builders of ancient and medieval cities found ways to proclaim the realities of their societies truthfully and beautifully, and to make them visible from a distance. Before the skyscraper, the builders of merchant cities could not do this. They could build beautiful buildings and beautiful streets, but they could not shape a skyline that was both compelling and truthful. The cathedral domes that rise above Florence and London are compelling, but they seem to say that these are sacred cities, like Rome or Jerusalem, when in fact they are cities of commerce and industry, with businessmen for priests, and lawyers and accountants for acolytes.

The New York Skyline c.1910.

Although Chicago built the first skyscraper (in 1884,) New York built the first compelling skyscraper skyline. The overcrowded island needed to colonize the air, and the businessmen of J.P. Morgan's New York, richer than Chicagoans and finally as rich as Londoners, had the money to embellish acres of vertical wall space artistically. They did not do so for sheer aesthetic pleasure; skyscrapers, like the flamboyant warehouse-palaces that they replaced, had advertising value. The President of the Singer Sewing Machine Company calmly stated that his spectacular 1908 skyscraper had paid for itself through additional sales in Asia alone.

It is hard to believe how many skyscrapers went up in Lower Manhattan between 1890 and 1914. Each one seems to have been the tallest building in the world for at least a week. The most remarkable thing about them, though, was not their individuality. It was something that no one had planned or designed. Somehow, jammed together at the sharp point of Manhattan Island, these individualistic spires formed a collective Cathedral of Commerce. They were the first thing that transatlantic passengers and immigrants saw of America, and almost everyone drew the moral that democracy and equality under law could unleash power and create magnificence. Every American city except Washington (which imposed height limits in the 1890s to preserve its political iconography) had skyscrapers by 1900, and Liverpool finished its dramatic Pierhead trio of tall buildings in the first years of the new century.

The new skyscraper downtowns, packed with people, required steady improvements in mass transit. Electric streetcars replaced horse cars in the mid-1890s, and the smokeless miracle of electricity brought a boom in underground railways, with multiple new lines in London and new underground systems in Boston and Glasgow, all in 1896. New York followed, massively, in 1904, Philadelphia more tentatively in 1907. Each of these improvements doubled the speed of travel and, rivers permitting, quadrupled the amount of land available for urban development. While each invention enabled more people to work downtown, it also allowed them to live farther and farther from downtown, on larger amounts of cheaper land, and each increase in speed allowed a wider range of people to commute. Finally, with electric streetcars and subways, the stable working class could get to new houses on cheap land.

That is why we can walk forever, in any row house city, through neighborhoods of orderly turn-of-the-century rows built for the stable working class. The houses are two stories tall and thirteen to fifteen feet wide, usually with three rooms on each floor. They were bigger than any houses in working-class history, and they had good artificial light, either gas or electric, and separate bedrooms for boys and girls. Many had proper parlors and dining rooms, like middle-class houses. Many, too, had indoor plumbing, a working-class first. If there was an outhouse, it was convenient and private, and it was connected to a public sewer. In America, houses were tolerably well heated. Even in Britain, long the land of chilblains and hot water bottles, stoves and grates improved enough for children to do their schoolwork. Though these improvements cost money – Lewis Mumford calculated that the nineteenth-century innovations of plumbing, heating, and lighting doubled the cost of a house –the stable working class was earning enough to pay for them. And the opening of this mass market finally made house-building a big business, with cost savings based on economies of scale.

These six-room houses usually look like small versions of middle-class houses built a generation or more earlier. In Brooklyn, Philadelphia, and Baltimore, they are usually flat-fronted and classical, often with the large cornices of the Renaissance Revival; in England, Washington, and the American Midwest they are more likely to have little gables or small projecting bays to suggest the Middle Ages or the English village. Artistically, these houses are at their best when their facades are treated simply, as good ornament was too expensive for the working-class market; but even in Washington, which built the most elaborate small houses in the North Atlantic world, decoration was almost entirely a matter of virtuoso bricklaying, and builders generally avoided cheap stained glass and clumsy machine-carved ornament, the Scylla and Charybdis of the Victorian Age. Now that educated middle-class people are rediscovering these houses, it is obvious that these are houses of middle-class quality, conceivably the first ever built for working-class families. Mary Ellen Hayward, one of the first architectural historians to take the working-class row house seriously, called the turn of the twentieth century "The Golden City Years".

Meanwhile, at the top of the social pyramid, people in London and the American cities also seemed to be enjoying golden years. Rich people from smaller places

Good Working-class Houses in London and Baltimore. By 1900, stable working-class families were acquiring marks of gentility, from tiny front gardens in London to white marble steps in Baltimore.

continued to gather in each city for Seasons of parties and plays, and the best neighborhoods continued to blossom forth with elegant houses. The patterns of coming and going, of seeing and being seen and checking in with friends, had changed little since the Long Eighteenth Century, and the rituals of that polite period – promenades, Assemblies and Cotillons, riding rings and carriage drives – continued to be useful. Not surprisingly, then, old fashionable neighborhoods, and new neighborhoods built on old patterns, continued to be famous and to attract both seasonal residents and strolling tourists. W.S. Gilbert, a reliable guide to the prosperous English mind, expected audiences to recognize Belgrave Square as a synonym for wealth and fashion in his 1882 hit *Iolanthe*; and William Dean Howells, two years later, in *The Rise of Silas Lapham*, could assume – successfully – that a broad American reading public would know, and care, about the social and financial nuances of the housing market in Boston's three fashionable row house neighborhoods.

But things were different in the merchant cities of England and Scotland. Gilbert and Howells would have had trouble finding an exemplary avenue or square in Birmingham or Glasgow in the 1880s. The rich were leaving the merchant cities – for the suburbs, for rural areas with good rail connections – if they had not already left them.

We can see the change by walking or driving out from the center of Liverpool on Upper Parliament Street and its fashionable extension, Princes Road. Despite a lot of twentieth-century demolition, there are still enough row houses of various sizes in the first few blocks to show that, although middle-class Liverpudlians were still building proper city houses into the 1880s, rich people had stopped building really big row houses after about 1860. By the end of Princes Road, at Sefton Park, the rows have stopped altogether, and big Victorian villas have taken over.

The same thing was happening in a curious way even in London, albeit less completely and less noticeably. Though the greatest London neighborhoods were still brilliant, that was mainly the work of noblemen, gentlemen, and high civil servants. The luster of those neighborhoods blinded many eyes to the gradual withdrawal of rich members of what Victorians called the commercial classes. By the 1880s, stockbrokers and shipping agents were surrounding the city with the big, stern free-standing houses that figure so often in the Sherlock Holmes stories, and theatre managers were shortening their programs so that suburban playgoers could make the last trains home.

Why did rich Americans, mostly business and professional people, remain loyal to their cities while similar people in their British sister-cities did not? Mainly, one suspects, because business and professional people enjoyed more prestige in America than they did in Britain. America was still – and still is, to a surprising extent – a connected group of regional economies and regional societies, each centered on a particular city. Americans spoke of "Boston Society" or "Baltimore Society". No one in England spoke of "Liverpool Society" or "Birmingham Society". The English spoke simply of "Society," a national hierarchy, centered on London, with noblemen and gentlemen at the top. When railroads made it easy to go from one part of England to another, gentry families deserted the little Assize towns and Cathedral cities, but it was London, a quick train jaunt from everywhere, that took up the slack, not Liverpool or Birmingham. And the lure of the land, with its associated pleasures of politics and sport, continued to draw successful merchants and their children into the rural gentry, as it had for centuries.

It was in this environment that a remarkable new approach to architecture flowered rather brilliantly, beginning in England but spreading rapidly to the United States. It was unlike anything before or since; it seemed odd to most people when it was new; and it went out of style in less than a generation. But that generation built a great deal, and their work had more influence in the next century than anyone would have expected.

To understand what they did, and why, imagine that you had been born in the 1840s or the 1850s. You would have grown up in cities whose architecture was accidentally eclectic. In any short walk, you would have seen Gothic churches, rows of Renaissance houses, and a *soupçon* of Haussmann's Paris. The people who actually did grow up in those decades found that they liked eclecticism and set out to make it intentional. In the process, they made it much more subtle and interesting.

As is generally the case with important movements in architecture, the intentional eclecticism of the 1870s and 1880s expressed a widely-felt cultural enthusiasm, in this case for something that contemporaries called Culture. They followed Matthew Arnold,

Eclectic Houses in the Back Bay, Boston.

their leading essayist, who taught them that the path to a free and open mind lay through the selection and recombination of excellent examples from different times and places, an eclecticism based on connoisseurship. While we still follow Arnold in our notion of what it is to have a liberal education, we do not try to embody liberal education literally in architecture. His generation did. A fashionable street from the 1870s or 80s might have a French chateau at the corner, then a tall brick house with a Flemish gable, then a house that combined a Romanesque turret with a classical doorway and a loggia straight out of Florence in the age of Dante.

The use of houses to express an often quite personal delight in the breadth of world history was peculiar to the North Atlantic cities and got little traction in the palace cities of continental Europe. Like Arnold's Culture, eclectic architecture spoke for openmindedness, freedom from prejudice, and a wide-ranging historical curiosity. Although a long row of eclectic buildings could seem fussy, many of the buildings themselves were excellent works of architecture. It is hard to find better architects than Richard Norman Shaw in England or H.H. Richardson and Stanford White in America, the most famous practitioners of cultured eclecticism. Their approach worked best, however, when a house could stand alone in a good landscape, not when it was connected to other houses in a row. The suburban flight of rich businessmen gave British architects

Bedford Park.

abundant opportunity, and Norman Shaw built dozens of enchanting pseudo-manors within commuting distance of London and other cities. American architects did their best work, in the so-called Shingle Style, at Newport and other fashionable summer resorts. Less fettered by national traditions than the British, Americans felt a greater freedom to mix and match, making eclectic design something of a high-wire act for architects, not all of whom had the right sense of balance. And, as in England, eclecticism worked imperfectly in long rows. But the best American eclectic work was very good. To love Richardson's Sever Hall, at Harvard, is a liberal education.

Although the eclectic impulse burnt out quickly among the rich, most of whom were not cultivated enough to understand its references, Norman Shaw and a few others inadvertently set the pattern for much of Britain's twentieth-century development by taking cultured eclecticism down-market and giving it a comfortably nationalist ideology that contemporaries called "Queen Anne" or "Early English". The prototype, Bedford Park, built in the 1870s with Shaw as its supervising architect, was an ideal village for arty middle-class people, forty minutes by train from the Bank of England. A half-timbered pub, The Tabard, was built beside the station. Houses were built in pairs and short rows, some half-timbered like medieval or Elizabethan houses, others with the proportions and red brick of the early eighteenth century. By the end of a short walk in Bedford Park, you will believe that the English past was a lovely and harmonious affair. All the straight lines and hard edges of Victorian medievalism are softened, and flowers bloom beside curving, tree-shaded streets. Someone in the 1880s said that walking through Bedford Park was like walking through a watercolor painting. It still is.

By the early twentieth century, thoughtful people in the North Atlantic world were more optimistic than they had been for decades. They had overcome the apparently insuperable challenges of the Industrial Revolution. In doing so, they had learned enough to fill the magnificent Eleventh Edition of the *Encyclopedia Britannica*, published in 1910, with their inventions and their discoveries, and they had put their knowledge to good use in every department of life. If you had visited the North Atlantic world in the summer of 1914, you would have found street after street, neighborhood after neighborhood, of well-built rows, with splendor and parties for the rich, comfort and beauty for the middle classes, decency and health for a very high percentage of the industrial labor force. You might have seen the slums, and they would have dismayed you as much as the quality of the smoky air and the horsey slush in the streets, but these things were not new, and they would not have shocked you. The shock of skyscrapers might well have been pleasant.

Unless you had local friends, you would not have seen the suburbs that were spreading farther than you could walk. Even if you had seen them, you would have thought them an augmentation of city life, not a threat to it. If you had gone to see

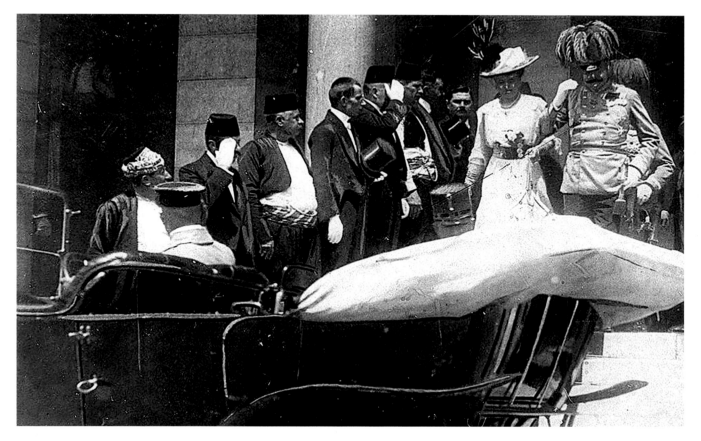

Bedford Park, the revolutionary ideal village of the 1870s, you might have had trouble finding it, or recognizing it when you were in it, because it had become typical, and tens of thousands of people now lived in places of similar design. If you had walked around the Manchester suburbs that were new in Engels's day, you would have noticed that Shaw's village-based eclecticism had spread beyond London and filtered down to all levels of the middle classes. The big villas and semi-detached houses of the 1830s and 40s were still there, with their names incised on their gateposts, but by 1914 they were intermixed with new rows and crescents of charming little gabled houses, many with diamond-paned windows and stuccoed gables, each with a garden in front and shady trees on the street.

You might, in short, have imagined that the North Atlantic tradition would continue forever, evolving slowly and giving more people a better life in predictable ways. But it was the summer of 1914. A fat Archduke and his wife were about to be murdered in an unpronounceable place, and no tradition was safe.

Franz Ferdinand and Sophie in Sarajevo moments before their assassination.

Chapter Six

WARS AND PEACES

If you had visited any one of the North Atlantic cities in the early summer of 1914, your hosts would probably have told you that their city had come through the storms of the nineteenth century with flying colors, and you would probably have believed them. Each city had survived the various life-threatening crises of the Industrial Revolution – the epidemics, the riots, the continual dislocations of progress and explosive growth – and all of them were now giving more people a better life than the world had ever seen. Everyone now had fresh water, all children went to school, life expectancy was beginning its astonishing twentieth-century climb. And the people of the North Atlantic communities had accomplished all these things without giving up the basic commitments that had marked the North Atlantic tradition for three centuries. People still valued freedom and privacy, nuclear families and the rule of law; they had not surrendered their freedoms to emperors or dictators; and rows and terraces of houses stretched for miles around every big-city train station. By the end of your visit, you would probably have predicted a flourishing of the North Atlantic tradition for the decades to come.

St. Paul's Cathedral in the Blitz.

We know what happened next, as your hosts in the spring of 1914 did not. We know about World War I, and we are used to smiling with sad irony at the various kinds of pre-war optimism. Everyone who writes about this period seems to tell us, sooner or later, that the civilized people of 1914 were like passengers on the *Titanic*, smug and over-confident, and did not foresee the horrors that awaited them. We know that the Tsar and the Kaiser fell, and that worse tyrants replaced them; and we have it in the back of our mind that the Great War, the War to End All Wars, marked the end of some historical period.

It is worth remembering that ocean liners continued to get bigger and faster after the *Titanic* hit her iceberg; they just sailed more carefully and carried more lifeboats. That is not a bad way of thinking of the effect of World War I on the North Atlantic nations. Although the war was terrible, particularly for the British, the governments of the North Atlantic nations survived without disruption, and their economies prospered. In short, the war did not bring sudden or fundamental change to the North Atlantic societies, as it most emphatically did to societies on the Continent. When peace came in 1918, North Atlantic growth and innovation returned to patterns that had been set before 1914.

There was to be much real growth in those two inter-war decades; and many innovations, both technical and political, would bring comfort and freedom to millions of people, often for the first time. The North Atlantic societies would be strong enough to win the next great war and generous enough to make their defeated enemies into allies. And the people of the North Atlantic cities in the inter-war years would build buildings and neighborhoods that we still admire and love.

Not until the 1960s would people notice that something was going wrong with their cities. Then, it sometimes seems, everyone woke up with a start and wondered if it was too late. There would be an urban crisis in the 1960s and 70s, often capitalized as the Urban Crisis. By 1975, people on both sides of the ocean would be wondering if their cities would survive, or even if they should – or if, like ocean liners in the age of air travel, they were best suited to the scrapyard.

Interwar Britain: Metro-Land

But 1975 was in the remote future when the guns fell silent in 1918. Continuity and progress appeared to walk hand in hand. In fact, in Britain, the decades between the World Wars were a triumph of the North Atlantic tradition, conceivably the best time since the Dutch Golden Age of the 1600s for people of small means to build good houses and pleasant neighborhoods. Architects and builders and government officials set a pattern of urban expansion that met the needs and desires of their people with affordable beauty and a small carbon footprint. From one end of the country to another – and in Ireland, an independent nation after 1921 – there arose a whole world of picturesque houses and terraces in the mold of Bedford Park, with curving roads, roofs of tile or slate, and flowers blooming in front gardens. Britain built four million houses in the twenty inter-war years, enough to house forty percent of the national population, and almost all of these new dwellings went to make good environments in the North Atlantic tradition. It is not easy to make mass-produced housing into art, and British inter-war achievement is worth analyzing.

To begin, there was a solid foundation of taste. The late-Victorian highbrow enthusiasm for Early England had filtered down through many strata of the middle classes in all parts of the country, and in Ireland, but the enthusiasm was not yet stale: those arch-highbrows Lord Peter Wimsey and Harriet Vane could still plausibly break into Early English folk song in a shop in the mid-1930s. There was also the solid old North Atlantic building culture of houses tied together in groups, at twelve to the acre or more, a culture shared by almost everyone, from sailors and coal heavers near the docks to noblemen and gentlemen near Parliament and the Court. It all added up to a national housing market that was remarkably united in its desires and collectively rich enough to attract good designers, not to mention the publishers of national magazines for architects, builders, and fashion-conscious housewives.

Ebenezer Howard.

Left. Letchworth Garden City.

Then, there was a great man. Ebenezer Howard was both an amateur and a bit of a crank, but neither of those qualities has ever been an insuperable barrier in the homeland of Christopher Wren and John Wood the Elder. Like most Englishmen in the 1890s, Howard was horrified by the filth and smokiness of the Victorian city; and he cherished a life-long passion for Early England. If he had been rich, he might have commissioned a pseudo-manor from Norman Shaw, and his name would be unknown today. But he was far from rich, and he had withal another typical 1890s passion, a fierce belief in social reform, honed by years of following Parliamentary debates as a drudging copyist for Hansard, the official Parliamentary record. In 1898, he published a little book called *Tomorrow: A Peaceful Path to Real Reform*, illustrated with geometric diagrams of concentric towns that he called Garden Cities. *Tomorrow* was exactly the kind of little book that has usually been the stopping place of most earnest cranks, even in England, but Howard was no ordinary crank. Like Wren and Wood before him, he could get people to believe in him. He formed an organization, aggregated capital, bought land, and lured in some of Britain's most talented young designers to turn his diagrams into a reality called Letchworth Garden City.

If Bedford Park brought Early English design to the middle classes in the 1870s, Letchworth brought it down another notch or two at the turn of the century. The time was right for doing this; Sir William Lever, a rich soap-maker in Liverpool, was building houses and streets of heart-breaking Early English beauty for his workers at Port Sunlight in exactly the same years. But Howard's Garden Cities were not essays in top-down benevolence. He was the prophet of a better world, and he meant to re-house the whole English nation. Not only did he provide a theoretical framework for an Early English utopia, he also put it on a solid business footing and brought it about on a large scale. And he built a great team. Under the guidance of his chief architects, Barry Parker

Hampstead Garden Suburb.

and Raymond Unwin, geniuses in small forms, Letchworth earned its reputation as a university of planning, design, and building.

To see what Parker and Unwin learned at Letchworth, go to their second big project, Hampstead Garden Suburb near Hampstead Heath in London. Not since Bath had Englishmen designed or built so well. Parker and Unwin led the team, and the great architect Edwin Lutyens contributed, among other things, one of the most exciting churches of the twentieth century. All in all, Hampstead Garden Suburb may be the best residential environment in Britain. It was well along by 1914, and most of its designers survived the war, ready to take up their pencils again in a good cause.

The final element of Britain's inter-war felicity was mass transport. This had been essential to the high-volume evolution of the North Atlantic tradition during the Industrial Revolution, and every British city was well served in 1918. Trams and motor buses sufficed for the cities of two million people: Liverpool, Manchester, Birmingham, and Glasgow. As for London, with eight million people and greater distances to travel, there was the Underground; and it was the good fortune of inter-war Londoners to enjoy the Underground's first golden age, when the Underground led the world in station architecture and revolutionized the mapping of complicated networks.

London developers worked closely with Underground companies so that rail extensions would support new developments to mutual advantage. One Underground line, the Metropolitan, owned a great deal of developable land along its right-of-way and turned itself into one of the country's largest developers. The Metropolitan called its developments Metro-Land and promoted them with gushy prose and dreamy pictures of embowered cottages. It is hard to look at a Metro-Land picture without wanting to buy an Underground ticket and go there. Every suburban town around every British city built new neighborhoods of the Metro-Land type.

Metro-Land Advertisement, 1921.

Left. Metro-Land Reality, Harrow

Metro-Land brought mass production to Howard's Garden City ideals. With the return of peace in 1918, Parker, Unwin, and the other graduates of Howard's informal university went to work with a will. Garden City principles guided the development of most of Britain's four million inter-war dwellings, and England's vast national Metro-Land still accounts for more than a quarter of all British dwellings. As always, mass production brought some coarsening of detail, and the inter-war Metro-Lands are different from a true, pre-war Garden City in a hundred potentially meaningful ways; but they are very good places to live, and a walk through any one of them – in London or Manchester or a hundred other cities – can give a visitor hours of sustained pleasure.

Houses in Metro-Land were built in terraces or pairs. Their architectural style was usually Early English, with half-timbered gables and ornamental bricks in walls of stucco – though the Georgian Revival, in smooth stucco or red brick, had an increasing influence as the years went by. Every house in the national Metro-Land had a garden in the front, most of them blooming with some kind of flower for most of the relatively mild British year. The result of it all was neighborhoods that looked like blossoming versions of Warwick after its rebuilding in 1694, where half-timbered Early English houses shared streets with classical houses in brick and stucco.

Metro-Land brought high-fashion design to people of what the British called the lower middle-classes, and did so without government subsidies or private charity. This, in its cozy English way, was something of a revolution, and pre-1914 England might have settled for it. But the War, the ghastly democracy of mechanized death in the trenches, had brought social classes more closely together; and the working classes – always described in the plural in this period, by friends and foes alike – now fully enfranchised, expected a reward for their efforts; and housing was close to the top of their political wish list.

Though working-class people could not afford Metro-Land, they wanted it, and His Majesty's government set out to make this possible. No sooner was the ink dry at Versailles than Lloyd George and his zealous Minister of Health, Christopher Addison, proclaimed a massive program called Homes for Heroes, in which government money would build middle-class houses and rent them to working-class veterans at subsidized rates.

Homes for Heroes was good news for British cities, and for the North Atlantic tradition. Although the houses in Addison's first year cost too much, and standards for government-financed developments were soon lowered somewhat, the quality of design and construction remained high, and new residents routinely told reporters and sociologists that they felt as if they'd been given rooms in Buckingham Palace.

It could have played out differently. Britain could have followed the lead of Germany and Austria, where Socialist and Communist collectives built giant working-class apartment complexes with excellent Expressionist architecture. These were well-known in Britain, and pilgrimages to Berlin and Vienna became obligatory for architects and city officials. But huge Expressionist buildings did not catch on in Britain. Metro-Land caught on.

Government-financed housing was successful in large measure because it respected, and even strengthened, English traditions of local government. Though the national government paid for new working-class housing, town and borough councils developed it and managed it, so that it came to be known, and is still known, as council housing. In all, the nation's councils built a million houses and apartments between the wars, a quarter of the national total. Councils had unprecedented money and power, and dynamic council leaders like George Lansbury and Herbert Morrison could rise to national prominence in Parliament and even enter the Cabinet, something new in British political history.

Whether built for workers or for managers, with private or public money, the new Metro-Lands were comprehensively planned. They had to be; unlike developments in earlier centuries, they depended on water, sewer, and gas lines that required sophisticated engineering. But they did not have to be planned for beauty or convenience, yet they usually were. Town planning – the design and building of entire urban districts that were beautiful and orderly – rapidly transformed itself from a movement into a profession. Schools of architecture began to offer Planning courses, like those pioneered by Patrick Abercrombie at the University of Liverpool, and good developers of large tracts were careful to take professional advice. These large pre-planned developments were Metro-Land at its best.

Of course, not all developers were good, or aesthetically ambitious, or well enough capitalized to plan and build entire neighborhoods. Many took advantage of England's excellent networks of trams and motor buses to line country roads with houses that backed onto fields and pastures – "ribbon development" – a cheap but ugly development pattern that became increasingly dangerous as car traffic increased. Planners led the fight against ribbon development, finally winning it after the next war.

It was in these inter-war years that the great Danish architect Steen Eiler Rasmussen celebrated London as "the spreading city" and urged his fellow Danes, and everyone in the apartment-house nations of continental Europe, to follow London's example. He could have expanded his praise to include the rest of England, as well as Scotland and newly-independent Ireland. Metro-Land saw the best coordination of planners with developers since the Amsterdam Canal Belt, and the best effort of mass-market housing in history. Although the Metropolitan's dreamy posters and gushy prose emphasized the rural feel of Metro-Land, the result was really urban, and urban at a high level within the North Atlantic tradition.

Interwar America: Automotive Suburbia

America should have been in a better position than Britain in 1918 to build well. Even before the war, the great coastal cities of the United States had been better places to live in than any British city except London, and the hardships of war had only accentuated the difference. America was richer than Britain, and it diffused its wealth somewhat more broadly, so that middle-class and working-class neighborhoods in American cities were uniformly better-built than their British equivalents. And American cities still had the allegiance of the rich. Every large American city was a social capital as well as a business center, with a Season of Assemblies and debutante parties to complement the workings of its skyscraper downtown. And the North Atlantic traditions still appeared to be holding. Most of America's North Atlantic cities were still building spacious middle-class row houses in 1914, and the glittering rituals of American Society were still concentrating "Society people" in rows and squares near the center of town.

But it was all a lot weaker than it looked. Most young Society people had already moved to the suburbs by 1914, leaving their parents behind in the world of terraces and squares, a world that was losing its function. America was becoming a more centralized country, both economically and politically, and New York and (to a lesser extent) Washington were displacing regional capitals like Boston and Philadelphia before 1914. Increasingly, the small-town rich bypassed the regional capitals, and the most prominent people of Philadelphia and Boston no longer had anyone to meet except each other. By 1914, they were wondering why they had to breathe the sooty air of a city and pay taxes to corrupt politicians when it was within their power to live in leafy suburbs, commute to work and shopping by train or streetcar, and rely on fashionable schools, fashionable resorts, and the newly-invented country clubs to bring about suitable matches for their children.

When Society's elderly died off, with their children already living in suburban towns or neighborhoods, the best central neighborhoods in one city after another collapsed almost overnight. In the five years between 1917 and 1922, the beautiful

Frederick Law Olmsted.

houses around Baltimore's Mt. Vernon Place went from eighty percent owner-occupied to eighty percent absentee-owned. As usual, middle-class families followed the lead of the rich, and very few middle-class families built row houses after 1918.

They did not, however, stop building. America's post-war building boom was enormous, a part of the greater economic boom known ever since as "the Roaring Twenties". We should be grateful to Roaring Twenties Americans for giving us the two greatest skyscrapers in the world, the Chrysler and the Empire State, but we should wish that they had built neighborhoods and cities as well as they built skyscrapers. If they had built spreading cities on the London model and created an American Metro-Land at twelve or fourteen families to the acre, American cities might not have gone into life-threatening crisis in the 1960s, and we might not be worrying about global climate change today. As it was, the most influential nation of the twentieth century began to build sprawling cities rather than spreading cities. American developers put far fewer families on an acre of land than their British contemporaries were doing. Although America's new pattern of residential development produced decent neighborhoods for millions and occasional oases of beauty, it did so at the cost of a ruinous amount of heating, cooling, and, above all, driving.

American sprawl and British spread came from the same complex of values and desires. It was all a matter of degree. People in both countries wanted beauty, privacy, freedom, and tradition, but Americans wanted more privacy with their beauty, more freedom with their tradition. And each country's development had a kind of a patron saint. In England, this was Ebenezer Howard. In America, it was Frederick Law Olmsted. Both men were born reformers. Both disliked the smoky cities of the nineteenth century and yearned for a union of Man with Nature. But Howard had a tradition within which he could work, the English village and the village-like suburbs of Victorian London. Olmsted did not, except what he had made from scratch by designing what may be the greatest city parks in the world. And the solitary Olmsted sought a more direct communion with nature than the more sociable Howard dreamed of. In the absence of a usable village tradition, Olmsted used his own parks as his model for ideal communities; and he wondered if, with his help, people could build houses in parks and live their whole lives in communion with the earth.

By the 1890s, when rich Americans were ready to experiment with year-round suburbia, Olmsted was an old man, but he threw himself with his customary energy into the design of park-suburbs, and he had two gifted sons working with him. When his mind failed, his sons stepped forward and created America's dominant firm of landscape architects. If we find ourselves in an American neighborhood with the word "park" in its name, we may infer an origin in the 1890s. If people tell us that their neighborhood was designed by "Olmsted," we should usually assume that his sons did the actual work.

Roland Park, Baltimore.

Just as Howard and Olmsted had much in common, so the American park-suburb had much in common with the English garden city. Both types of development hoped to place daily life in a setting of pleasant nature, and both favored curving streets, preserved trees, and architecture that comfortably evoked the past. But there was a vital difference. Garden cities were a movement of social reform, an urgent attempt to improve the lives of people in the working classes and the lower-middle classes. America's park-suburbs were built for the rich.

These suburbs were, and are, very beautiful. Every city in America's temperate zones has good examples of them, from Brookline and Chestnut Hill in Boston to Windsor Farms in Richmond. Americans used to say that their country was raw and uncouth until it became civilized in the first third of the twentieth century, and we can see what they meant if we wander through Bronxville, just outside of New York City, or along the Main Line of Philadelphia.

The best example of Olmsted design on a large scale is in Baltimore, in Roland Park and the other neighborhoods developed by Edward Bouton. He was neither a reformer nor, at the beginning, an artist; he was a hard-nosed business man from the booming cow town of Kansas City who came to the old-money politeness of the North Atlantic world as an outsider on the make. But the work brought out things in him that may have surprised him. In a career that lasted from 1891 to the eve of World War II, Bouton bought and brilliantly developed more than two square miles of land on Baltimore's northern outskirts, combining in a seamless way the design of buildings with the design of landscapes. The Olmsteds landscaped his neighborhoods after 1901, and he spared no expense to turn their plans into reality. Together, the Bouton-Olmsted team tackled difficult topography, preserved mature trees, and graded ruthlessly when their vision required it. They invented the cul-de-sac, and made it beautiful. Hiking trails snaked beside private gardens, and a generation of architects received a mix of smiles and frowns from Bouton that called forth thousands of excellent designs.

In the vast Bouton-Olmsted tapestry, each neighborhood was distinct, but all flowed together seamlessly; and they had, between them, enough people of compatible tastes and budgets to support schools, churches, and shopping. There were big houses and (relatively) small houses, formal mansions and picturesque cottages, apartments for childless people and common playing fields lifted directly from the work of Parker and Unwin. In the end, Bouton, a westerner with a cattle-drive vocabulary that must have amused his patrician customers, achieved his stated goal of "corralling half of the Baltimore *Blue Book* [the register of people in Baltimore Society] onto the lands of the Roland Park Company".

The problem with the great park-suburbs was not that they were poorly designed or ineptly planned, but that they set a bad example of wasteful sprawl. And, since they were built for the rich, who had the power to set fashion, their example was followed. Though middle-class people could not afford custom architecture or sensitive Olmstedian landscapes in the years after 1918, an enormous number of them could afford to buy half an acre of land, or a fifth of an acre, and put a house in the middle of it. They did so.

The results of their labor are harder to like than the park-suburbs of the rich. Like all suburban environments, the middle-class neighborhoods of the Roaring Twenties needed good landscaping, but good landscaping was too expensive for middle-class house buyers. Their developers chopped trees indiscriminately, leveled valleys, buried streams in pipes, and laid streets in grids. The new suburbs were as barren as they look in the chase scenes of silent movies. If middle-class Americans had been willing to live on smaller lots, in semi-detached houses or in terraces, they could have pooled the cost of better landscapes, as the British were doing in Metro-Land. Bouton himself produced a charming English-style garden city, Dundalk, for shipyard workers during World War I. But American fashions were set by the rich in their free-standing houses, and even barren lots were powerful status symbols in the middle-class suburbs of the Roaring Twenties. Americans could have softened their new neighborhoods if, like the British, they had discovered the pleasures of gardening. Instead, they planted grass and mowed it. Americans still do not refer to the plots of land in front of their houses and behind them as "gardens". They call them "yards" – as in barnyards or railroad yards. The people of America's North Atlantic cities are no different in this respect from Midwesterners and Californians.

Anyone who wanders the middle-class suburbs built around America's North Atlantic cities in the 1920s will notice that most of the houses are made of wood, and that their outlines have little or nothing to do with the traditions of Amsterdam, London,

Middle-class American Suburbia. A 1920s Bungalow in Baltimore, built at a density of five houses to the acre.

or the Long Eighteenth Century. While some of them echo the American adapters of Shaw's Early English, most derive from prototypes that evolved in the American Midwest and were publicized by America's middle-class magazines in the first third of the twentieth century. American magazines had little to say about row houses. Like media moguls today, publishers in the years around 1918 played to the largest market, and most middle-class Americans lived in free-standing houses made of wood. Even *The Ladies' Home Journal*, written and edited on an elegant square in the heart of Philadelphia, printed hundreds of house plans without offering a house that was designed to be built in a row. The most common published house types, with names like "bungalows" and "foursquares," proliferated on the outskirts of all American cities, the North Atlantic cities among the rest, until the Great Depression ended building in 1929.

By 1930, then, in the United States, the North Atlantic tradition had lost both the rich and the middle classes. Almost everyone who could afford to live at low density was doing so. With so few houses per acre, there were hardly ever enough people within walking distance of any single place to support a neighborhood shopping district or a public school. How did people made a life for themselves under such conditions? They bought cars.

If you have to pick only one reason for the divergence between the North Atlantic cities of Britain and America between the wars, you should pick cars every time. Even in 1913, when Henry Ford brought assembly line production to the auto industry, the rate of car ownership was already two and a half times higher in America than in England. By 1930, when British carmakers finally installed their first assembly lines, the pattern of Britain's national Metro-Land was already set. Thus, most of the four million new homes built in Britain between the wars were, and are, good places to live without a car, while their American equivalents were, and are, not.

For all that, America's North Atlantic cities continued to build row houses by the thousand, mostly for working-class families. Many of the buyers were first- or second-generation immigrants from countries with radically different traditions in building. They did not drive cars or read national design magazines. What they knew of America was what they saw in the port-of-entry neighborhoods of their cities, the bottom edge of the North Atlantic tradition; and they made of it what they could. The builders and developers who catered to them worked almost entirely without the guidance or inspiration of good architects. No Ebenezer Howard inspired them. No Barry Parker, no Raymond Unwin designed for them.

By the 1920s, American row houses had become a mere regional survival, almost a folk art. As happens with folk arts, each region did its best to become a sub-region. Each of the row house cities developed its own styles in isolation from the others. It takes no training or experience to notice that row houses built in Washington after about 1880 are planetarily different from row houses of the same size and vintage in Baltimore, forty miles away. This augured poorly for the North Atlantic building tradition in America.

To us, it may appear that America's Society people, the clients of Bouton and the Olmsteds, the tastemakers and fashion-setters of America's North Atlantic cities, betrayed their urban and architectural heritage by moving to park-suburbs. Having inherited beautiful urban environments in the tradition of Amsterdam and Bath, they tossed them carelessly aside and built themselves irresponsible enclaves, segregated by class and race, miles away from the people whose lives they controlled. Not surprisingly, they did not see it that way. Rather than thanking their parents and grandparents for building great terraces and squares, young Society people abused their parents for making houses and lives that were stiff and dark and repressive. The best of the young, the Progressives, went further and castigated their Victorian forebears for abandoning political virtue in a relentless scramble for high-volume money. For them, great nineteenth-century quarters like Philadelphia's Rittenhouse or Boston's Back Bay were mere spoils of corruption, products of the dark industrial decades when America had sold its birthright of political purity for a mess of industrial pottage. A Boston guidebook of 1912 felt obliged to apologize for the bad taste of the Bostonians who had commissioned H.H. Richardson's magnificent Trinity Church in the 1870s.

Informality, light, political reform – all these things came together in American buildings that revived the architecture of the Long Eighteenth Century. So did snobbery:

A Georgian Revival House.

Society people were eager to celebrate their connection to America's heroic past as a way of distinguishing themselves from the new rich and from America's immigrant masses. Progressive or not, they restored manor houses in the Chesapeake country and saltboxes in New England, and they adorned Olmsted suburbs with houses inspired by those originals. They saw little, however, to restore or copy in their cities.

This did not prevent them from doing some good urban work. It was they who rebuilt the center of Washington, turning a messy set of afterthoughts into the Mall and creating the grandest urban environment in the country. They expanded Jefferson's Virginia Capitol in Richmond and created a beautifully-scaled ceremonial boulevard with the not-yet-incorrect aim of honoring the leaders of the southern Confederacy. They even launched a movement, the City Beautiful, and adorned American cities with marble court houses and tree-lined boulevards, most spectacularly in Philadelphia. To train the next generation of civilized people and political reformers, they brought Colonial architecture and City Beautiful planning to many of their greatest colleges and universities. Harvard took the lead with some individual Colonial Revival buildings in the early 1890s. Then came Columbia and Johns Hopkins with whole new Colonial/City Beautiful campuses. The campus reform movement reached a stately conclusion with Harvard's River Houses, finished in the mid-1930s, on the same schedule as the Mall in Washington.

This was impressive, and the Progressives accomplished great things in many fields, but their understanding of cities was incomplete. They had too much faith in political

Eliot House, Harvard.

and administrative reform, too little sense of what cities were or how they worked. In the end, the Progressives thought they could make great cities without living in them.

By the end of the Roaring Twenties, middle-class people were eager to follow their lead. The discovery of cottages on Cape Cod and the restoration of small wooden houses in Williamsburg furnished affordable models with impeccable colonial credentials. Though few small colonial houses were built before the music stopped in 1929, the desire to build them survived and strengthened, awaiting its opportunity.

Enter the Apartment House

All the while, as millions of people on both sides of the ocean were stampeding out of their cities in hopes of more private space than the North Atlantic tradition provided for, millions of others were hoping for less. They wanted to live alone, in apartments.

The apartment revolution came, not from architecture, but from changes in cooking. This had been a full-time job since the dawn of time, and it had never been possible for an employed person to live alone. Wives and servants had spent many hours over a hot stove; unmarried people had lived with their parents or their employers, or boarded with another family, or shared the cost of a cook in a boarding house. Gas stoves and prepared foods changed all that at the beginning of the twentieth century. There should be a monument to the first person who ever came home from a full day's work and cooked dinner.

This provoked a real estate crisis in the North Atlantic cities. No one wanted to live in a boarding house or a lodging house any more, but every row of large houses had at least one of them, most of them presided over by widows like Sherlock Holmes's

Park Avenue, New York.

Mrs. Hudson. Boarding and lodging houses vanished with astonishing speed after the war, leaving thousands of Mrs. Hudsons in houses that they could no longer afford to keep up. Like Society people, they sold out to absentees, and it soon happened that entire neighborhoods were owned by people who lived somewhere else and viewed their houses only as a source of income. Houses and neighborhoods usually began a downward spiral. Maintenance fell victim to profit. A coat of "tenement tan" paint often did duty for elegance indoors

Things tended to be better in the big new apartment buildings that became common after the war. These were often well designed. Purpose-built apartments had proper sitting rooms, distinct dining rooms, and ample light from ample windows – and a building superintendent, or even a doorman, to take care of maintenance and receive packages and visitors. In the years after World War I, apartments ceased to be prisons for the poor or luxuries for the rich. They became a rational and liberating choice for working people, single and married – both men and, increasingly, women.

The result is most obvious in New York, long America's unique outpost of apartment living. To look down Park Avenue or West End Avenue is to see a new kind of city. Buildings that would count as skyscrapers anywhere else, twelve to fifteen stories tall, here are merely sections of the long walls that frame the street. They form solid rows of red brick and pale stone. If they were not so large, we might think we were in any good street of Georgian terraces.

Palatial Apartments, Grosvenor Square, London.

And what a lot of them got built so quickly! On Manhattan's Upper West Side, apartment houses went up at a rate of twenty-five to thirty per year all through the Roaring Twenties. Across Central Park, on the Upper East Side, builders wallpapered fifty blocks of Park Avenue with harmonious leviathans between 1917 and 1929; and almost all of the extravagant Gilded Age mansions in Fifth Avenue opposite Central Park gave way to apartment houses of fifteen stories or more, some with multi-level apartments as big as the houses they replaced.

While no city in the North Atlantic world came close to New York for the volume or quality of apartment construction, the two large national capitals, London and Washington, did their best. In the best streets of both cities, developers sacrificed hecatombs of elegant houses to make way for elegant apartment buildings. The loss was more serious in London, where most of the best Georgian houses on the great squares of St. James and Mayfair disappeared in the twenties and thirties, replaced in most cases by massive Georgian Revival apartment buildings. It is perhaps a measure of the confusion built into unplanned eighteenth-century London that there was little outcry over the destruction of so many irreplaceable masterpieces at precisely the moment when their historical style was most in fashion.

In New York, the acceptance of apartment living as a good thing for upper-class and middle-class people – mainly childless people and families with second houses – eased the development of expansive apartment-house quarters for working-class families. By 1918, most of the people in Jacob Riis's "Other Half" could finally get off Manhattan Island on a splendid system of subways and bridges. Manhattan's population declined

The Grand Concourse. The Bronx, New York.

rapidly after 1920 as the "outer boroughs" of Brooklyn, Queens, and the Bronx grew to equal Manhattan itself in population. When working-class families got to the urban frontier, they found clean air, parks, and thousands of apartment houses, generally ranging from five to ten stories, many designed by competent architects. Every room had a window, every apartment a bathroom. Many streets were spacious and orderly, and avenues like the Grand Concourse in the Bronx were impressive.

Too many buildings and streets, however, too many entire neighborhoods, were dreary and hard-edged. Only people conditioned to accept New York's tenements would have embraced them so eagerly. To create more humane environments for poorly-paid workers would have required large government investments, as it did in Britain; but the administrations of Harding and Coolidge were not interested in anything that smacked of Socialism. That left New York to solve its own problems, which it did to the best of its ability. The city's property tax abatements were generous enough to call forth six hundred thousand housing apartments during the inter-war years, an astonishing total; but the abatements were not enough to build graciously.

The only attempt to create a bit of Metro-Land in New York in the Roaring Twenties, Sunnyside Gardens in Queens, shows what might have been. The streets are quiet and well-shaded. Rows of simple, two-story houses frame the streets, and there are common green spaces for everyone. Sunnyside Gardens was exciting when it was new, and it is decidedly pleasant today. But it took charitable investment to build Sunnyside Gardens, and there was nowhere near enough charity, even in New York, to house six hundred thousand families pleasantly.

Sunnyside Gardens. Queens, New York.

Working-class apartment development arrived in England a little later, in the 1930s, through the desire to clear slums and rehouse slum populations. The desire was certainly understandable, as much Victorian housing was shoddy when it was new, and hardly any of it had been updated with modern inventions like plumbing. Ambitious councilors wanted to clear substandard housing, and residents were anxious to live in better places; but residents often did not want to leave their neighborhoods, and councilors wanted to retain voters for whom they had done a favor. This posed a conundrum: how to replace overcrowded slums with new neighborhoods that accommodated the same number of people? Developments of the Metro-Land type, aiming for twelve houses to the acre, could not meet this demand.

The answer, it seemed, was building council flats instead of council houses. There was renewed interest in Socialist and Communist housing experiments in Berlin and Vienna, and, this time, enthusiasm for council flats was not confined to the political Left: New York and Mayfair were setting fashions on the Right as well. The two strands of opinion met in Liverpool, where a Conservative council took the lead in building council housing along German and Austrian lines. Under an energetic City Architect named Lancelot Keay (eventually Sir Lancelot,) Liverpool cleared acres of old slums and built big new complexes with dramatic Expressionist architecture. Leeds came next, with a gigantic Bauhaus development called Quarry Hill Flats. Soon everyone was building council flats, even Birmingham, which resisted longer than any other large community. Most councils, however, shied away from fancy architectural statements. London's inter-

Gerard Gardens, Liverpool, 1935.

war council flats were typical, simple five-story walkups with brick facades on the street and balconies at all levels on the rear. They are unobtrusive until you learn to recognize them, and they appear to be good neighbors in almost all parts of town.

No one in any British city seems to have considered preserving and renovating the existing housing stock. This was understandable in many cases, but it was carried too far. Zealous councilors demolished many old houses of historic and artistic value. There was an unmistakable element of emotional release in destroying bad places and starting life afresh. There was also the quite rational realization that terraced houses did not always divide well into apartments. Floors were often too big or too small. Staircases were often in the wrong place. Upstairs tenants had no access to the rear yard or garden – a serious inconvenience if rubbish was picked up at the back, not to mention if there was a shared outhouse, as there still so often was. The good old houses had been built for lower densities, and had adapted poorly to higher-density demands as their neighborhoods decayed. They were not allowed a second chance.

By the time the next World War broke out, in 1939, the North Atlantic tradition of row houses at moderate density seemed to be obsolescent. The city of the future, it appeared, would have two parts: a core of high-density apartment houses for the rich and the poor and a corona of low-density suburbs for the middle classes.

World War II

The Second World War did what the First had not: it dramatically affected the North Atlantic nations and drastically changed their cities. On the European side of the ocean, the changes were wrought by bombing and politics. On the American side, they occurred as the result of massive wartime industrialization and associated internal migrations.

Bombing was certainly the most obvious of these. The first city to be bombed was Rotterdam, the Dutch port that had risen in the late 19th century to become the busiest harbor in Continental Europe. On May 14, 1940 – perhaps by mistake – the *Luftwaffe* destroyed the entire center of the city, leveling a square mile of buildings and making 85,000 people homeless. Things got even more serious ten days later, when the *Luftwaffe* accidentally dropped bombs on a few houses in the London suburbs. Churchill and the RAF retaliated against Berlin the next night, and the Nazi leadership prepared for revenge. The bombing of London began on September 7 and lasted, with lapses and changes in weaponry, until the end of the war, four and a half years later. The first months were the worst, with bomber runs day and night. We have all seen countless pictures of the London Blitz: buildings collapsing, people sleeping in the Underground, Spitfires and Hurricanes, the dome of St. Paul's rising indomitable above the smoke. By the time the last V-2 rocket fell, more than forty thousand Londoners had been killed, more than two million houses damaged or destroyed.

We have seen fewer pictures of bomb damage in Britain's other cities, but things were no better there. Liverpool, the destination of almost all supply convoys from America and the world, was hit proportionately as hard as London. Docks were smashed and Foster's great Customs House gutted in raids that killed more than four thousand civilians and left acres of desolation. Belfast was caught unawares, with horrific casualties and a hundred thousand people made homeless in one night. Bristol, blitzed again and again in 1940 and 1941, lost much of its downtown, and Coventry's roofless Cathedral became the national symbol of horror and loss. These cities were all ports or industrial centers, and as such "legitimate" targets in the logic of modern warfare; but both sides also bombed sites of cultural importance in a misguided attempt to break morale. Much beauty was smashed in Bath, Norwich, and other historic towns simply because it was beautiful.

Britain put four million of its citizens, about eight percent of the total population, into uniform and still managed to produce a high percentage of the ships, planes, tanks, and guns that British servicemen used. As in the First War, women took the places of men on farms and in factories.

America mobilized women too – Rosie the Riveter is still something of a national icon – but there were not enough women to staff America's war effort, which was considerably greater even than Britain's. Sixteen million Americans, more than twelve percent of the total population, served in the armed forces. All the while, America stepped up the production of arms and materiel to a degree scarcely conceivable. While British factories were making much of what Britain needed to fight the war, America's factories were making the rest, plus everything America needed, plus much of what was used by the Soviet Union, the Free French, and the other Allies. Car plants retooled to make tanks, steel mills flared night and day, shipyards sprang up from nothing. By the end of the war, the Navy had so many Liberty Ship freighters that sailors loaded them with mattresses and used them to clear minefields. A mattress-laden Liberty Ship could detonate five mines before quietly sinking, giving its skeleton crew ample time to get off in a lifeboat and man the next mattress-laden ship.

Ships, planes, mattresses – mattresses? There were nowhere near enough men and women in America's industrial cities to make it all. It was lucky for the Allied war effort that the farmers of the American South, long the most primitive and labor-intensive agricultural region in the developed world, picked the years around the war finally to mechanize their operations. "My daddy farmed this land with five hundred black guys," said a farmer in the Mississippi Delta in the 1980s. "I farm it with three black guys, three white guys, five tractors, and me." If five tractors could put four hundred ninety-seven black guys out of work on one farm, it is no wonder that roughly ten million African-Americans left the rural South in the years during and just after the war.

They went to the industrial cities of the North to make ships, planes, and mattresses for the war effort; and they stayed when the war was over, joining with returning GIs to maintain the unprecedented flood of manufactured goods that rolled off America's assembly lines for the next thirty years. Historians now speak of "The Great Migration" of blacks from the South to the North. It showed a strength that war planners in Berlin and Tokyo had overlooked, and it helped mightily to win both the war and the peace.

What made for success overseas, however, made for local disorder in America's cities. White Americans were not disposed to welcome ten million new black neighbors. Their culture had taught them – in the North as well as in the South –that "the Negro" was biologically inferior to "the White Man." White children had absorbed racial lessons as children absorb the lessons of their culture, and white adults during World War II took for granted a war effort in which factory assignments and the Army itself were racially segregated. It was eccentric to believe that all men had been created equal.

As black populations grew, many American cities attempted to maintain racial segregation in housing; there were "white blocks" and "black blocks" in newspaper ads and even on the statute books. Edward Bouton, the greatest of suburban developers, took the lead in segregation, as in so many better things. But ten million people take up a lot of space, and virtually no housing was built for anyone during the war. By 1944, blacks were bursting out of their little pre-war ghettoes, using their good industrial paychecks to rent or buy houses in white neighborhoods; and their new white neighbors were as deeply shocked as Romans had been when the frontiers of their Empire began to give way.

The Great Migration from South to North in the 1940s sparked fear and tension. William Manchester's novel about Baltimore in those years is called *City of Anger*. Unscrupulous real estate men made fortunes out of racial prejudice. The technique known as "block busting" was representative: a speculator would move a black family into a white block and would then induce a wave of panic selling, allowing him to buy the rest of the houses in the block at low prices and sell or rent them at sky-high rates to black families desperate for a place to live. Overcrowding for people of all colors added to the tension. As soon as building began again after the war, middle-class white city-dwellers sold their houses and moved as far from the city as their cars would take them. The white working classes, suddenly earning middle-class incomes in a global economy where American factories had little competition, bought cars and took off after them.

The Great Migration did not cause the suburbanization of white America. This was already well under way in the days of Bouton, the Olmsteds, bungalows, and foursquares. But it sped suburbanization and made it less reversible. The typical white family of American television in the 1950s and 1960s lived happily in a tidy suburban house in a tree-shaded neighborhood without racial or ethnic diversity. Real white families in the new white suburbs often nursed bitter grievances. They pined for their lost neighborhoods like victims of ethnic cleansing.

Rebuilding, with a Big Public Sector

The end of the war in 1945 brought euphoria on both sides of the Atlantic. Everything seemed possible to high-hearted people; and mass production, which had won the war, would bring what General Electric called "a big, bright, beautiful tomorrow". Everyone understood the importance of planning – planning of production, planning of invasions, planning of wages and prices and mattresses and just about everything else.

This was most visible in Britain. For one thing, the ruined cities of Britain needed large numbers of replacement buildings; for another, Britain's new Labour government of 1945, avowedly Socialist, was committed to using the power of the state to plan the economy in such a way as to raise the poor, lower the rich, and end the class system. This meant a great deal of housing and a very great deal of planning. Patrick Abercrombie, long a teacher of Town Planning in Liverpool, became Sir Patrick, a national figure, responsible for replanning the whole of metropolitan London.

We might now think him an odd choice for shaping one of the biggest cities in the world. He was hardly a lover of big cities. In his Liverpool years, he had commuted across the Mersey from a picturesque village in Cheshire; and his first big foray into practical planning had to do with preserving the beauty of the countryside from ribbon development. To his contemporaries, however, these were good qualifications for the planner of a great city. Planned rural informality, the legacy of Capability Brown and Ebenezer Howard, was still the national ideal.

Abercrombie's London was to be a denser Metro-Land, an alliance of villages, each with about ten thousand people, "segregated" from each other by parks, railways, and motorways. Every resident of London was also to be a member of some smaller and quite self-contained community. Overcrowded places were to become less crowded, and a network of new satellite towns, twenty to forty miles away, would accommodate the "overspill" of about a half-million people. All the while, a vast Greenbelt, rural land on which nothing could ever be built, would encircle the Metropolis. Never again would London spread, and every Londoner would live within a cheap train jaunt of refreshing countryside.

Of the various elements of Abercrombie's London plans, the ones that seem to us most difficult tended to get built, while the ones that seem easier generally did not. The satellite towns, which required a seemingly impossible expenditure of time and money, slid down the ways like battleships, one after another, for thirty years and more, under Labour and Tory governments alike. Similarly, the Greenbelt, which sounds to us like a ploy by prosperous suburbanites to keep poorer neighbors away at public expense, received most of its support from the working-class leaders of the Labour Party. It swelled rapidly during Britain's Socialist enthusiasm of 1945-51 and survives today more or less as Abercrombie envisioned it. Chief among the things that did not get built were motorways. Because London traffic had already become nightmarish before the War, Abercrombie did not create immediate controversy when he called for three big ring roads and a number of other large arterials. But the first of his London motorways aroused so much opposition that the rest were eventually cancelled – an enduring nuisance to drivers, an enduring pleasure to residents and pedestrians, and a lasting testament to the excellence of London's system of mass transport. One of the glories of modern London is that motorways hardly ever "segregate" one neighborhood from another.

That left housing. There was bound to be a lot of it, if only to replace bomb damage, but the boom in post-war British housing was bigger than simple calculations of household growth and housing production can explain. Despite progress in the twenties and thirties,

The Lansbury Estate.
Poplar, London.

most working-class Britons were still overcrowded in houses and flats without modern conveniences and in neighborhoods without parks; and they believed that their second bout of wartime sacrifices had earned them larger and more modern quarters. Though a massive increase in council housing was initially a rallying cry of the left-leaning Labour Party, Tories knew how to compete for votes, and council housing quickly became a cross-party objective. Private house-building became virtually a thing of the past as councils built almost all new housing, in all parts of the country, for roughly thirty years. By the early 1970s, the stock of council housing had grown from its pre-war total of one million housing units to four million, and councils were the landlords for one in three British households.

Initially, the Metro-Land vision seemed to be holding. The Lansbury Estate in East London, a council development finished just in time for the Festival of Britain in 1951 and intended to be a model for post-war rebuilding, featured moderate densities and a stripped-down version of the Georgian vernacular. So did the "overspill" New Town of Stevenage. But post-war was not inter-war. The cultural background of Early English and Georgian Revival architecture had withered. Jazz had replaced folk songs, the jitterbug had taken over from Morris dancing. In architecture and planning, it was finally time for the continental innovations of Modernism to cross the Channel. Theories and practices from France and Sweden and Germany, from Gropius and Mies and Le Corbusier, made

*Robin Hood Gardens.
Poplar, London.*

short work of the Early English defenders and conquered the academies in which architects and planners were trained. Modern Architecture, reviled before the war as *furrin* and *Bolshie*, gained post-war prestige from the fact that the Nazis had hated it. Besides, it was cheap, or was said to be cheap; and England had a lot of housing to build in a hurry, after a war that had exhausted the national wealth.

Thus it was that the brick terraces of Lansbury and Stevenage were described, not as Georgian – they could have been – but as Swedish. Ah, Sweden. Peaceful, productive, socialist, and egalitarian, Sweden offered the first vision of a new, post-war Britain. Architects with a Swedish bent described their approach as "the New Humanism". Unfortunately, there is a certain English machismo that takes comparisons with peaceful Sweden as a threat to British virility, and many English architects viewed Sweden, not as an ideal nation whose level England might someday reach, but as a namby-pamby nonentity nation to whose level England might someday lazily sink. The calm, cheap Metro-Land of the New Humanists stirred fears of emasculation among a number of young British architects, some of them women. Their response was a specifically English version of Modernism that recalled, in spirit, the principled harshness of Victorian Gothic. They called it Brutalism, a name that their enemies were only too happy to adopt.

Like Ruskin and the Victorian Gothicisits, the Brutalists wanted to affirm architecture

Tower Blocks, Liverpool.

as a high art by making buildings that could express the full range of human emotions. The result was a large number of apartment blocks that allowed residents to experience feelings of pity and terror as they attempted to come home with their groceries. Anyone who knows the 1960s television series *The Avengers*, or the movie version of *A Clockwork Orange*, has felt the anomic fear that Brutalist buildings can inspire.

Brutalism was eye-catching, for better and for worse. Brutalist monuments like Robin Hood Gardens and the nearby Balfron Tower in London's East End were noteworthy when they were new and became household words when they started to fall apart; and many British voters eventually turned against council housing because Brutalism was their image of it. Brutalism, however, was a great deal less common than people thought. Most post-war council housing was, in architectural terms, pretty tame New Humanist stuff. Much of it was low-rise, a decaffeinated Metro-Land. But, again, post-war was not inter-war. For the first time, the British built high-rises (tower blocks, in British English,) and they built a huge number of them.

This was the biggest change in British city-building since the classical revolution of the seventeenth century – bigger, perhaps, as it was a change of substance as well as of style. There would have been less trouble if the new tower blocks had been dedicated to single people or childless couples. Childless people in the middle classes had made the leap to apartment living between the wars, as soon as gas stoves and canned soup allowed them to do so, and working-class people liked elevators and expansive views as much as anyone. But the new working-class tower blocks too often filled up with families and children. For the first time, British families were asked, as a general rule, to have neighbors above them and below them, to share doors and corridors with strangers, to divorce themselves from the life of the street, the calm of a garden, and the ability to keep an eye on their children while doing something else. Tenants were unquestionably happy, at first, with sunlit rooms and modern mechanical systems; but it was anyone's guess whether they would be happy once the novelty had worn off.

Since big cities usually have higher densities than smaller cities, we might expect London to have built more tower blocks than the second-tier cities. The reverse was true. Much of central London was still respectable, some of it downright fashionable; there was less need for slum clearance, and no money to buy expensive property for redevelopment. The second-tier cities had not held together so well. They had failed to attract noblemen and gentlemen a century before and, as a result, had long since lost their own richest citizens to manor houses and suburban villas. Most of their central neighborhoods – those that had not become central business districts – had long since lost their fashion and turned into slums. The land was inexpensive, and the buildings had few articulate defenders.

Birmingham proudly cleared all but eleven of its twenty-nine thousand back-to-back houses. Manchester seems to have preserved only two Georgian terraces. The northern city of Newcastle, whose proudest boast is a magnificent late-Georgian district called Grainger Town, wantonly tore down half of Richard Grainger's major square for a shopping center and a parking lot. But the worst losses were in Liverpool. The first of the merchant cities had the most to lose and lost the most. This cannot be blamed on the *Luftwaffe*, which had left most of residential Liverpool intact. Even Foster's Custom House, gutted by bombs, could have been rebuilt. But Liverpudlians had long since lost interest in their city's architectural history. Fine old streets had become grimy and overcrowded, and demolition continued even as preservationists awakened to the beauties they were losing. The Duke's Warehouse and the Seaman's Home were already famous when the wreckers did them in; and local authors mourned the wholesale destruction of their city in books with titles like *It All Came Tumbling Down* and *The Agony of Georgian Liverpool*.

In place of historic Liverpool arose tower blocks, something like sixty-five of them. They were not eye-catching in a Brutalist way, or any other way. Nor was there any attempt to connect them to Liverpool's distinctive building culture. They were exercises in International Modernism, meant to look like buildings of their period all over the world. They had flat façades and flat roofs, with a lot of metal, concrete, and glass. And they were cheap, as befitted a country where wartime rationing continued for ten full years after the coming of peace. Like similar buildings built throughout Britain, many of them took advantage of new materials and experimental construction techniques that had been tested in drier climates, with results that would become apparent later. Monty Python's *Architect Sketch* of 1970 caught the mood of the people as flaws of design and construction became obvious.

Liverpool's tower blocks were typical, not only in their architecture, but also in their relationship to the city around them. Following the dictates of Le Corbusier, British councils and their architects tried to set their tower blocks in parks. If this idea is in fact workable, it certainly did not work very well in Britain. By the early 1970s, large parts of every British city had become odd places indeed. Where once there had been neighborhoods of terraced houses, with people on the streets and shops at the corners, now there were tall, bland towers floating in space, dwarfing the pedestrians who scuttled about in search of neighbors or purchases or something to do.

And hardly anyone had money. In a nasty bit of irony, post-war Socialism, which was supposed to break down the barriers between social classes, wound up reinforcing them by turning the centers of entire great cities into means-tested council estates for the working classes. As for middle-class people, Socialism did not treat them as badly as they had feared. They remained secure in Metro-Lands and villas, worried about taxes but untroubled by low-class neighbors or idealistic planners with the power of eminent domain.

Things were similar in Holland. The obliterated center of Rotterdam returned to a cool, angular life in the 1950s, to general applause, and tall apartment blocks soon surrounded the historic centers of many Dutch cities. Even Delft, a city of fewer than thirty thousand people, acquired high-rise neighborhoods, one of them apparently the densest area in the Netherlands.

Although the United States had suffered neither bombing nor occupation, it too had an acute housing shortage at the end of the war. No one had built housing in any quantity since the Crash in 1929. Meanwhile, the population had grown by something like fifteen million people, and an additional ten million had moved from the South to the North. In the national capital and the great industrial cities – including all of America's North Atlantic cities – the influx of war workers, mainly from farms and plantations in the South, had strained housing markets to the breaking point.

Like the British and the Dutch, post-war Americans had faith in planning and mass production. And they had faith in their government: Roosevelt's New Deal consensus, though a pale reflection of British Socialism, brought Americans as close as they have ever come to a general belief in public-sector activism. But Americans did not ask for Modern Architecture or towers in parks; nor did they want to rent houses from the government, or from anyone else. They wanted what they had wanted before the Crash of 1929, automotive suburbia, and they asked their government, not for dramatic planned environments, but for insured mortgages that would allow them to buy the houses of

Simple Colonial Houses, Baltimore.

their choice from private builders. Their government obliged them on a grand scale.

Because one of the purposes of US government intervention was to increase housing production and end the nation's housing shortage, government mortgages were generally restricted to newly-built houses. It was hard for anyone to get a government mortgage for an old house anywhere in any city. And because America was still overtly racist, black Americans were excluded from government mortgage programs, and thus effectively barred from post-war suburbia. The result of this double bias – in favor of new houses and against black homebuyers – was that white people bought new suburban houses with cheap mortgages while black people got stuck with old houses and expensive mortgages in the centers of cities. This would have been bad enough if the new black city-dwellers had commanded as much income and wealth, or as many marketable skills, as the whites they replaced. But three centuries of slavery and Jim Crow oppression had insured that this was far from the case. All told, the *Luftwaffe* could hardly have done more damage to American cities than was done by the double bias of federal mortgage policies.

No one at the time, white or black, seems to have put the whole picture together. Instead, white post-war Americans, like Mr. Blandings in a hilarious 1948 movie, set about building their dream houses. Although they disliked Modern Architecture, they wanted the kind of democratic informality that Modernism promised, and they got it by simplifying traditional forms. Their style, like the style of Society people before 1929, was the Colonial Revival, but it was the simple Colonial Revival of cottages in Williamsburg and on Cape Cod.

It is tempting to dismiss post-war simplicity as a sign of declining taste or the thoughtlessness of the mass market. Post-war brickwork and woodwork were cruder than pre-war work. Shutters were often fake, screwed into the wall. But post-war simplicity had strong positive values. It celebrated the marriage of America's great colonial traditions with modern mass production and the improvisatory can-do spirit that had won the war. It also expressed the respect that men and women of all social classes had developed for each other in foxholes and on factory floors. The post-war rich no longer felt as different from other Americans as their parents and grandparents had felt. Most Americans, in fact, now thought of themselves as middle-class people. They wanted a free-and-easy life of backyard cookouts, Little League baseball, and endless upward mobility. Although they were proud of their national heritage, they cast aside elaborate moldings and artistic brickwork as they cast aside hats, vests, and corsets.

All this simplicity left little room for architects. Any competent draftsman could design a simple colonial house, or copy a plan from a magazine, and fancy work like doors and staircases was bought ready-made. Pre-1929 architects, trained in the traditions of French classicism and steeped in the details of Georgian craftsmanship, faded from view. Their replacements, trained in the International Modernism that captured American schools of architecture in the years around the war, had the zeal that characterized their counterparts in Britain and on the Continent, but they did not have Socialist governments. They got to build schools and hospitals for America's endless new neighborhoods, but little more; there were few or no opportunities for tall apartment buildings, and we can drive a long way through post-war American suburbia without seeing a Modern building.

Landscape architects had even less influence. With high tax rates for the rich, no one could afford sensitive earth-sculpting of the Olmsted type, and the curving streets of post-war suburbia, like the straight streets of pre-war suburbia, were usually designed by engineers. Since landscape architecture is a more important element of beauty in suburbia than is the architecture of houses, this was a more serious loss than anything that happened in the realm of architecture.

But American egalitarianism had its limits. Even after the bonding experiences of Depression and War, America was not Sweden, and successful Americans wanted their dwellings to reflect their success in some visible way. If architecture sent its messages too forcefully, and landscape architecture was too expensive, what was left? Unfortunately, acreage itself. Sprawl became an expression of snobbery. Where Bouton and the Olmsteds had put elaborate houses on small lots, their post-war successors put simple houses on large lots. The richer the people, the larger the lots. Residents of subdivisions with half-acre lots sneered quite undemocratically at people in quarter-acre subdivisions, and zoning regulations required large lots in the best locations. The size of the average building lot crept steadily upward.

Needless to say, as houses got farther away from each other, it took more linear feet of paved street to get from one house to another – to get anywhere, in fact – and more driving. A typical suburban housewife in the sixties thought nothing of driving fifty or a hundred miles a day. There was no controversy over this. Driving was fun, gasoline was cheap, and no one was measuring global temperatures.

The North Atlantic tradition put forth some brave new shoots in Baltimore and Philadelphia, as builders used government mortgages to finance an often-charming American Metro-Land for people in the very middle of the housing market. Their simple colonial row houses, built of red brick with small-paned windows painted white, looked very much like the real things from the Long Eighteenth Century. It is a pity that architecture and city design are arts in which fashion moves down from the top. The buyers of simple colonial row houses could not inspire richer people to emulate them.

Instead, America went on its gas-guzzling way. There were no row houses in the neighborhoods built by the most prolific of the post-war developers, William Levitt, whose "Levittowns" on the outskirts of New York, Philadelphia, and Washington offered small free-standing colonial houses on curving streets to tens of thousands of white families with government mortgages. Levitt's competitors differed from him only in scale, and every American city was soon ringed with curving streets of simple colonial houses. The immensity of it thrilled some, horrified others, and generated a lively pro-and-con literature throughout the 1950s and 60s. To read those books, one would imagine that post-war suburbia was something entirely without precedent in human history. It was not, in fact, very different from pre-war suburbia. There was just a lot more of it.

And it was even more completely automotive. The gaudy 1950s cars that people parked in front of their bland colonial cottages excited people more than their houses did. Teenagers slow-danced to ballads about sweethearts killed in crashes and lost their virginities at drive-in movie theatres while James Dean played "chicken" on the screen.

Meanwhile, federal and state agencies worked together to build almost fifty thousand miles of broad, smooth, high-speed interstate highways. City governments got in on the act too. All governments planned, and most built, the kind of segregating motorways that Londoners had stopped. Philadelphia's Schuylkill Expressway spoiled much of the riverfront in America's largest city park. Boston's Central Artery, towering noisily above the central business district, cut most of the city off from its riverfront.

But it was in New York that the most work, and damage, was done. The supremely energetic Robert Moses, an automotive Haussmann, received both credit and blame for ramming massive highways through one part of the city after the other, displacing

American Public Housing.

hundreds of thousands of people and crippling the neighborhoods of millions. His projects took years to build – years in which condemned buildings stood vacant, years in which construction disrupted almost every aspect of neighborhood life. When his projects were finished, countless New Yorkers lived in the shadow of monstrous, roaring overhead expressways, many of them approach roads to bridges of astonishing size and beauty. Although historians argue over what Moses himself actually did, everyone agrees that he became the icon of urban road-building, the god or devil of opposing sides in some of the most contentious political fights in America's urban history. Wherever he and his followers prevailed, more cars moved, and citizens used them to flee their wounded cities. The only successful post-war television show to be set in a row house was *All in the Family*, a comedy about an aging working-class white man who hates every other kind of person under the sun. He was the kind of person you could find in a row house. People who were kind, or successful, lived in suburban houses or fancy New York apartments.

Outside New York, although apartment development accelerated in the 1960s, apartments were not viewed as emblems of success. Post-war homeowners viewed apartments with class-based suspicion. Apartment dwellers were their inferiors, not their children or their parents. Homeownership, they thought, bred responsibility, and renting was a sign of weak character. Government policies reinforced this prejudice. Zoning laws limited the scale of apartment developments and restricted their location, generally to unattractive sites next to major roads, where apartment dwellers would not cause traffic on the streets of homeowners.

Unfortunately, the most noticeable apartments in post-war America were the worst, the government developments called Public Housing. This was the only instance in which American governments have ever acted as residential developers. American public housing bore a superficial resemblance to council housing in Britain, in that it was rental housing, built and managed by local bodies with finance from the national government, and with architecture that was unstintingly Modern. From then on, however, everything was different. British council housing was intended to provide lifetime dwellings for a high percentage of the population, and architects were expected to do the best they could with the money at their disposal. American public housing was explicitly meant to offer temporary shelter to a relatively small number of stable families who had suffered in the Great Depression, and public housing developments were designed to be ugly and demeaning lest residents be tempted to stay after they had put their finances back in order. Invariably called "the Projects," America's public housing developments were the first residential buildings since the workhouses of Victorian England to be unpleasant on principle.

Luckily, the scale of the American effort was much smaller than in Britain. By the end of the high days of project construction, in the early 1960s, public housing projects were accommodating only about three percent of the American people, as opposed to a third of the people in Britain. And there were few of the notorious high-rises: Baltimore built seventeen of them, while a British city of comparable size, Birmingham, was building four hundred sixty-four. But the American projects did much less good, and much more harm, than council housing. Once America's private developers began to work off the post-war housing shortage, stable families in the Projects bought houses with government-insured mortgages, as they were supposed to do; but the buildings and their managerial bureaucracies did not go away. By the late 1950s, public housing was becoming something no one had ever intended to be, permanent housing for the long-term poor.

British managers of council housing consider that a housing estate is in trouble if more than twenty percent of its adults are unemployed, or if more than twenty-five percent of its residents are children. In American public housing, by the early 1960s, almost all adults were unemployed, and children usually outnumbered adults by at least two to one. By that time, too, almost all residents of public housing were African-Americans, whites having moved up and out. This did not bode well in a racist country with a general contempt for people who receive public charity. And American projects were disproportionately visible, inasmuch as they tended to get built through slum clearance in the oldest neighborhoods, which were closest to downtowns. By the early 1960s, then, the business downtowns of every American city were hemmed in by large complexes of intentionally ugly buildings that were home to a population despised both for poverty and for race. The Projects were bad environments for their residents, and they made non-residents think of new ways to shop and work without going downtown.

The Urban Crisis

People on both sides of the Atlantic remember the 1950s and the early 1960s as a happy time. Work and money were plentiful, streets were safe from crime. Working-class people in all countries were improving their lot rapidly, and every year seemed to bring some new piece of tangible progress: a television, a dishwasher, a shirt that looked good enough without ironing. Snug in their new dwellings, whether council flats or simple colonial cottages, war heroes and their formerly-riveting brides settled down to create and manage the post-war baby boom. Most people seem to have thought it would go on forever. Their cities had other ideas. Each bit of progress – mass-produced cars, slum clearance, high-rise construction, highways and motorways – had come with a hidden cost. The bill came due with shocking speed in the decade after 1965.

By that time, the North Atlantic cities had lost their most useful residents, the people best able to pay taxes, sustain an economy, and inspire their children to do well in school. These people, the middle-class backbone of middle-class nations, had fled *en masse* to one kind of suburbia or another, British Metro-Land or American Levittown, leaving vast central areas to people with less money and fewer marketable skills. The new suburbs, moreover, in both countries, were usually in different political jurisdictions, so that cities lost tax revenue when they lost taxpayers. Government at all levels had encouraged this, both by facilitating the spreading and sprawling of suburbs and by redeveloping the centers of cities in ways that turned them into preserves for people who were relatively or absolutely poor. Bulldozers had forced millions of people from their homes, and tens of thousands of neighborhood businesses had failed when their customers moved away. When new city neighborhoods finally arose from the rubble, often after years of delay, residents too often confronted bleak vistas of mass-produced housing with few shops, jobs, or middle-class neighbors. While Americans did a particularly awful job of this with their public housing projects, the greater scale of the British effort magnified its smaller mistakes.

The people who ran the North Atlantic cities seem to have believed that they could lose all their middle-class residents without any harm to their commercial downtowns. They were soon disabused. The change was felt first and most sharply in America, where the shift from mass transportation to private cars made downtowns obsolete. Downtown retailers could not build parking fast enough, or cheaply enough, and whole downtown shopping districts went vacant after suburban developers in the 1950s invented the shopping mall. Office buildings and their owners came next. Many office tenants – insurance agents, medical doctors, accountants, and the like – were effectively retailers, needing a middle-class walk-in trade as much as any seller of hats or shoes; and they followed their clients to small suburban office buildings with free parking. Larger companies, with enough office workers to fill entire skyscrapers, soon found homes in suburban office parks, some with beautiful landscaping. These were convenient to the places where senior executives already lived, and workers further down the corporate pecking order soon followed. By the middle of the 1950s, the only healthy downtowns in the North Atlantic world were the four – London, New York, Boston, and to a lesser extent Philadelphia – whose mass transport systems were good enough to compete with the private car. Every other city center was emptying out.

Though there were differences between one country and another – more cars in America, more high-rise apartment buildings in Britain and Holland – the pattern was unnervingly consistent: low-density suburbs for the prosperous, high-density city centers for the poor. Urban life, once a symbol of elegance and sophistication, was now stigmatized as a sign of failure. Middle-class women began to boast that they never went downtown. There were obvious implications in this for their children, and for the future.

With cities so drastically weakened, almost any serious shock could have pushed them into full-blown crisis. There were two such shocks.

The first, race, was felt first in America. The Great Migration had brought the issue of race out of the silence of the southern countryside, and the Civil Rights movement of the early 1960s had created, or freed up, as much resentment as relief in people of both races. No sooner had the first struggles for brotherhood and equality been won, it seemed, than angry black orators began to talk about violence leading to "Black Power", and angry white orators began to talk about repressive measures that they called "law and order." Bloody riots, televised against a background of burning streets and looted stores, began in the summer of 1964 and lasted through the spring of 1968. It was no comfort to white people to realize that black activists had justice and human nature on their side. Nor did it help that the sudden upsurge of black aggression occurred just as American rates of crime and murder were rising for the first time in a couple of generations. By the late 1960s, with young black men in American cities dying at rates that suggested casualty lists in a major war, white people found it irresistibly tempting to scapegoat black people. "White Flight," the exodus of white people from the city and from blacks, accelerated with every call for "Black Power."

Ignoble as flight was, it was not the only ungracious response to the situation. White Philadelphians elected, and re-elected, an openly racist mayor in the early 1970s. In Boston, white parents in the early 1970s rioted against racial integration in the public schools. And, wherever schools were integrated, white parents moved to different, whiter, school districts in the suburbs. By 1970, the public schools of Washington were more than ninety percent black, making a mockery of dreams of racial integration. By 1980, for too many white Americans, the word "city" had become synonymous with "ghetto."

Racial strife came somewhat later to Britain and the Netherlands, as an import from former colonies overseas. Most people date the beginning of race issues in Britain to a campaign by London Transport to hire workers from the Caribbean. By the early 1970s, every British city had districts that were predominantly black, and riots in the London neighborhoods of Brixton and Notting Hill suggested parallels with America. There were larger streams of immigrants from India and Pakistan, stirring white racist skinheads to go on rampages of "Paki bashing." In the Netherlands, immigrants from former Dutch colonies in South Asia and the Caribbean were blamed, at first, for increases in crime in Amsterdam and Rotterdam, and Dutch politics are dominated to this day by concerns over immigrants and immigration.

Though the shock of race and racism hit British cities more gently than their American cousins, the second shock, which we still call by the awkward term "de-industrialization," hit British cities first and hardest. It is hard to believe, in an age largely ruled by the beneficed interpreters of economic statistics, that the collapse of British factories and ports could have hit the country unawares, like a hurricane in the days before weather satellites. But so it was. Into the late 1960s, the businessmen and bureaucrats who guided Britain's factories were still preparing for high-volume production, and port authorities in Liverpool and London were planning new docks. By the early 1970s, the ports were largely empty, and much of the country's industrial base had disappeared. Manchester no longer made cloth. Birmingham no longer made aircraft. Glasgow no longer made ships. The world no longer exchanged its surpluses at Liverpool and London. Foreigners were supplying foreign markets directly, and British families were buying foreign cars. Whole towns lost their reason for being. Whole pieces of great cities became places without work. Frustrated young people turned to crime, racial hatred, and senseless acts of vandalism. Everyone blamed everyone else as the gears of politics seemed to freeze up in Tory and Labour governments alike.

The effects of economic collapse were felt most among industrial workers, and in the council estates where many of them lived. These were already showing signs of physical decay. Many had been poorly built, and almost all of them, it seems, had been poorly maintained; Britain's local councils, usually eager to build and often quite good at building, proved less adept at routine maintenance. Their paymasters in the national government approached matters in no better a spirit, economizing on expenses for maintenance and management while setting ever more ambitious targets for new construction. This had consequences both in the steady dripping of untended pipes and in the disappearance of the social workers who had originally helped residents to build and maintain community in strange new buildings. By the early 1970s, when the people of the British working classes fell into economic crisis, they were left to face it alone, in big, shabby buildings where locks and faucets took a long time to get fixed.

The South Bronx, 1970s.

America was not far behind. Japanese cars and televisions were better and cheaper than domestic products by the early 1970s, and the Oil Shock of 1974 drove gasoline prices high enough to turn buyers away from the big inefficient cars that Detroit was still making. The city of Detroit itself, after decades of pro-automotive planning, became the national symbol of de-industrialization. Detroit's job losses and racial tensions began the free-fall that would lead it to bankruptcy in 2013. But America's North Atlantic cities were not far behind. Baltimore and Philadelphia lost two-thirds of their manufacturing jobs. New York's garment industry, which still had six hundred thousand employees in the 1960s, evaporated more or less overnight. Ports continued to carry high tonnage, but they became so efficient that hardly anyone worked in them any more. Young black men, groomed to take the places of aging white factory workers, found themselves with few good options.

To drive across New York City in the mid-1970s was a harrowing experience. To drive through it over and over again, and watch large parts of the city fall apart, was both harrowing and heartbreaking. New Yorkers had run the busiest north-south highway in the country through the South Bronx, which promptly fell into a spiral of decay and abandonment under the horrified gaze of millions of drivers and passengers from all over the country.

The South Bronx is a big place. Driving across it took a long time, particularly in the crawling traffic that was usual in the 1970s on the elevated highway that bisected it. Most South Bronx buildings were apartment houses from the 1920s, five to seven stories tall, of a type familiar to New Yorkers but strange and unpleasant to most other Americans. As year succeeded to year in the 1970s, before the eyes of millions, South Bronx tenants and landlords abandoned one building after another. Windows disappeared; blackened bricks showed the scorch marks of insurance fires; and armed gangs fought wars over turf.

The South Bronx came to stand for New York in the minds of millions, as Times Square and the Empire State Building had done in happier times. And not without reason: almost three thousand New Yorkers died of murder every year in the 1970s. True, there were still plays on and off Broadway, and Sutherland and Sills and Bernstein at Lincoln Center, and plenty of jobs for bankers and lawyers with college and graduate degrees; but what were New Yorkers to do if they had only high-school degrees, or if they didn't? Giant mechanized cranes unloaded ships in New Jersey. The nearest garment jobs were in Asia.

What was happening in New York was happening, with local inflections, in Philadelphia, Baltimore, Washington, and Boston. East Baltimore and North Philadelphia shocked rail passengers with empty factories and crumbling row houses. Boston's Roxbury mocked the good intentions of America's best-educated city. Washington had the nation's highest murder rate. Every American city, it seemed, was on the road that leads to Detroit.

So, for that matter, was every British city except London. Though murders were fewer, there were race riots in Liverpool and Birmingham, and we can hear the collapse of British industry in the musical shift from the hedonism of Rock to the nihilism of Punk. Things appeared to be even worse in the Netherlands, where Amsterdam lost its downtown office district, its big corporations, and its middle-class families with children. The population of the city fell by an unprecedented seventy-five percent, worse by far than Detroit.

The North Atlantic cities had beaten the Kaiser and the Nazis, but they could not beat their own suburbs, and they had now to compete with the entire world. Most thoughtful people were pessimistic about their prospects. For that matter, thoughtful people were pessimistic about the prospects of cities in general. They believed that cities existed to facilitate business and manufacturing, and it was obvious to them that neither business nor manufacturing still required high-density concentrations of people in first-world countries. Telephones were cheap; cars were fast; and the poor nations of the world teemed with willing workers.

Besides, by the 1970s, most thoughtful people lived in the suburbs. They did not like cities, or have a feel for them, and they could not see why anyone else would like them. They liked lawns and trees, both at home and in the beautifully-landscaped corporate campuses that were draining one downtown after another; and the so-called Principle of Consumer Sovereignty, as taught at the Harvard Business School, stated that people should be free to choose how they wanted to live and work. Jane Jacobs, who liked cities and explained her reasons in vigorous, readable prose, was a lonely voice.

In 1975, New York City, the center of the world financial system, ran out of money. It had at last given its suburbs too many of its middle-class residents. Its taxpayers could no longer maintain its roads and bridges, much less give hope and teach skills through its schools. The city had lived by borrowing for a while, but now its lenders would no longer lend. The Mayor appealed to the President, Gerald Ford, for a bailout. The President's refusal provoked an immortal *Daily News* headline: "Ford to City: Drop Dead".

It was in 1975 that Robert Caro, a very thoughtful person, published *The Power Broker*, a massive biography of Robert Moses. The subtitle of the book was *Robert Moses and the Fall of New York*. Caro did not say Decline. He said Fall.

Ford to City: Drop Dead.

Chapter Seven

WORKS IN PROGRESS

From the vantage point of 2018, when these words are being written, it is apparent that the North Atlantic cities hit bottom in 1975. That was a long time ago, even by the standards of cities, and much has happened since. Many people now believe that the Urban Crisis of the 1960s and 70s is over, and there are places in the North Atlantic world where such a belief is defensible. In London, Boston, Brussels, and all the Dutch cities, the troubles of the 1960s and 70s are vague memories. In New York, once the emblem of the Urban Crisis in America, the murder rate has fallen to virtually nothing, and the population has grown by a million people. The city has put its finances in order, and most experts seem to think that it will be able to weather its next crisis. Even in the many cities where the Urban Crisis persists, many improvements have been made, some of them very dramatic, and life for many people in our cities is better than observant people in 1975 could have predicted.

From 1975 on, I have been a participant in the story of the North Atlantic cities. In this chapter I will be writing about things that I have seen, some of them quite recently, and occasionally about things in which I have been involved. I probably have my biases. The best I can do is use the so-called perpendicular pronoun, "I", as a kind of navigational marker to help you know when and where you should be on your guard.

By a stroke of good luck, I finished undergraduate college in the hit-bottom summer of 1975 and moved into the center of Baltimore, a North Atlantic city that was then in the depths of the Urban Crisis. I lived in a pleasant old row house at the top of a natural outcrop called Federal Hill, which commands the city and the harbor and has been the place to go for the official view of Baltimore since at least 1752, when a farmer named Moale looked across the water from Federal Hill and sketched the oldest surviving drawing of any American town.

What I saw from Federal Hill in 1975 was a fairly imposing skyscraper downtown surrounded by rotting piers, dying industries, and vacant land. If I wanted to walk downtown, I could do it in about ten minutes, but it was no fun. After passing through a couple of blocks of tired old row houses, many of them coated with a dreary grey imitation stone called Formstone, I would come to a big blank space of empty ground, something like sixty acres of it, with a little clump of windowless vacant houses in the middle. My

Baltimore from Federal Hill, 1972.

Baltimore's Waterfront Today.

father, a World War II veteran, said that the vacant houses reminded him of a little Belgian town after a battle. A heavy rain could turn it all into a checkerboard of big mud pies, and a strong wind in the dry days of late summer could raise clouds of dust that looked like sandstorms. There were no traffic lights in those blocks, nor any traffic to light.

When I go to Federal Hill today and take in the official view of Baltimore circa 2018, it is hard for me to believe that I am looking at a place with the same name. It takes mental effort to remember that the 1975 skyline was only about five blocks across. Today, there are tall buildings for about two miles without much of a break, and I can walk for more than seven miles around the urban waterfront on handsome brick promenades in reviving neighborhoods. The old row houses on Federal Hill have shed their drab Formstone coats and are now trim and elegant in their birthday suits of warm red brick. If I want to walk downtown from Federal Hill, I can take my choice of pleasant routes. I can walk along the waterfront and share a joyous promenade with thousands of tourists from all over the world. Or I can walk on tree-shaded streets of well-restored houses. The vacant houses and lots that reminded my father of war-torn Belgium have become Otterbein, a lovely and civilized district of historic houses and excellent infill buildings.

Back in 1975, I tried to estimate how many people were living in the center of

Otterbein Before and After.

Baltimore voluntarily – that is to say, how many people were living in the center of town even though they could afford to live in the suburbs. I came up with about three thousand people. Today, by my count, there are about sixty thousand. No one in 1975 would have believed that Baltimore could do so much in forty-one years.

But the Urban Crisis is not over. While we Baltimoreans were achieving so many successes, we were also failing in some pretty dramatic ways. Our city is generally considered to be the heroin capital of the United States. Our murder rate is usually in the top five among American cities. Our public schools do a particularly bad job, and factory employment has collapsed from three hundred thousand people in 1975 to about a hundred thousand today. If you are wondering where poorly-educated people can find work in a city without manufacturing, the answer, too often, is nowhere. A well-made television show called *The Wire* has taught millions of people to think of Baltimore as an urban dystopia.

And the economics of running the city are very trying. The city proper, home to about a quarter of the people in its metropolitan area, has about eighty percent of the metropolitan poor. As a result, the tax rate in the city is twice as high as in any of its suburban counties, and the city government still has too little money to maintain its roads, bridges, and water and sewer lines, the oldest in the metropolitan area. As for meeting the needs of a needy population, or helping the poor to get out of poverty, the city can only seek funds from other sources. Its finances are far too dependent on the whims of politicians in Washington and Annapolis, the state capital. An incompetent Mayor, an unfriendly Governor, a depression, or simply a run of bad luck could put us where New York was in 1975.

But that is better than most people would have predicted. Although the Urban Crisis is far from over in most of the North Atlantic cities – even in some cities that think they have put it behind them – all of them are in better shape than they were forty years ago, and some of our cities have worked their way out of the Urban Crisis altogether.

The key to success has turned out to be something that few city leaders in 1975 considered important: our cities have begun to recapture the residents they lost in the first three quarters of the twentieth century. Millions of people are now choosing to live in cities even if they can afford to live in the suburbs.

This is readily visible. Hundreds of miles of old row houses have been restored, and the tallest skyscrapers in many North Atlantic cities are residential. And our thinking about cities has evolved to fit our new facts. No one still thinks that a city can survive and prosper if it is merely a job base surrounded by slums and suburbs. Today, in fact, our most popular cities worry that they may be too popular, and thus too expensive for their people.

In the process of rediscovering and rebuilding our cities, we have learned, often unconsciously, to measure urban success by whether we can walk for miles and be in good, safe, satisfying urban environments every step of the way. And that is right. The freedom to move around – on foot, or on a bike, without the protective armor of a car – is the essence of a great city. It is why a great city is as potent an image of freedom as a redwood forest or a sailboat.

We are now getting a lot of help from professional scholars. Urban History has become an established academic discipline since 1975, with the result that we can understand how cities come to be, how they get built, and how, at various times, they have worked or failed to work. We are the first humans in history who have been able to do these things.

Perhaps more important, we are getting help from the people who write serious non-fiction for a general audience. Every year seems to bring a new book that tells us why cities are good and how they are getting better. Jane Jacobs's 1961 *Death and Life of Great American Cities*, a wise and spirited manifesto for cities and city-ness, is now received (sometimes too gullibly and with a superstitious reverence) as gospel.

Even writers about architecture, who have traditionally restricted their interest to buildings designed by famous architects, are beginning at last to shed this outmoded elitism and pay attention to the buildings and neighborhoods of which cities are made. Coffee table books celebrate the terraces and squares of Dublin, and Stephan Muthesius has made the everyday terraced houses of Victorian Britain the subject of serious scholarly work. Every city in the American branch of the family has at least one book devoted to its row houses – except, curiously, Philadelphia, which has more row houses than any city in the country. This is all new. As late as 1973, two passionate lovers of Baltimore, writing a guidebook to the city's architecture, could write: "What the skyscraper is to Chicago, the lowly row house is to Baltimore". No one calls row houses lowly today – in Baltimore, London, or any other city with a North Atlantic housing stock.

We are even getting help from popular culture, at least in the United States. A hit television show called *Sex in the City* was a good sign in a world where sex proverbially sells. Equally hopeful were the sitcoms *Seinfeld* and *Friends*, which presupposed that choosy young people would choose to live in cities. I should probably be glad that I can no longer sip a leisurely beer in my favorite Boston bar from student days. A few years after I left, it became the set for a popular sitcom called *Cheers* and is now mobbed by souvenir-buying tourists.

All in all, this is a good time to take stock of what has worked and what hasn't. If we can learn from our successes, we may be able to tackle our abiding failures. And these are still severe. Americans are still sprawling across their once-beautiful countryside. Britons are still wringing their hands over a national housing shortage and trying scattershot schemes of regeneration in the bedraggled doughnuts of old council estates around their city centers. Too many neighborhoods are unsafe and/or unpleasant. Too many people have been unemployed for too long. And we seem unable to strike the right balance of supply and demand in urban real estate. It often seems that city neighborhoods, sometimes whole cities, become too expensive as soon as they cease to be dreary and dangerous.

Why We Need Cities Today

To begin, we need to understand why we need cities today. Cities are a technology for bringing large numbers of people together, but the reasons for bringing people together have changed several times. There were cities of worship and warfare, with temples and cathedrals surmounting battlements, and cities of commerce and industry, with skyscrapers lording it over factories and docks. Most of us grew up in cities of commerce and industry, and many of us think that we still need cities primarily to mobilize large labor forces.

The empty docks of Liverpool and the vacant factories of Philadelphia say otherwise. They say that commerce is done electronically rather than in coffee houses and exchanges, and that auditors, rating agencies, and global law enforcement have replaced the personal relationships on which merchants once relied. They say that low-skilled laborers abound in low-cost nations, that mechanization has done on our docks and factory floors what it did a century ago on our farms, and that our high-cost cities will never again have large industrial labor forces. This is a painful message, and many prefer not to listen. Brexit passes, and Donald Trump tweets from inside the White House.

But we still need cities today, as much as people have ever needed them. We are in a new era of urban development.

Two demographic facts make this era – our era – different from every previous age. The first is that a uniquely high percentage of us – thirty to fifty percent of adults in the North Atlantic nations – have university educations. The second is that most of us, on any given day, are living in households that do not contain children. Sixty-five percent of American households do not contain children, up from fifty percent in 1950. These are the two most important facts in any intelligent discussion of cities today.

And this is good news for cities. Well-educated adults without children at home tend to want places to go, things to do, people to see – things that cities are good at providing. And they do not care much about the things in which most of our cities are still lagging, principally good schools and safe play spaces. It has taken educated adults a long time to understand how they want to live when they are not raising children. But they are beginning to understand it now, and cities are benefiting.

Not surprisingly, then, the most successful cities today are the ones that have done the best job of giving independent adults what they need and want. Bars and clubs abound in large areas, and mass transit – backed by taxis, Uber, and Lyft – is often good enough to banish thoughts of car ownership. Within the North Atlantic world, London and New York probably still lead the field, but they no longer have the field to themselves. Boston and Washington, Rotterdam and Amsterdam, Manchester and Dublin are formidable competitors, and every one of our cities has at least one great university that is driving revival.

In many ways, our cities now need to do what polite towns needed to do in the Long Eighteenth Century. They need to attract people who have the freedom to live, work, and play elsewhere. Like the gentry capitals that built Malls and Assembly Rooms, our successful cities are first and foremost good places for civilized private life. Young people, and a good many older people, need to find new friends, keep up with old friends, and do things with friends. Young people, and a good many older people, need to find mates. Our most successful cities are splendid places for meeting, keeping up, courting, and all that follows.

But they are not mere resorts, like Bath. They are economic centers, every bit as much so as the miasmatic cities of the Industrial Revolution. Wherever tens of thousands of talented, educated people have come together, met, and taken each other's measure, they have built dynamic economies. The skills that make for friendship and courtship are useful in the invention of new technologies, the formation of new businesses, and the launching of new political and social movements.

Is there a name for the new kind of city that we are building? If a city is not about worship and warfare, or commerce and industry, what is it about? I would suggest, not in jest, that we are building cities of friendship and love.

A Second Golden Age in the Netherlands

Who is doing the best job of building cities of this new kind? The Dutch, hands down. After three centuries in the shadows, they are making a second Golden Age. They are doing the best work, shaping the best environments, and perhaps living the best lives in the North Atlantic world today.

Their country has grown, and grown rich, in the decades since World War II, creating along the way an enormous demand for buildings of all kinds. If the Dutch had been Americans, they would have paved half of their country and mowed grass on the other half. If they had been British, they would have run up hundreds of leaky tower blocks. As it is, they have accommodated dramatic growth without ruining their cities or despoiling their countryside. Dutch cities are still the pleasantest in the world, and farms and villages are still close by.

At the heart of the Dutch achievement is an astonishingly good system of public transportation. Inter-city trains run as frequently in Holland as city buses do in most British or American cities.

The importance of Dutch public transportation first hit me in a place called Hoofddorp. Hoofdorp is something like an American-style office park, but it is very, very large, and it appears to be in the middle of nowhere, surrounded by plowed fields. Hoofddorp may have as much office space as there is in the center of Liverpool or Richmond, but there is no city around it, just a small old town and a few streets of inoffensive post-war row houses on small canals. Its official population of 78,000 is far from large enough to use its office space. Why, then, is the office space there?

The reason why – and the key to the modern Dutch Golden Age – is that Hoofddorp has a station on the best railway system in the North Atlantic world. Because of that station, it is fifteen minutes away from Amsterdam, Leyden, and many other well-peopled places – not to mention Schipol Airport. Anyone can work in Hoofddorp and get home to Amsterdam or Leyden in less time than most Americans and Britons spend in commuting around a single city.

Meanwhile, the Dutch have been restoring their historic cities, and they defend them with development regulations that make it almost impossible to change old buildings or put up new ones in historic districts. This fidelity to the most basic of the North Atlantic traditions is the most obvious sign of the Dutch achievement. But they do not stop at preserving historic urban areas. They are building new neighborhoods that could easily be mistaken for old towns.

Not long ago I went to a new Rotterdam suburb called Berkel Westpolder. It took me twelve minutes to get there by subway from the center of Rotterdam. Most of my journey

Berkel Westpolder.

was above-ground through open country, and Berkel Westpolder itself was surrounded by farmed fields. Next to the station was a tiny downtown, with a food store, a few little shops, and three stories of apartments overhead. From then on, everything was row houses and the occasional pair of semi-detached houses. If I had not seen houses under construction and developer's advertisements at the station, I would have assumed I was in an established town.

The houses were pleasant. The water in the little canals was calm and clear. The afternoon was hot, and children were running around in bathing suits, drenching each other with the big squirt guns that American kids call Super Soakers. There was almost no traffic, and the kids were playing without noticeable supervision. It looked like an ideal place to be, or raise, a child.

But the Dutch are not stuck in the mud of history. The final element of the new Dutch miracle is an embrace of cutting-edge contemporary architecture. On the old wharves behind Amsterdam's Central Station, five minutes' walk from the great Golden Age canals, a vast new quarter has been built that feels like a different planet. In design, the buildings are full-throated Starchitecture, with angled walls and space-age materials. If they had been plopped down one-by-one between the canal houses in the Herengracht, the work of both periods would have been diminished. As it is, the city fathers have allowed each kind of building to form its own kind of environment without compromise, and each kind of place is excellent in its own way.

New Apartment Buildings in Amsterdam.

It is no accident that this new quarter is close to a train station. With train service so good, it makes sense to live as close to a station as possible, and every old rail yard behind every station is now blossoming forth with contemporary buildings. Many of these are tallish apartment buildings, and I was afraid, at first, that the Dutch had continued their unfortunate post-war habit of building high-density housing for families with children. But I learned not to worry. The tenants in these buildings are not families who might prefer quieter surroundings. They are independent adults, many of them young, who want places to go and things to do within walking distance. Perhaps someday they will want to live in Berkel Westpolder, but not now.

All in all, the Dutch seem to be having their cake and eating it too. Their cities are lovely and active, their countryside relatively unspoiled. Childless people and families with children seem to be getting what they want – and getting it at the highest level of design and construction. And it is all done with an extraordinarily low carbon footprint. The Dutch use their excellent trains, they walk a lot, and, of course, they ride bicycles. The train station in Utrecht, which is connected to the biggest shopping mall in Europe, has recently built a parking garage for twenty-two thousand bikes.

Although no North Atlantic nation is firing on as many cylinders as the Dutch are, we are all trying to accommodate growth and prosperity without ruining our cities and landscapes or accelerating climate change. Each of us is doing remarkable things, albeit with less coordination than among the Dutch, and with inferior results.

Georgetown, Washington.

Rediscovering Historic Buildings and Places

Until very recently, most people in the North Atlantic world preferred new buildings and places to old ones, and our old buildings and places were a problem that often seemed insoluble. The movement called Historic Preservation has made them an opportunity.

The first example of an old North Atlantic neighborhood revived through a conscious appeal to the historic past was Beacon Hill, Bulfinch's great Federalist-era neighborhood in Boston, which began its revival in 1895. Beacon Hill had begun to lose its luster by then, but it was not so far gone as to be unsafe, and young Society people could move there without personal risk. In a pattern that would repeat itself countless times in the second half of the twentieth century, an energetic realtor and two young architects (one of them the soon-to-be-famous Ralph Adams Cram) took the lead. They stressed the grandeur of Boston's early history and did not scruple to invent, under the guise of rediscovery, colonial and federalist traditions that have since caught on widely, including the Christmas customs of outdoor caroling and placing a single white candle in each window. By 1910, the little neighborhood had a critical mass of respectable people and was strong enough to grow; and two new squares, small but stylish, were built in Bulfinch's style just before 1914.

The first urban district where the lure of history and historic buildings attained city-shaping scale was Georgetown, a neighborhood in Washington that had been an independent town in its early years and had an authentic Early American pedigree. Georgetown was cheap and run-down by the 1920s, and three quarters of its residents were black, hardly an inducement to fashionable re-settlement in America in the Jim Crow era. But the neighborhood had enough old houses and streetscapes to stimulate the imagination, and a hard core of resident patricians made it their mission to recruit respectable newcomers and offer them access to Washington Society. Georgetown also had a good location, next to the most fashionable neighborhoods in the city, Dupont Circle and Kalorama, with only a little stream to separate them.

The combination of history, charm, cheapness, and location made Georgetown the Beacon Hill of Washington. As Georgetown's earnest young men rose in the world, Georgetown itself became the most fashionable neighborhood in town, a place where power and charm went well together. Writers and government officials formed the "Georgetown Set" in the 1950s, and John F. Kennedy moved from Georgetown to the White House in 1961.

Beacon Hill and Georgetown were, however, unusual. Most historic neighborhoods, in America as in Britain, were much poorer than Beacon Hill and Georgetown ever became. Young people from respectable families were afraid to visit them, much less

Society Hill, Philadelphia.

live in them. Baltimore was not unusual in destroying its greatest Federal-era neighborhood in 1917, at the height of the Colonial Revival, as a slum-clearance project.

The first city to make preservation and row house restoration a part of its publicly-funded redevelopment strategy was Philadelphia, where Edmund Bacon, the head of the City Planning Commission, realized as early as 1950 that the lure of history and old houses could help to revive his troubled city. Bacon was able to organize a coalition of public agencies and private groups to restore the oldest neighborhood in the city, which had become a slum and a messy wholesale fruit market. His team gave the district a catchy name, Society Hill, and convinced some heavyweights from business and Society to restore old houses and move into them. By the early 1960s, sensitive infill development by I.M. Pei and others added Modern distinction (and density) without spoiling the neighborhood's charm, and adjoining neighborhoods sought to benefit from spillover.

Many people today would use the word "gentrification" to describe what happened in Georgetown and Society Hill. The word, however, was coined in London, and that is a significant fact. It was in London that the revival of historic neighborhoods first acquired real force. As soon as the worst of the post-war housing shortage began to abate, in the late 1950s, Londoners who had the luxury of choice began to choose old terraced houses in neighborhoods that had gone shabby without becoming dangerous, and things moved fast. Georgian neighborhoods were the principal beneficiaries of this movement, the visible sign of which was the appearance of antique shops in neighborhood shopping streets. Eventually, even down-at-heel districts such as Notting Hill and Islington – which had dangerous parts – began to feel the warmth of desire.

Outside London, things began to stir in the New Town of Edinburgh and the West End of Glasgow; and Bath, which a local cabbie described to me 1973 as "the only graveyard in the world with streetlights", was already beginning bounce back as he spoke. I remember watching deliveries of new-cut pilasters and capitals to replace originals ravaged by war and weather. Everything is fresh and clean now, and house prices are reminiscent of London.

Things were not so easy in England's merchant cities. Liverpudlians began to speak of Rodney and Hope Streets and Falkner Square as "Georgian Liverpool", but they kept their bulldozers busy all the while, and a brisk walker today can take in most of Georgian Liverpool without feeling a great loss of time. Manchester and Birmingham had few Georgian neighborhoods left to preserve or restore by the late 1950s.

Preservation is first and foremost a marketing strategy, a way of getting people to like old buildings. It is a lot like an advertising campaign for a consumer product – except that no company has a patent on old buildings, so no profit-motivated outfit will ever pay to run ads for them. This makes Preservation inevitably an affair of volunteers, non-profits, and government agencies. All of these kicked into gear during the Urban Crisis. When too few people saw any reason to live in our cities, Preservation offered a reason, and it was reason enough for some.

Preservation has won great victories since then. Though many people still prefer new houses to old ones, many now prefer old ones, and many more can go either way. This seismic change in taste has helped us to attract the skilled, well-paid people of whom every North Atlantic city – even London – faced a shortage in 1975.

And Preservation is cheap. Rich in the time and talent of unpaid enthusiasts, it has always given value for money. We could never have afforded to lure millions of useful people back into our cities by tearing everything down and starting over – even if (and it is a big "if") our skill in architecture and planning had been equal to the task. Thanks to Preservation, millions of people have decided that they want what our cities already have.

Not surprisingly, then, Preservation has become public policy. Every city has seen the benefits of attracting skilled residents without expensive new development, and every North Atlantic nation now protects historic buildings and neighborhoods, sometimes entire historic cities, by laws and regulations of considerable strength. I have been told that eighty percent of all buildings in central London are protected against demolition or insensitive repair. The percentage must be higher in the centers of Amsterdam and Edinburgh and must approach 100% in Delft and Leyden. Liverpool's Victorian downtown is a UNESCO World Heritage site.

In America, the federal government and many cities and states now spend hundreds of millions of dollars every year on tax incentives that reward the restoration and re-use of historic buildings. They do not do this because Americans have become a history-mad people, but because preservation incentives are a very efficient way of ending the Urban Crisis. I have devoted much of my career to the use of preservation incentives, and I can say that they are a very good use of the taxpayer's money.

Perhaps the most useful triumph of Preservation is the rediscovery and re-acceptance of small row houses. Built for working-class people, sometimes for the poor, these houses were frequently overcrowded when they were new, and they made easy targets for well-meaning bulldozers in the twentieth century; but many of them are left, and they are just the right size for today's small, childless households. It helps that they are often built densely enough to support walkable neighborhood shopping.

Predictably, the Dutch outdistance everyone else in the race to love and use small houses, but London is never far behind, and whole neighborhoods of working-class Bristol are now bursting forth in bright colors. Little row houses in the back alleys of Baltimore and Philadelphia now command higher per-square-foot prices than mansions in Olmsted suburbs.

Thanks to Preservation, almost every Georgian building in the North Atlantic world can sleep soundly at night, and we should be very glad that preservationists have expanded the range of their tastes – and helped us to expand ours – to include the Victorian buildings of which our cities are mainly comprised. Cultivated people were ashamed of Victorian architecture for most of the twentieth century, and their shame powered many a bulldozer. It took some remarkable individuals to change the taste of millions. When I walk past Victorian terraces that have been restored in the past generation, I always try to offer silent thanks to John Betjeman, who began to champion Victorian architecture in the 1950s, when most cultivated people liked Victorian buildings only in the cartoons of Charles Addams. I also try to thank A.S. Byatt, whose 1990 best-seller *Possession* crystallized the fascination of the Victorian world for millions of readers.

As an American, a citizen of the country that has always valued newness for its own sake, more than any other, I feel a special delight, even an occasional burst of national pride, as I walk our cities today and survey the triumphs of Preservation. Nowhere do I feel this more than in the Back Bay of Boston, a magnificent Victorian quarter which faced demolition in the 1950s and was still shabby when I was a student in the 1970s. Even at its dingiest moments, the Back Bay always had interest for architectural historians, but now it is so well restored that its beauties are obvious to the non-specialists who buy houses, rent apartments, and unconsciously decide whether cities will succeed or fail.

Even tough, dangerous neighborhoods have often bounced back. Boston's South End, the biggest of the city's three row house neighborhoods, had rows of burnt-out vacants when I first saw it in 1970, but it is now chic enough for sidewalk cafes and

The South End, Boston.

stratospheric condo prices. Similar things have happened in huge swathes of tough old neighborhoods in Philadelphia and Baltimore; and walking through Harlem today – or tonight – is as easy and urbane as wandering through any part of Paris that tourists don't know. In Washington, where Georgetown used to be an island of safety and decorum in a sea of dilapidation and violence, people now walk comfortably for miles through neighborhoods of picturesque Victorians, corbeled and turreted and front-gardened, as charming an urban environment as I know.

Downtown, Midtown, and Center City

If our cities are to be about friendship and love rather than commerce and industry, our all-business downtowns, those proud creations of the North Atlantic nineteenth century, will need to become more like the mixed-use centers of cities in Continental Europe. They are, in fact, doing this. They are not, however, copying Paris. They are copying Midtown Manhattan, the most influential urban district of the twentieth century.

As the name implies, Midtown is midway between Downtown – Wall Street and the rest of New York's old central business district – and Uptown – the rich residential neighborhoods on both sides of Central Park. It first became a distinct area in the early years of the twentieth century, and its middle-ness was both geographical and functional.

It had offices like Downtown and apartment buildings like Uptown. And it had much more – hotels, department stores, Clubland, the Great White Way of Broadway. And, uniquely in the North Atlantic world, it had a variety of things in each street, sometimes in each building. You could rent an apartment above a dress shop, a grocery store, or Carnegie Hall. You could work in a skyscraper, live next door, and stroll to the theatre after work. After the play, you could booze it up and/or dance the night away in any one of dozens of nightclubs, then stumble home without crossing too many streets. It was in Midtown that New York became "the city that never sleeps".

Downtown was merely a place to work, Uptown merely a place to live. Midtown was everything. The most beautiful of skyscrapers were built on 42nd Street (the Chrysler Building) and 34th Street (the Empire State Building). Rockefeller Center, a complex of tall buildings and spectacular public amenities, showed that large-scale planning could increase profits while creating landmarks. Times Square became the Main Street of the United States.

The fifteen-year building moratorium imposed by the Great Depression and World War II slowed the spread of Midtown's influence, but those fallow years gave America's architects, planners, and civic leaders plenty of time to envy Midtown and absorb its lessons. When building started up again after the war, and the business leaders of American cities realized that suburbia was threatening the survival of their downtowns, they turned to Midtown for ideas and techniques.

One city, Boston, tried to emulate New York directly by creating a new mixed-use area at some distance from its central business district. This was understandable: Boston's downtown was almost as cramped as Lower Manhattan, and the city was just big enough, and just vibrant enough, to make the creation of a second major business district possible. And – perhaps most important – Boston had an excellent subway system, as good for a city of Boston's size as New York's larger system was for that far larger city.

Noticing that New York's Midtown had arisen in the city's most fashionable Victorian residential district, the brownstone paradise centered on Fifth Avenue, Boston's leaders planned to demolish their equivalent neighborhood, the Back Bay, and replace it with skyscrapers. Bostonians, however, pride themselves on respecting tradition more than New Yorkers do, and Boston preservationists saved the Back Bay after years of bitter wrangling in the 1950s, the first major triumph for American preservationists in any big city-shaping fight. In the end, the two sides shook hands over a plan called the "High Spine", in which a line of skyscrapers would be built on an old rail line that ran parallel to the Back Bay streets.

The High Spine worked, and works, brilliantly. Its big new buildings concentrate enough people to support a full range of restaurants and shops, to which the residents of the lower-density row houses in the Back Bay and the South End can walk in minutes.

The High Spine, Boston.

It accomplishes what New York's Midtown accomplishes even though it does not look or feel very much like it. What it resembles most, in fact, is the juxtaposition of historic city centers with rail-based contemporary architecture in the Netherlands.

Boston's attempt to create a second high-intensity district turned out to be unique in the North Atlantic part of the United States. Philadelphia set the model for the rest of America's cities by attempting to turn its traditional downtown into a Midtown on the Manhattan model. Philadelphia was, and is, a big city, a third as big as New York. Philadelphia's downtown had enough skyscrapers to turn the streets into Manhattan-style canyons, and it had a ready-made mix of uses: the city's department stores and theatres were still downtown, while the famous Philadelphia Orchestra and the fashionable apartment houses of Rittenhouse Square were an easy walk away. Philadelphia also had an excellent system of suburban trains, and these came together downtown.

Philadelphia also had Edmund Bacon. Like Inigo Jones in London or Charles Bulfinch in Boston, Bacon was a man with a mission, and his mission was the creation of a Manhattan-style Midtown in the center of Philadelphia. He realized that Philadelphia's downtown already had most of what it needed; he and his team just needed to expand it, enrich its mix of uses, and improve the declining neighborhoods around it. They got to work early, while the war was still in full swing, and they designated a very large area, the whole of Penn's original town, about three miles long and a mile wide. And they coined a valuable new phrase, "Center City", to express both the scale of the area and its importance.

Much of the area that Bacon defined as Center City was a mess, but Bacon was lucky enough to have time for long-range plans. He gained the confidence of one mayor after another, and he worked tirelessly into the early 1970s. No shrinking violet, he made the cover of America's biggest magazine and became the one name that Americans thought of when they heard the words "city planning". The list of his achievements was impressive: the building of Penn Center, the restoration of Society Hill, the creation of Independence Mall, the integration of the region's commuter rail lines.

But was it enough? The issue was long in doubt. It usually takes more than thirty years to change a big city, and America's Urban Crisis had sunk its teeth deep into Philadelphia. Center City was still a work in progress when Bacon retired in the 1970s and did not reach critical mass until thirty years later. But things then began to move fast. People quite suddenly noticed that they could walk for miles through dense urban districts and be glad they did, and Center City became so powerful a magnet for talented and skillful people that the city as a whole began to turn itself around. After losing population in every Census after 1950, Philadelphia gained thirty thousand people between 2000 and 2010.

The most dramatic enlivening of any civic center in my experience has taken place in Washington. America's capital city has a big downtown and armies of well-paid office workers, but the enlivening of downtown Washington did not happen organically. It began in the mid-1970s with the opening of a wonderful subway system. Washington's traffic had been appalling for decades, and the creation of Metro was a necessary first step. Then, in the mid-1980s, the city's government set a goal of adding five thousand housing units to the downtown mix and required developers to create several floors of apartments within each office building. By the time Washington developers made the city's five-thousand-unit quota, downtown living had caught on, and developers began to build housing because they wanted to. A virtuous cycle was created, in which every new apartment building meant more restaurants and stores and theatres and offices, which attracted more residents, and so on. Washington has now rewoven its office district into the fabric of the surrounding neighborhoods and created a Center City. You can walk for miles in safety and with pleasure.

This is the pattern. Most downtowns in the North Atlantic world are now becoming center cities. The highest compliment you can pay to the center of a city today is to say that it is a "24/7 place" – that is, that it is lively twenty-four hours a day, seven days a week. Many now warrant that accolade. All of them still have as many office workers as they ever did, often more, but they also have residents and the things that residents want and need.

Center City, Philadelphia.

Docklands, London.

The area around Wall Street, long a workplace pure and simple, now has 68,000 residents and a notable restaurant scene. The streets around the Bank of England, once pin-drop quiet on weekends, now have neighborhood shops and neighborhood shoppers on Saturday afternoons. The tallest buildings in Manchester and Birmingham are expensive downtown apartment towers. There are a thousand new apartments in the center of Liverpool, and downtown Baltimore is the fastest-growing residential neighborhood in the metropolitan area. These new residents are supporting the theatres, bars, clubs and venues that are turning these old central business districts into 24/7 center cities.

So great is the prestige of the successful center cities that developers are now building new center cities far from traditional downtowns. Unlike the auto-centric "edge cities" that Joel Garreau, twenty-five years ago, promoted as the inevitable future of all cities, most of today's newly-created center cities depend on mass transit.

Some of these new center cities result from an intensification of old low-density suburbs. Washington has done more of this than anyone else, using its splendid Metro system – and many tools of law and regulation – to turn post-war strip-mall districts like Bethesda and Silver Spring into impressive secondary center cities. As in the Netherlands, the most dramatic new center cities are being built on abandoned rail lines and dockyards. London, with its immense Docklands and its beautiful King's Cross, is setting the pace for this kind of development.

Salford Quays, Manchester.

It should be no surprise that the largest cities are the best at creating new center cities. Only they have enough jobs, people, and activities to go around; and only they have transit systems robust enough to move tens of thousands of people to more than one central place. If a smaller city embarks on an ambitious new 24/7 district, it will probably just weaken its downtown without strengthening the city as a whole.

The great warning is Manchester's Salford Quays development, a complex of large new buildings stretched out along a mile or so of disused industrial canals about two miles from the center of the city. Salford Quays is beautiful. It has some spectacular buildings, and it is Britain's second-largest center of television production. But the two miles that separate it from the center of Manchester are impenetrably chaotic, and the single light rail line that glides through Salford Quays is inadequate to the district's ambitions. As a result, this rather glorious place is failing to be urban. It is an automotive edge city, with the biggest parking garage I have ever seen in Britain, and it is positively tranquil after 5 pm on a working day. If Edmund Bacon had been running Manchester, he would have added all the good things of Salford Quays to the city's downtown, and the center of Manchester would by now have grown out to embrace the city's great universities and form a true center city.

Organized Bohemia

Although Dutch cities are famous for their Golden Age painters, it is only in the past decade or so that the builders of North Atlantic cities have given attention to the needs and wants of working artists. Our Victorian ancestors, having located Bohemia in Paris, were emphatically anxious to keep it there. But this has been changing for decades and is now changing rapidly. Artists and the arts are now such an important part of reviving cities that all of our cities are working to create arts districts.

The origins of self-conscious North Atlantic Bohemia appear to lie in London's Bloomsbury and New York's Greenwich Village, both of which acquired something of a loose and arty reputation before 1914. These were neighborhoods of the Long Eighteenth Century that had gone to seed, and the first Bohemians had things in common with the first Preservationists: Virginia Woolf, who incorrectly thought of wallpaper as a Victorian invention, was thrilled to paint a wall in her Bloomsbury house instead of papering it.

The Villagers and Bloomsberries whose names we know today – Theodore Dreiser and Edna St. Vincent Millay, Willa Cather, the Woolfs and the Bells, Lytton Strachey and John Maynard Keynes – were hard-working, high-minded people, and self-disciplined in a way that would have seemed austere if it had involved sexual repression. Eventually, however, their example attracted much larger groups of people who were less austere and a great deal more fun to watch. By 1925, the goings-on of Villagers had become a part of the New York tourist itinerary, and Rodgers and Hart could sing:

We'll go to Greenwich,
Where modern men itch
To be free.

So things bubbled along until the 1960s. By that time, New York had become the center of the art world; American artists like Jackson Pollock and Andy Warhol had become celebrities of something like Hollywood caliber; and rich people wanted to party with Bohemians and even live among them. It was not, however, in New York that Bohemia gained recognition as a city-shaping force. That honor goes to San Francisco, where Beatniks morphed into Hippies and declared 1967 the Summer of Love. Love of different kinds followed soon thereafter, and San Francisco displaced Greenwich Village as the capital of Gay America – just in time for people to notice that San Francisco was becoming the richest city in the country and so must obviously be doing something right.

From then on, the border between Bohemia and the Bourgeoisie lost its guards and its passport controls. Many educated baby-boomers, having rebelled against bourgeois convention in their youth in the late 1960s, wanted to believe that they had retained their rebelliousness after settling down to steady work. An acute cultural critic called them BoBos, for Bourgeois Bohemians.

The resulting "scenes" were greenhouses for the city of friendship and love, albeit with the unintended consequence that BoBo lawyers and bankers sooner or later priced working artists out of their neighborhoods. A pattern became established in which artists more or less unwittingly become the shock troops of neighborhood revitalization, opening up one long-forgotten neighborhood after another and then getting priced out of it. This happened so quickly and so visibly in New York's SoHo that artists and developers call it "the SoHo effect".

Today, many North Atlantic cities are fostering the growth of districts for artists. No one calls artists Bohemians any more, or giggles at the thought of what their private lives might be. There are attempts, both cynical and altruistic, to exploit the SoHo effect for civic improvement, and there is a growing recognition that artists are valuable for their own sake. Artistic training now has more economic use than ever, and thousands of art school graduates in dozens of cities now make good livings in new fields like web design and computer gaming. Foundations and even city governments are trying to create art-centered districts that will stand the test of time.

Predictably, New York and London have had the most success in attracting artists and forming arts districts. But other cities are coming up fast. Boston's art scene is so solidly established that the SoHo Effect is bringing new life to abandoned mills in the deindustrialized cities of Lowell and Providence, forty miles away. Philadelphia, ninety miles from New York, is attracting New York artists who call it "the sixth borough". A top-flight art college is putting Baltimore on the artistic map. Artists in the small Dutch industrial city of Eindhoven have turned a large vacant factory into an internationally-renowned art center that seems to be bringing broader life to the whole community.

Arts districts are not necessarily pretty or urbane. Artists tend to favor, and have the money for, abandoned warehouses and factories, often in places where it is possible to walk a long way without seeing a human face. I can remember when New York's SoHo was like that; my best college friend was shocked in 1972 that so many handsome old buildings in the middle of New York City could be vacant – and more shocked when he found that people were living in them. If you want to see a young arts district that is handsome and urbane without having sold its soul, I recommend Manchester's Northern Quarter. Not only does it have some good architecture, it also plays a useful part in Manchester's center city, rather than loitering miles away in some post-industrial wasteland.

I have never seen anything like an accurate count of the artists who are living in the centers of our cities, but my own work in Baltimore suggests that it is beginning to be fairly significant. Baltimore's Station North, whose buildings were more than fifty percent vacant ten years ago, now has living and working space for about a thousand artists, most of whom would probably be living and working in some other city if Station North had not happened. Artists, arts institutions, and developers like me have invested more than $150 million in new and renovated Station North buildings during the past five years.

Openness

The North Atlantic cities would not exist without many historical waves of immigration. This has always been a source of tension in the short run and of energy in the long. One of the triumphs of the North Atlantic cities, in fact, has been their ability to work through painful ethnic differences. The people of our cities were not born with that ability. They had to learn it, and the learning was often slow. But they have that ability now – we have it now – and it is as much a strength of our tradition as the row house or the underground train. As early as 1911, a London guidebook could boast that London "has more Irishmen than Dublin, more Poles than Warsaw, more Jews than Jerusalem, and more Catholics than Rome". It says a great deal for London in 1911 that this was a boast.

Today, it is obvious that the most dynamic cities in the North Atlantic family are the ones that are most open to foreigners. An easy acceptance of diversity – and a ready willingness of immigrants to watch their children become natives – has made it possible for London and New York to become the twin capitals of today's global world. Boston, Amsterdam, and Washington are not far behind.

Two things are worth noting. The first is that immigrants go to dynamic cities and make them more dynamic. Cities with more sluggish economies have trouble attracting immigrants. Whatever jingoistic politicians may say, immigrants are good for local economies. The second is that, when it comes to racial and ethnic groups, three's company and two's a crowd. I can remember when every American city was a black-and-white movie, with only two races. Now, many cities are movies in Technicolor. Real diversity – the presence and interaction of people from many different cultures – removes a lot of pressure. New York can boast of mayors of named Bloomberg and DiBlasio. London can boast of a Mayor Boris and a Mayor Sadiq.

Mass Transit

Mass transit was one of the great inventions of the North Atlantic cities in the century before 1900. The car-crazy twentieth century cut ridership and budgets, often disastrously, but transit is on an upswing now in many of our cities, and our hope for continued revival depends on its improvement. Because public transit is usually provided and maintained by some level of government, it is the element of urban development in which politics is usually most important, and thus something of a barometer of the political health of a community.

This is where the Dutch come into their own. Because the very existence of the Netherlands depends on thousands of miles of dikes, built and steadily maintained for as long as history can remember, the Dutch have long since learned to do patient committee work and inglorious maintenance. They are used to taking the long view and working together without a raging thirst for individual glory. If their cities are now the best in the North Atlantic world, as I think they are, it is because Dutch habits of dealing with water have taught them to envision and build a great system of national rail and local transport.

This is why the Dutch have been able to become rich without destroying their wonderful old small-scale cities. Every city in the so-called *Randstad* is within easy reach of every other, and each city is effectively a part of a great conurbation with a population of eight million. Those who want big-city hustle and bustle can have it among skyscrapers in Rotterdam or museums and bawdy houses in Amsterdam. Those who want peace and quiet can stroll beside historic canals in Leyden or Delft, or new canals in Berkel Westpolder. Most people, of course, want both from time to time, and they can have both.

London is not far behind. It too has about eight million people, and it is to a great extent a group of settlements, each with a strong local identity, connected by a transit system that is beginning to give the Dutch a run for their money.

In the past fifteen years or so, Londoners have made heavy investments in signaling, ticketing, and rolling stock, with the result that the Underground runs twice as many trains and carries twice as many passengers as it did in 2001. If people hear an approaching train as they are walking down to an Underground platform, they no longer run, as they used to; they are confident that the next train will be along in two minutes or less, and they walk without breaking stride. And a new high-speed line, Cross Rail, is about to cut the time of a cross-town journey in half. If London had a poorer transport network, its people would have to sprawl and drive like Americans, or clump closer together and walk like Continental Europeans. As it is, London's transport renaissance is allowing London, as it grows, to remain itself, a unique tapestry of very different places, the city of Docklands, Belgravia, Metro-Land, and everything in between.

It would be hard to overstate the importance of subway systems in the revival of Washington and Boston. Lucky Boston, with a system dating back to the 1890s, has used the "T" to shape its booming recent growth intelligently. Washington has reaped enormous rewards from its magnificent Metro system. In both cities, it is easy to live without a car in very large areas, and suburban growth is beginning to focus intelligently around stations.

Things are not so good elsewhere. Manchester and Birmingham have outgrown their systems, as have Baltimore and Philadelphia. I have come to believe that every metropolitan area of two million people or more should have, or should be planning, an underground system with a minimum of three or four lines. The first new lines should probably be short, serving only the urban areas that are already dense enough to support frequent service.

And then there is New York. Once the home of the greatest subway network in the world, New York has let its system stall and stagnate since World War II. In the past forty years, while London has finished several entirely new lines and built most of Cross Rail, New York has added only a handful of new subway stations – at curiously vast expense – and still fails to provide a direct connection to any one of the city's three airports. Maintenance, too, is a front-page issue in the New York papers, and no one seems even to be thinking of the kind of improvements that have doubled the capacity of the London Underground. With an inadequate route map and tens of billions of dollars of deferred maintenance, New York's subway may turn out to be the city's Achilles heel.

That leaves inter-city rail service, the backbone of the Dutch achievement. Despite a fair amount of chaos in nationalizing, privatizing, re-nationalizing, and re-privatizing tracks and rolling stock, the British are serving their much larger country almost equally well. America is the laggard here, and the failure of the American government to provide decent rail service along the East Coast weakens every one of America's North Atlantic cities. If the Dutch ran America's East Coast railroads, there would be five times more passenger trains than there are, they would go twice as fast as they do, and millions of people who now drive around in suburbia would sell a car and move closer to the centers of their cities.

The other side of transportation is traffic. I cannot think of any city that has pulled itself out of the Urban Crisis without taming the private car and restoring calm to city neighborhoods and freedom to pedestrians and cyclists. Good transit systems can help people to drive less, but achieving a good transport picture takes sticks as well as carrots. The Dutch tax cars and gasoline as if they were luxuries, with the result that they are. Speed limits are kept low, parking is kept scarce, and pedestrians and cyclists insist upon the right of way.

Most Americans have never seen such things and cannot imagine them – or would view them as infringements on personal liberty. As a result, millions of Americans sit in traffic for untold hours, while millions of other Americans live on streets that are raceways for speeding commuters. My own Baltimore is a prime offender in this regard. Our city government has used many row house streets as commuter raceways for decades. Neither the roadways nor the buildings are big enough to stand up to the assault of cars. As a result, these streets are much less popular than they would be if traffic were better managed, particularly among families with children. Traffic makes these streets weak, and weak streets weaken the neighborhoods around them.

But all is not hopeless. Although no place in the North Atlantic world penalizes auto-dependence as severely as the Dutch do, New York has achieved miracles in the past decade. With inspired leadership from Mayor Michael Bloomberg and his traffic commissioner, Janette Sadik Khan, New York has cut speed limits, given traffic lanes to bikes, even eliminated parking spaces. Times Square itself, once the most gridlocked set of streets in America, is now a pedestrian precinct, mobbed at all hours with people. The number of cars on the streets of Manhattan has fallen so drastically that Uber can predict accurately how long a car will take to reach its destination.

Wherever we have tamed traffic, we have rediscovered the pleasures of walking on streets and promenading in public places. Jane Jacobs taught us that busy streets are safe, William H. Whyte taught us that they are fun, and we have learned their lessons whether or not we have read their books. The expression "street life", which used to denote gangsterism and destitution, is now a compliment.

Times Square Pedestrianized.

Bryant Park, New York.

Parks and Open Spaces

What is true of streets is also true of public spaces. At the height of the Urban Crisis, we often feared riots so much that we were unwilling to make places that would bring crowds of people together. Things are better now. We now have, and use, and love, an astonishing variety of public places. Many of these are quite small, like Post Office Square in Boston. Many have been reclaimed from vagrants and drug dealers, like Bryant Park in New York. The best offer food, drink, and a range of things to do. Bryant Park, the best example of a new-style city park, has five different places to get refreshments and something like seventeen different things to do, ranging from sitting alone to playing ping-pong, all in one city block with no sense of crowding.

These places conform to our normal idea of a park as a green space surrounded by other things, but many of our favorite new places are not green at all. The High Line in New York, a mile and a half of abandoned rail line about twenty-five feet above ground, breaks every possible rule of good traditional park design. It is not very wide, it is hard-surfaced for most of its length, and it is difficult to get to. Once people get there, they cannot get food or drink, play ping-pong, or do much of anything else. Yet it is jammed with people all the time. Similar, if more conventionally elegant, are the brick promenades around the Inner Harbor of Baltimore. The pleasure of such places is the pleasure of social walking in a polite public place with a comforting frame of urban architecture. In them the Long Eighteenth Century returns to life, albeit in tee shirts and tank tops.

The big Victorian parks remain a bit of a problem. They were designed for a vanished world in which most city-dwellers had no other escape from buildings and streets. Now that middle-class families have vacations, televisions, air conditioning, and backyard grills, there is little political pressure to spend public money on the activities that made these big parks destinations in the first place, and most of them are empty most of the time.

A few lucky parks in dense middle-class areas have attracted big volunteer efforts and raised lots of money for park improvements and maintenance. Central Park in New York, perhaps predictably, took the lead in this. It was the first big park to have a Parks Conservancy and is now the model for public-private partnerships that bring charitable money to bear on parks. When I want to see this kind of thing in action in Baltimore, I wander over to Patterson Park, a hundred acres of green in the midst of a very dense row house district that is gentrifying and becoming ethnically diverse at the same time. Deserted and dangerous twenty years ago, the park is now full of people at most non-working hours. A volunteer group has raised money and badgered public officials into making it usable – and local bar owners have financed sports leagues that now have thousands of members.

Not all urban green space needs to be active. Much of it has the simple function of being green and soft in an environment that is red or grey and hard. When I walk through terraced neighborhoods in London, I seem to have trees and grass beside me for a high percentage of the time, and this is pleasurable, even though I never walk into the green spaces that I pass, and probably could not if I wanted to, not having a key. If looking at nature were not enjoyable, there would be no landscape painters.

In fact, our most frequent "uses" of urban open spaces come when we are not actually using them at all. We walk past them with a little smile, or pay a bit extra to have a window that overlooks them. Most of these spaces are small. When people use them, there is hardly ever a program, a budget, or a burly fellow with a whistle. Children throw balls for each other, adults throw balls for dogs, and parents and dog-owners get to know each other while their charges play informally. If there is any kind of polite public space that our cities need today, it is small, informal spaces, the more frequent the better.

Parks are not the only kinds of spaces that count as polite public places. Jane Jacobs was right to insist that neighborhood businesses are an invaluable kind of polite public place. This is sometimes forgotten when academic planners try to revive abandoned neighborhoods that have acres of vacant land. If planners preserve too many vacant lots as "open space", the neighborhoods wind up without enough residents to support businesses, and that is a great impoverishment. Residents are often wiser. My favorite neighborhood planning process, conducted by seventeen volunteer residents in a neighborhood that was more than fifty percent vacant, concluded that their neighborhood needed three kinds of public spaces: a playground, a dog park, and a coffee shop.

Rebuilding Britain's Cities

Not long ago, I tried walking from the center of Manchester to Chorlton, the charming Manchester Metro-Land in which I was staying. The walk wasn't long, only a mile or two, but it was consistently unpleasant. I walked alone, on narrow sidewalks, inches from fast-moving traffic. Every now and then I would come to a cross street on which I could see people congregating, and I turned into them to see what was going on. But this was not the thing at all. What appeared to be quiet cross streets turned out to be cul-de-sacs, each one the center of an isolated and self-isolating little community. Time and again, I found myself in a dead end with people looking at me as if I had come to steal their money, so back I went to traffic and solitude on a main street.

This was a perfectly typical walk through the acres and miles of council housing estates that surround the center of Manchester and every British city except London. I wish I could say that these were Brutalist relics from the 1950s or gimcrack tower blocks from the mass-production years of the 1960s. The failures of such developments are widely acknowledged and often corrected. In fact, these were some of the corrections, replacements of earlier council developments, and their architecture was red-brick traditional. The problem was that each estate had been planned to be an inward-turning village, walled off from its surroundings. As a result, strangers are made to feel uncomfortable and go away, as I obligingly did.

Jane Jacobs says that great cities help strangers to feel like neighbors and fellow-citizens. Too many of Britain's' council estates, new and old, do the opposite. As these estates get redeveloped, local governments should insist that they form a coherent street plan. They should connect one estate to another gracefully, make it easy for residents to get where they need to go, and generally knit the centers of these great cities back together.

There is no shortage of good models, from William Penn and Edmund Bacon in Philadelphia to the Wide Streets Commissioners in Dublin, from the New Town of Edinburgh to Howard's Garden Cities and the New Urbanism in the United States. It would be nice to think that, within a generation or two, Britain's great merchant cities could connect their admirable downtowns to their charming Metro Lands with pleasant and useful neighborhoods.

Unfortunately, although the need for sensitive re-planning and redevelopment is most pressing the merchant cities, most work will probably occur in London. This is not because London has the worst examples of council housing – on average, it has the best – but simply because London has a higher demand for housing, and there are powerful pressures to increase population densities. As a result, huge tracts of post-war council housing may soon be demolished and redeveloped in all parts of the Metropolis.

Create Streets, London.

The debate over how to redevelop these huge tracts is shaping up to be the most interesting urban debate in the North Atlantic world.

There are two basic sides. The first – and the stronger, it would appear, in numbers and financial heft – wants to build residential skyscrapers. I have seen plans for mixed-income tower blocks of forty and sixty stories on the site of current two-story council estates across the Thames from Docklands. On the other side is a small, brainy group called Create Streets which argues that developers can achieve high-rise densities by building traditional North Atlantic low-rise buildings in traditional North Atlantic streets. Create Streets is akin to the New Urbanist movement in the United States. Its design team has replanned a number of old council estates to produce neighborhoods that look like traditional London neighborhoods, with terraced houses fronting on public streets. If I were British, I would give money and volunteer time to Create Streets. They are a voice crying in the wilderness, and that voice should be heard.

But there is an elephant in the room of the British housing market. The whole country is facing a painful housing shortage that is getting worse every year. The arithmetic is simple enough: the country is growing by two hundred fifty thousand households per year while building only fifty thousand houses and apartments. Everyone acknowledges this, but no one seems to think he or she can do anything about it. Everyone blames some other person, party, or philosophy. This makes everything hard, and it may make the redevelopment of Britain's poorly-planned urban areas impossible.

After all, given that Britain has a chronic housing shortage and no plans for solving it, why should the current residents of council estates favor any redevelopment schemes at all? Current residents will surely be displaced, probably for years, and told to find apartments that do not exist. They are, moreover, voting citizens, and they have principled, intelligent people on their side, like John Boughton, whose blog and book called *Municipal Dreams* champion council housing with a humane intelligence worthy of Orwell. Until the British can get beyond the fundamental absurdity of an insoluble housing shortage, it is hard to see how there will be a lot of good redevelopment in British cities.

There is a ray of hope for two British cities. London and Birmingham may be able to solve some of their housing problems in the best North Atlantic fashion. London's problem is that it does not have enough housing for the people who want to live there. Birmingham's is the reverse. Each would benefit from some kind of union of their real estate markets. This has never been even remotely feasible, as the two cities are a hundred miles apart, but plans are afoot for a high-speed rail line that will link them to each other at commuting speed, and a global bank has already moved a thousand employees from high-cost London to the cheaper city a hundred miles away. This is the North Atlantic tradition at its best, using public transport to create a humane metropolis at moderate density.

A Persuasive Alternative to American Sprawl

Although America's cities have a version of the British doughnut problem, this is the result of structural racism rather than poor planning. Buildings and street plans in the half-abandoned neighborhoods of Philadelphia and Baltimore are usually no different from those in more expensive neighborhoods, except that African-Americans have moved up and out to better neighborhoods, and everyone else is afraid to go there. Little will be gained by wholesale clearance and replanning.

Although urban blight is shocking and obvious in many American cities, it is not actually America's biggest physical-development problem. That is automotive sprawl.

A few years ago, I wanted to understand how big a problem sprawl was. I decided to estimate how much land it would take to house the entire population of metropolitan Baltimore under several different assumptions about population density. I started by looking at my own part of the city, a pleasant Anglo-Dutch mixture of three-story Victorian row houses and twentieth-century high-rise apartments with a density of approximately twenty thousand people to the square mile. I knew that metropolitan Baltimore had 1.1 million households, and it was easy to calculate that all of us could fit into about ninety square miles if we lived in places like my neighborhood. I tried the same test with several city neighborhoods and got similar results.

I then went out to a suburban planning department on the outskirts of the city and asked my friends there to show me the plans of the ten most typical new neighborhoods they had approved in the past year. Not the best, not the worst, just the most typical. They gave me roll after roll of plans and a room with a big table, and I had a day of fun with various measuring devices. It turned out that the average house lot took up about three-quarters of an acre. At that very low level of density. Baltimore would need to extend to a point somewhere between the White House and the US Capitol in Washington. The four million people of metropolitan Washington would presumably resist our incursions.

My calculations revealed a second problem. Even if we could find enough land to make sprawl universal, the expense would be ruinous. The typical three-quarter-acre lot on these subdivision plans was at least a hundred feet wide. This meant that somebody – the homeowner or the taxpayer or both – would have to build and eternally maintain a hundred feet of road, a hundred feet of sidewalk, and a hundred feet of water lines and sewer lines just to take care of each house. Even big row houses, like those in the crescents of Bath or on the great Amsterdam canals, need only twenty or twenty-five feet.

Sprawl also fails to meet the needs and desires of the childless adults who make up most modern households. It has everything they don't want – maintenance, driving, loneliness – and nothing they do want – things to do, people to see, convenience. This did not seem important a hundred years ago, when most childless people lived with their parents, their children, or Sherlock Holmes's Mrs. Hudson, but it is crucial now. Childless adults have a legitimate need for the things that a good city provides in rich measure, and a sprawling suburb cannot provide them at all.

But the real curse of sprawl is the damage that it does to the earth and its inhabitants. American-style suburbia shares with coal-powered China the honor of being the leading cause of global climate change. Even today, surprisingly few Americans understand the connection between climate change and sprawl. They look at a leafy suburb and assume that it is "greener" than a hard-edged city neighborhood. Appearances, alas, are deceiving. A free-standing house in sprawling suburbia, exposed to heat and cold on all sides, takes a great deal more energy, and has a much bigger carbon footprint, than a house in a row, which can share heat with its neighbors – or an apartment, which can share heat vertically as well as horizontally.

And that is only the beginning. The real problem is driving, as it has been in American suburbia for a hundred years. Because there are never enough people within walking distance of any one place to support a store or a school, American suburbanites drive everywhere – to work, to the doctor, to stores, to parties, to churches and synagogues. Even Orthodox synagogues sometimes have parking lots.

Suburbanites cannot, for instance, walk to a neighborhood hardware store, as my dog Spot and I have already done twice today. It's true that our little hardware store is smaller than the hardware behemoths in the suburbs, but it has everything my neighbors and I need on an average Saturday, and we can support it with very little driving and just a few parking spaces. If Spot and I lived in sprawling suburbia, our two little trips would have taken up twenty miles of driving – and the uniformed attendants at a giant store would never have allowed Spot to pass through their electric doors, much less given him a treat, as Micky and his team have done twice today at our neighborhood store.

Things have reached such a point that most American parents consider it a sign of negligence to allow children to walk to school, and few suburban children are allowed to play in their neighborhoods without supervision. Suburban parents log countless billions of miles in quest of soccer fields, play dates, music lessons, and all the other things that children used to get to independently on foot, on bicycles, or on the bus. The Olmsteds would feel that they had lived in vain.

Back when most pollution came from the belching smokestacks of coal-burning factories, polluters could claim to be economically useful. Sprawl, the source of most of today's greenhouse gases, cannot do this. It is a technology of consumption, not of production.

The Value of the North Atlantic Tradition Today

The people of the North Atlantic cities have been experimenting with buildings and places for more than four hundred years. After thousands of trials, and not a few errors, they have developed an approach that works very well for large numbers of people with a small carbon footprint. The key elements are: row houses, apartments, parks, and public transportation. At its best – and it is often at its best – it offers convenience and delight.

Many of these elements have already come together in successful center cities and expansive districts of old moderate-density housing. But what about the doughnuts of council developments that separate Britain's city centers from their middle-class neighborhoods? And what about the American sprawl that endangers our very survival?

If you have ever walked down Kensington High Street in London or Connecticut Avenue in Washington, and then walked around them, you have seen what a good first step would look like. Each of those streets is wide and busy. They are lined, for most of their length, by large apartment buildings, many of them with shops on the ground floor. But the streets that surround them are small and quiet, and are lined with houses – 19th-century row houses in London and 20th-century suburban houses in Washington.

This is such an obvious win-win that it is hard to imagine why more cities do not routinely do what London and Washington have done. People who live alone, or in childless couples, find thousands of well-designed apartments on the busy avenue. People who have children at home find thousands of houses on the quiet streets. Thanks to the high densities in the apartment buildings, there are enough people to support all kinds of commerce on the big streets – and robust public transportation on it or under it. This Avenue-and-Streets pattern works even though densities on the streets behind Connecticut Avenue are quite low.

Britain's merchant cities could use the Avenue-and-Streets model to shape the redevelopment of the dull, chaotic doughnuts that surround their downtowns. Manchester would be a great place to start. Good development along Oxford Road, tying

A Busy Avenue and Quiet Streets. Connecticut Avenue from the Air.

the city center to the universities and the "Curry Mile," would house thousands of people and give them a good life. And it must be possible, somehow, to connect the center of Manchester with the isolated magnificence of Salford Quays.

In America, every suburban area could use the model of Connecticut Avenue to add density, vitality, and urbanity to the sad and obsolescent strip-mall streets that disfigure every American suburb. Bethesda, a Washington suburb, is doing this now, replacing parking lots and strip malls with apartment buildings that have shops on the ground floor. A good test case in a more typical city might be the Harford Road in Baltimore.

Meanwhile the North Atlantic world is full of places that are already delightful, and there are plenty of places that could be delightful with a modest amount of money and work.

My own neighborhood, which has some tall apartment buildings but consists mainly of three-story row houses from various parts of the nineteenth century, is a pretty good advertisement for the basics of the North Atlantic tradition. On one of our trips to the hardware store today, Spot and I stopped at the corner to talk with our neighbors Val and Sarah. Val is a retired lawyer in her seventies. She lives in one of the only two early-Victorian suburban villas that survive in the center of Baltimore, and she is usually to be seen watering the flowers in her beautiful front garden. Sarah is about twenty-five, an artist and art teacher who came to Baltimore for college and now lives with her Indian-born fiancé on the second floor of the house next to mine. Val and Sarah are very close, despite the difference in their ages and dwelling types. I do not see how they could ever have met each other if they had lived in sprawling suburbia, with its rigid separation of houses like Val's from apartments like Sarah's. They would have missed so much.

As the three of us were talking, kids played in the quiet street, and several grownups wandered along as grownups do on a Saturday. And there we were: young and old, two-legged and four-legged, dwellers in houses and apartments, with and without children, on a quiet Saturday in a typical neighborhood in a North Atlantic city.

We have a good tradition, strong and flexible, time-tested on two continents. If we build on it, we can live good lives and lessen the coming ecological catastrophe.

THANKS AND REGRETS

Writers often complain that theirs is a lonely trade, but this book has been delightfully sociable.

First and foremost, I would like to thank Orest Ranum, my *cher maître* in the making of this book, It was – it is – a deep delight to share this adventure with him.

Alex Garvin gave unstintingly of his time, his wisdom, his photo collection, and his inimitable brightness of eye.

Tim O'Donnell has done more than anyone else to shape my thoughts about buildings, cities, and people. This book is a first attempt to put our forty years of debate and observation to work.

Jeff Cohen, Jim Grubb, and Barbara Trimble read the manuscript at various stages, and Kathrin Rosenfield read each chapter while still hot from the oven. Their criticisms have been valuable, their support and encouragement invaluable.

George Scheper of the Odyssey Program at the Johns Hopkins University offered me a chance to give a course on the North Atlantic Cities while this book was still finding its form. The course and the students were tremendous fun, and the process of preparing illustrated lectures on deadline brought things into focus quickly.

Nicholas Noyes graciously contributed beautiful photographs while enhancing my understanding of both London and New York.

My colleagues at Jubilee Baltimore have taught me much, and our work has allowed me to face the physical and social realities of a representative North Atlantic city. I am glad to be part of a great organization that considers scholarship and teaching to be integral parts of planning and development.

Of the many people who have helped me to explore and understand their cities, none has been so comprehensively helpful as Colin Wilkinson of the Bluecoat Press. I met Colin many years ago by e-mailing him a question about Liverpool. He became a guide, a friend, and now, happily for me, my publisher.

Michael March, graphic designer with an address in Liverpool's beautiful Rodney Street, has turned a mass of words and pictures into something so beautiful that you have wanted to pick up this book and keep reading until you get to these words.

I have enjoyed few things more than roaming London with John Boughton, Leeds with John Thorpe, or Dublin with Anngret Simms – or taking huge road trips with Johns Hopkins in America and Koert Vonderhorst in the Netherlands. My thanks to them, and to many other good companions.

I regret that I cannot give a paragraph, or even a sentence, to so many who have helped and cheered me along the way: Bob Belknap, Joe Bergin, Nicholas Boys Smith, Jay Brodie, Paul Brophy, Tom Casey, Tracey Clark, Jennifer Crewe, Amy Davis, David Dickson, Andrew Dolkart, Ann Giroux, David Gleason, Peter Guillery, Mary Ellen Hayward, Greg Heller, Neil Hertz, Eric Holcomb, Sabine Hummerich, Lance Humphreys, Alan Kahan, Rob Kanigel, Volker Kirchberg, Kathleen Lane, Laurence Le Quesne, Alan Mallach, Robert Mankin, Ellen Lupton, Jim Marrow, John Martin, Stan Mazaroff, Joe McNeely, Karl Means, Jeannette Meijer, Martin Millspaugh, Paul Muller, Gerard Noel, Rob Noel, Will Noel, Valerie Olson, Peter Pearre, Kennon Pearre, Sallye Perrin, Lee Riordan, Dan Rose, Emily Rose, Constance Rosenblum, Ed Rutkowski, Heather Scanlan, Walter and Nancy Schamu, Tamara Schellander, Patrick Shaffrey, Gráinne Shaffrey, Steve Shen, Frank Shivers, Natalie Shivers, Jean Stevenson, Damie and Diane Stillman, Jillian Storms, Gary Vikan, Jim Wollon, Sarah Wright, and Arthur Ziegler. Thank you, all of you.

I regret also that I cannot thank the hundreds of people who invited me into their homes, told me about their neighborhoods, and showed me nooks and crannies that I would otherwise have missed. Cities are great when their people love them.

It seems to be customary for authors to thank their spouses and children at the end of their lists of acknowledgements. I am more than content to follow such a fine old custom. Lydia and Robert have endured enough city exploring and city talk to drive most people into a pastoral retreat. And Lydia has wielded her red pencil with surgical skill. I owe them, at the very least, a lifetime of looking with interest at conifers and machines.

BIBLIOGRAPHY

Armitage, David and Braddick, Michael J., *The British Atlantic World 1500-1800*, New York, Palgrave MacMillan, 2009

Ayris, Ian, *A City of Palaces, Richard Grainger and the Making of Newcastle upon Tyne*, Newcastle, City of Newcastle, 1997

Baker, T.M.M., *London, Rebuilding the City after the Great Fire*, Chichester, Phillimore & Company, Ltd., 2000

Baltzell, E. Digby, *The Protestant Establishment, Aristocracy & Caste in America*, New York, Random House, 1964

Barbour, Violet, *Capitalism in Amsterdam in the Seventeenth Century*, Baltimore, Johns Hopkins University Press, 1950

Barker, Felix and Jackson, Peter, *The History of London in Maps*, London, Barrie & Jenkins, 1990

Beier, A.L. and Finley, Roger, eds., *London 1500-1700 The Making of the Metropolis*, London and New York, Longman, 1986

Bergdoll, Barry, *Mastering McKim's Plan: Columbia's First Century on Morningside Heights*, New York, Columbia University Press, 1998

Blackmar, Elizabeth, *Manhattan for Rent, 1785-1850*, Ithaca, Cornell University Press, 1989

Bloom, Nicholas Dagen and Lasner, Matthew Gordon, eds., *Affordable Housing in New York*, Princeton, Princeton University Press, 2016

Borsay, Peter, *The English Urban Renaissance*, Oxford, Oxford University Press, 1989

Borsay, Peter, *The Eighteenth Century Town*, London and New York, Longman, 1990

Borsay, Peter and Proudfoot, Lindsay, eds., *Provincial towns in Early Modern England and Ireland*, Oxford, Oxford University Press, 2002

Brady, Joseph, and Simms, Anngret, eds, *Dublin Through Space & Time*, Dublin, Four Courts Press, 2007

Breidenbaugh, Carl, *Cities in the Wilderness, The First Century of Urban Life in America 1625-1742*, London, Oxford University Press, 1971

Breidenbaugh, Carl, *Cities in Revolt, Urban Life in America 1743-1776*, New York, Capricorn Books, 1967

Briggs, Asa, *Victorian Cities*, New York, Harper & Row, 1970

Bunting, Bainbridge, *Houses of Boston's Back Bay*, Cambridge, Harvard University Press, 1967

Bunting, Bainbridge, *Harvard, An Architectural History*, Cambridge, Harvard University Press, 1985

Burgers, Jacqueline, *Wenceslaus Hollar: Seventeenth-century Prints from the Museum Boymans-van Beuningen*, Alexandria, Art Services International, 1994

Burke, Gerald L., *The Making of Dutch Towns*, London, Cleaver-Hulme Press, Ltd., 1956

Burrows, Edwin G. & Wallace, Mike, Gotham, *A History of New York City to 1898*, New York, Oxford University Press, 1999

Campbell, Colen, *Vitruvius Britannicus*, Mineola, NY, Dover Publications, 2007

Caro, Robert A., *The Power Broker: Robert Moses and the Fall of New York*, New York, Alfred A. Knopf, 1974

Casey, Christine, ed., *The Eighteenth-century Dublin Town House*, Dublin, Four Courts Press, 2010

Chalklin, C.W., *The Provincial Towns of Georgian England*, Montreal, McGill-Queen's University Press, 1974

Chalklin, Ch.W., *The Rise of the English Town, 1650-1850*, Cambridge, Cambridge University Press, 2001

Charles, Prince of Wales, *A Vision of Britain*, London, Doubleday, 1989

Cherry, Gordon E., *Town Planning in Britain since 1900*, Oxford, Blackwell, 1996

Clark, G. Kitson, *The Making of Victorian England*, New York, Atheneum, 1976

Clark, Kenneth, *The Gothic Revival*, Harmondsworth, Penguin, 1962

Clark, Peter and Gillespie, Raymond, eds., *Two Capitals: London and Dublin 1500-1840*, Oxford, Oxford University Press, 2001

Clark, Peter, ed., *The Cambridge Urban History of Britain, Volume II*, Cambridge, Cambridge University Press, 2000

Clifford, Joan, *Capability Brown*, Aylesbury, Shire Publications, Ltd., 1974

Coles, Robert, *The South Goes North*, Boston, Little, Brown & Company, 1971

Cook, Robert, *More of Milton Keynes*, Stroud, The History Press, 2013

Corfield, P.J., *The Impact of English Towns 1700-1800*, Oxford, Oxford University Press, 1982

Craig, Maurice, *Dublin 1660-1860*, London, The Cresset Press, 1952

Cummings, Abbott Lowell, *Massachusetts & its First Period Houses*, Boston, Colonial Society of Massachusetts, 1979

Curtis, Mark H., *Oxford and Cambridge in Transition, 1558-1642*, Oxford, Oxford University Press, 1959

Davies, David William, *Dutch Influence on English Culture*, Ithaca, Cornell University Press, 1964

De Vries, Jan, *The Economy of Europe in an Age of Crisis, 1600-1750*, Cambridge, Cambridge University Press, 1976

Dickson, David, *New Foundations Ireland 1660-1800*, Dublin, Irish Academic Press, 2000

Dolkart, Andrew Scott, *Biography of a Tenement House in New York City*, Charlottesville, University of Virginia Press, 2012

Dolkart, Andrew Scott, *The Row House Reborn*, Baltimore, Johns Hopkins University Press, 2009

Dollinger, Philippe, *The German Hansa*, Stanford, Stanford University Press, 1971

Dorsey, John, *Mount Vernon Place*, Baltimore, Maclay & Associates, 1983

Elliott, J.H., *Empires of the Atlantic World*, New Haven, Yale University Press, 2006

Engels, Friedrich, *The Condition of the Working Class in England*, Stanford, Stanford University Press, 1968

Everitt, Alan, ed., *Perspectives in English Urban History*, New York, Barnes & Noble, 1973

Farrar, Emmie Ferguson, *Old Virginia Houses Along the James*, New York, Bonanza Books, 1957

Faucher, Leon, *Manchester in 1844*, London, Frank Cass & Company, Ltd., 1960

Fisher, F.J., *London and the English Economy, 1500-1700*, London and Ronceverte, The Hambledon Press, 1990

Forman, H. Chandlee, *Maryland Architecture*, Cambridge, Tidewater Publishers, 1968

Frampton, Kenneth, *Modern Architecture, A Critical History*, New York, Oxford University Press, 1981

Gans, Herbert J., *The Urban Villagers*, New York, The Free Press, 1962

Gans, Herbert J., *The Levittowners*, New York, Vintage Books, 1967

Girouard, Mark, *The English Town*, New Haven, Yale University Press, 1995

Girouard, Mark, *Sweetness and Light, The Queen Anne Movement 1860-1900*, New Haven, Yale University Press, 1984

Green, Alan H.J., *The Building of Georgian Chichester*, Chichester, Phillimore & Company, Ltd., 2007

Guillery, Peter, *The Small House in Eighteenth-century London*, New Haven, Yale University Press, 2004

Haley, K.H.D., *The Dutch in the Seventeenth Century*, London, Thames and Hudson, 1972

Hamlin, Talbot, *Benjamin Henry Latrobe*, New York, Oxford University Press, 1955

Harvey, David, *Birmingham, The City Center*, Great Addington, Silver Link Publishing, 2002

Harvey, David, *Birmingham in the Age of the Tram*, Great Addington, Silver Link Publishing, 2003

Hayward, Mary Ellen and Belfoure, Charles, *The Baltimore Rowhouse*, New York, Princeton Architectural Press, 2001

Hayward, Mary Ellen and Shivers, Frank R., Jr., eds., *The Archtiecture of Baltimore*, Baltimore, Johns Hopkins University Press, 2004

Heijenbroek, Jacqueline and Steenmeijer, Guido, *A Walk along the Houses Designed by Philips and Justus Vingboons*, s-Gravenhage/Maarssen, SDU, 1989

Heller, Gregory L., *Ed Bacon*, Philadelphia, University of Pennsylvania Press, 2013

Herman, Bernard L., *Town House*, Chapel Hill, University of North Carolina Press, 2005

Hexter, J.H., *Reappraisals in History*, Evanston, Northwestern University Press, 1961

Hobhouse, Hermione, *Lost London*, Boston, Houghton Mifflin Company, 1972

Hofstader, Richard, *The Age of Reform*, New York, Vintage Books, 1955

Holcomb, Eric, *The City as Suburb, A History of Northeast Baltimore since 1660*, Santa Fe, Center for American Places, Inc., 2005

Hollinghurst, Hugh, *Classical Liverpool*, Liverpool, Liverpool History Society, 2008

Holloway, Marguerite, *The Measure of Manhattan*, New York, W.W. Norton & Company, 2013

Hoppen, K. Theodore, *The Mid-Victorian Generation, 1846-1886*, Oxford, Oxford University Press, 1998

Howell, Peter and Sutton, Ian, *The Faber Guide to Victorian Churches*, London, Faber and Faber, 1989

Huizinga, J.H., *Dutch Civilisation in the Seventeenth Century*, New York, Harper & Row, 1968

Hutton, William, *An History of Birmingham (1783)*, Creative Media Partners, LLC., 2015

Inwood, Stephen, *A History of London*, London and New York, MacMillan, 1998

Ison, Walter, *The Georgian Buildings of Bristol*, London, Faber & Faber, 1952

Jackson, Kenneth T., *The Crabgrass Frontier*, New York, Oxford University Press, 1985

Jefferies, Dr. Henry A., *A New History of Cork*, Dublin, The History Press Ireland, 2010

Kanigel, Robert, *Eyes on the Street, The Life of Jane Jacobs*, New York, Alfred A. Knopf, 2016

Killiam, Tim, *Amsterdam Canal Guide*, Amsterdam, Cityboek Productions, 2006

Kirker, Harold and Kirker, James, *Bulfinch's Boston 1787-1817*, New York, Oxford University Press, 1964

Knapp, Mary L., *An Old Merchant's House*, New York, Girandole Books, 2012

Kouwenhoven, John A., *The Columbia Historical Portrait of New York*, New York, Harper & Row, 1972

Kuyper, W., *The Triumphant Entry of Renaissance Architecture into the Netherlands*, Leyden, W. Kuyper, 1994

Kuyper, W., *Dutch Classicist Architecture*, Delft, Delft University Press, 1980

Lemann, Nicholas, *The Promised Land: The Great Black Migration and How it Changed America*, New York, Alfred A. Knopf, 1991

Lennon, Colm and Montague, John, *John Rocque's Dublin*, Dublin, Royal Irish Academy, 2010

Lewis, Michael J., *The Gothic Revival*, London, Thames and Hudson, 2002

Liedtke, Walter, *Vermeer and the Delft School*, New York, The Metropolitan Museum of Art, 2001

Line, Paul Leslie and Baggett, Adrian, *Maps & Sketches from Georgian & Early Victorian Birmingham*, Walsall, Mapseeker Archive Publishing, 2013

Lloyd-Jones, Thomas, *Liverpool Old and New*, East Ardsley, E.P. Publishing, Ltd., 1975

Lounsbury, Carl R., *Essays in Early American Architectural History*, Charlottesville, University of Virginia Press, 2011

Lukas, J. Anthony, *Common Ground*, New York, Alfred A. Knopf, 1985

MacLaran, Andrew, *Dublin the Shaping of a Capital*, London and New York, Belhaven Press, 1993

Mak, Geert, *Amsterdam*, London, The Harvill Press, 1999

Marchand, Bernard, *Paris, histoire d'une ville*, Paris, Editions de Seuil, 1993

Marsan, Jean-Claude, *Montreal in Evolution*, Montreal, McGill-Queen's University Press, 1981

Maxwell, Constantia, *Country and Town in Ireland under the Georges*, Dundalk, Dundalgan Press, 1949

McCusker, John J. and Morgan, Kenneth, eds., *The Early Modern Atlantic Economy*, Cambridge, Cambridge University Press, 2000

McKellar, Elizabeth, *The Birth of Modern London*, Manchester and New York, Manchester University Press, 1999

Metcalf, Priscilla, *Victorian London*, New York, Praeger Publishers, 1974

Minchinton, W.E., ed., *The Growth of English Overseas Trade in the Seventeenth and Eighteenth Centuries*, London and New York, Methuen & Co. Ltd., 1969

Montias, John Michael, *Vermeer and His Milieu*, Princeton, Princeton University Press, 1989

Montias, John Michael, *Artists and Artisans in Delft*, Princeton, Princeton University Press, 1982

Morrison, Hugh, *Early American Architecture*, Mineola, Dover Publications, Inc., 1987

Moss, Dr. William, *Georgian Liverpool*, Lancaster, Palatine Books, 2007

Murray, James H., *Bruges, Cradle of Capitalism*, Cambridge, Cambridge University Press, 2005

Murray, John J., *Amsterdam in the Age of Rembrandt*, Norman, University of Oklahoma Press, 1967

Murray, John J., *Antwerp in the Age of Plantin and Brueghel*, Norman, University of Oklahoma Press, 1970

Mustafa, Sam A., *Merchants and Migrations: Germans and Americans in Connection 1776-1835*, Aldershot, Aldgate, 2001

Muthesius, Stefan, *The English Terraced House*, New Haven, Yale University Press, 1982

Neudenburg, Elisabeth, *Hendrick de Keyser, Beeldhouwer en Bouwmeester van Amsterdam*, Amsterdam, Scheltema & Hobkema, 1930

O'Brien, Gillian and O'Kane, Finola eds., *Georgian Dublin*, Dublin, Four Courts Press, 2008

Olsen, Donald J., *Town Planning in London*, New Haven, Yale University Press, 1964

Olsen, Donald J., *The City as a Work of Art: London, Paris, Vienna*, New Haven, Yale University Press, 1986

Osman, Suleiman, *The Invention of Brownstone Brooklyn*, New York, Oxford University Press, 2011

Papenfuse, Edward C., *In Pursuit of Profit*, Baltimore, Johns Hopkins University Press, 1975

Parkinson-Bailey, John J., *Manchester, An Architectural History*, Manchester, Manchester University Press, 2000

Parrott, Kay, *Pictorial Liverpool, The Art of WG & William Herdman*, Liverpool, The Bluecoat Press, 2005

Pearce, David, *London's Mansions*, London, B.T. Batsford, Ltd., 1986

Pinkney, David H., *Napoleon III and the Rebuilding of Paris*, Princeton, Princeton University Press, 1972

Plumb, J.H., *The Growth of Political Stability in England*, London, Penguin Books, 1973

Price, Stephen J., *Birmingham Old and New*, East Ardsley, E.P. Publishing, Ltd., 1976

Purdue, A.W., *Newcastle, The Biography*, Stroud, Amberley Publishing, 2011

Ranum, Orest, *Paris in the Age of Absolutism*, University Park, Pennsylvania State University Press, 2002

Rasmussen, Steen Eiler, *London: the Unique City*, Cambridge, The M.I.T. Press, 1967

Reddaway, T.F., *The Rebuilding of London after the Great Fire*, London, Edward Arnold & Co., 1951

Riis, Jacob A., *How the Other Half Lives*, New York, Charles Scribner's Sons, 1909

Rodger, Richard, *Housing in Urban Britain 1780-1914*, Cambridge, Cambridge University Press, 1995

Roper, Laura Wood, *FLO, A Biography of Frederick Law Olmsted*, Baltimore, Johns Hopkins University Press, 1983

Rosenberg, H.P.R., *Architectur Den Haag 1800-1940*, s-Gravenhage, SDU Uitgeverij, 1988

Rosenberg, Jakob, Slive, Seymour, Ter Kuile, E.H., *Dutch Art and Architecture, 1600-1800*, Baltimore, Penguin Books, 1966

Rud, Peter, ed., *Glasgow, The Forming of the City*, Edinburgh, Edinburgh University Press, 1993

Ruff, Julius R., *Violence in Early Modern Europe*, Cambridge, Cambridge University Press, 2001

Rybczynski, Witold, *Home*, New York, Viking Penguin, 1987

Saint, Andrew, *Richard Norman Shaw*, New Haven, Yale University Press, 1977

Saint, Andrew, ed., *London Suburbs*, London, Merrell Holberton Publishers Ltd., 1999

Schorske, Carl E., *Fin-de-siecle Vienna*, New York, Vintage Books, 1981

Scully, Vincent J., Jr., *The Shingle Style*, New Haven, Yale University Press, 1971

Shaffrey, Patrick, *The Irish Town, an approach to survival*, Dublin, The O'Brien Press, 1975

Shaffrey, Patrick and Shaffrey, Maura, *Buildings of Irish Towns*, London, The Architectural Press, 1984

Shand-Tucci, Douglas, *Built in Boston, City and Suburb 1800-1950*, Amherst, University of Massachusetts Press, 1988

Shorto, Russell, *The Island at the Center of the World*, New York, Vintage Books, 2005

Spence, Craig, *London in the 1690s*, London, Centre for Metropolitan Research, Institute of Historical Research, University of London, 2000

Stanton, Phoebe B., *The Gothic Revival & American Church Architecture*, Baltimore, Johns Hopkins University Press, 1968

Stanton, Phoebe B., *Pugin*, New York, Viking, 1972

Stilgoe, John R., *Borderland: Origins of the American Suburb, 1820-1939*, New Haven, Yale University Press, 1988

Stone, Lawrence, *Social Change and Revolution in England 1540-1640*, London, Longmans, Green & Company, Ltd., 1966

Summerson, John, *The Unromantic Castle*, London, Thames and Hudson, 1990

Summerson, John, *Heavenly Mansions*, London, The Cresset Press, 1949

Summerson, John, *Architecture in Britain 1530-1830*, New Haven and London, Yale University Press, 1993

Summerson, John, *The Architecture of the Eighteenth Century*, London, Thames & Hudson, 1986

Sutcliffe, Anthony, *London, An Architectural History*, New Haven, Yale University Press, 2006

Tames, Richard, *Soho Past*, London, Historical Publications, Ltd., 1994

Tatum, George B., *Philadelphia Georgian*, Middletown, Wesleyan University Press, 1976

Taylor, A.J.P., *English History 1914-1945*, Oxford, Oxford University Press, 1965

Van Deursen, A.Th., *Plain Lives in a Golden Age: Popular Culture, Religion and Society in Seventeenth-century Holland*, Cambridge, Cambridge University Press, 1991

Van Nierop, H.F.K., *The Nobility of Holland*, Cambridge, Cambridge University Press, 1993

Vigier, Francois, *Change and Apathy: Liverpool and Manchester during the Industrial Revolution*, Cambridge, MIT Press, 1970

Wade, Richard C., *Slavery in the Cities, The South 1820-1860*, Oxford, Oxford University Press, 1969

Wade, Richard C., *The Urban Frontier*, Chicago, University of Chicago Press, 1976

Waine, Peter and Hilliam, Oliver, *22 Ideas that Saved the English Countryside*, London, Frances Lincoln, nd

Waller, Maureen, *London 1945*, London, John Murray, 2004

Ware, Caroline F., *Greenwich Village, 1920-1930*, Berkley, University of California Press, 1994

Warner, Sam Bass, Jr., *Streetcar Suburbs: The Process of Growth in Boston 1870-1900*, New York, Atheneum, 1973

Weber, Adna Ferrin, *The Growth of Cities in the Nineteenth Century*, Ithaca, Cornell University Press, 1967

Weigley, Russell F., ed., *Philadelphia: A 300-year History*, New York, W.W. Norton & Company, 1982

Westermann, Mariët, *Art and Home: Dutch Interiors in the Age of Rembrandt*, Zwolle, The Denver Art Museum, The Newark Art Museum, Wanders Publishers, 2001

White, Jerry, *London in the Twentieth Century*, London, Viking, 2001

Wilson, Charles, *The Dutch Republic*, New York, McGraw-Hill Book Company, 1968

Wittkower, Rudolf, *Palladio and English Palladianism*, London, Thames & Hudson, 1989

Wolmar, Christian, *The Subterranean Railway*, London, Atlantic Books, 2005

Young, Arthur, ed. Henry Morley, *A Tour in Ireland 1776-1779*, London, Paris, New York, Melbourne, Cassel & Company, Limited, 1897

Young, G.M., *Victorian England, Portrait of an Age*, Oxford, Oxford University Press, 1969

Zumthor, Paul, *Daily Life in Rembrandt's Holland*, Stanford, Stanford University Press, 1994

---, *The Georgian Squares of Dublin*, Dublin, Four Courts Press, 2007

INDEX

ILLUSTRATIONS

Allen, Nick CC: Eliot House, Harvard.
amsterdamplanner.nl: Canal Belt from the Air.
Author: Lanvale Street; A Dutch canal; Hendrick de Keyser House 170-172 Herengracht; West Church interior; Coymans House; Mauritshuis; Sint Sebastiansdoelen; Rapenburg houses; The King of Poland; Amsterdam gables; Weavers' Houses; An Amsterdam Canal; van Brouckhoven Hofje – Leyden; Same – courtyard; Silver Age street in the Hague; Walpole's Town House; St. James, Piccadilly; London and St. Paul's; Edes House; Oxmantown Mall, Birr; Wooden row, Baltimore; Hamilton Street, Baltimore; Abercromby Square; Louisburg Square; Pittsburgh, Old Allegheny; Natural History Museum; Johns Hopkins Hospital; Bremen row houses; The Free Trade Hall, Manchester; Eagle Insurance Buildings, Manchester; Commercial Ornament, Manchester; Union Square; Boston streetcar suburb, Dorchester; Good working-class row; Good working-class row; Back Bay; Metro-Land Reality; Roland Park; Middle-class 20s American suburb; Georgian Revival House; Simple colonial house; Berkel Westpolder; Rotterdam; Amsterdam, new apartments; Georgetown; Center City, Philadelphia; Salford Quays;
Berit CC SA 2.0 Generic: Houses of Parliament.
Cadman, Steve 2.0 Generic: Robin Hood Gardens
Boughton, John and Municipal Dreams: Gerard Gardens, Lansbury Estate. CC SA 2.5 Generic: Beau Nash.
ChrisO CC ShareAlike 3.0: Banqueting House, Whitehall.
Charles Center Inner Harbor Management, Co.: Otterbein 1975, Otterbein 1985.
ChristophedeNuit Public Domain: Abercromby Square.
cnbr SA 3.0 Unported: Watts Warehouse.
Create Streets/Gluckman Smith Architects: Create Streets.
Dixon, David CC SA 2.0: Manchester University.
Diggingspace ShareAlike 4.0: Castletown House.
Downer, Chris CC SA 2.0: Park Circus
Dragoni, Dora CC 3.0 Unported: Palazzo Madama
Edinburgh World Heritage: New Town from the Air.
Frick Collection: St. James's Park, 1783.
Garden City Collection: Ebenezer Howard.

Garvin, Alexander: Palazzo Rucellai; Via Giulia; Amsterdam City Hall; Petworth House; Charlotte Square; Mount Street Upper; Bedford Square; Belgrave Square; Cumberland Terrace; Beacon Hill; Washington Sq, NY; Parliament; Thornhill Crescent, Islington; Official Washington; Letchworth; Hampstead Garden Suburb; Park Avenue; Grand Concourse; South Bronx, 1970s; Baltimore in 1972; Baltimore waterfront today; South End; High Spine; Society Hill; Glasgow tenements; Docklands; Times Sq. pedestrianized; Bryant Park.
GDFL SA 3.0 Unported: The Four Courts.
Government of the District of Columbia, Office of Planning: Connecticut Avenue from the Air.
Grim, Cordelia, Mount Vernon Place.
Hanselpedia CC SA 3.0: Rotterdam.
Harvard Art Museums: Charles Bulfinch.
Healey, Liz, Warwick Visitor Information Centre: Warwick pre-Fire.
Henderson, Jim CC: Brownstone row.
Historic American Buildings Survey: The Stuyvesant, Waterloo Row.
Ian Christopher Weston CC SA 4.0: Houghton Hall.
Hammond Harwood House Association: The Hammond-Harwood House.
jameslwoodward CC SA 3.0 Unported: Paul Revere House.
Joy of Museums CC SA 4.0 International: Queen's House, Greenwich.
Library of Congress: Broad Street and Federal Hall; New York skyline from South Street; Washington row. houses: Covent Garden.
Maryland Historical Society: Baltimore Cathedral.
Metropolitan Museum, New York: Dining Room, Lansdowne House; London and St. Paul's; New York seen from Union Square, 1849.
Munckton, Richard CC 2.0: Highclere Castle.
Municipal Department for the Preservation and Restoration of Historic Buildings and Sites: Canal Belt from the Air.
Musik Animal CC SA 4.0: New York City Hall.
New York Daily News: Ford to City: Drop Dead.
NotFromUtrecht CC SA 3.0 Unported: Circus, Bath.
Noyes, Nicholas: Addison Avenue, Early English in Melbury Road, Haughwout Building, Park Avenue, Royal Crescent, St. Ann's Villas, St. James Gardens.

Phelan, John CC SA 2.0: Massachusetts Institute of Technology.
Phelan, John CC SA 3.0 Unported: Boston Streetcar Suburb.
Public Domain: A city palace, Archduke at Sarajevo, Chiswick House, city of London before the Fire, Clarendon House, Contrasts, Convents around Paris, Cumberland Terrace from *Metropolitan Improvements*, Dutch New York, Execution of Charles I, Frederick Law Olmsted, Great Fire of London, John Pym, John Wood the Elder, Lower East Side Tenements, Metro-Land magazine, Queen Square, Elfreth's Alley, St. Giles RC Church, St. James's Square, St. Paul's in the Blitz, The North Atlantic Ocean, Versailles, Wren Plan of the City of London, George Wade, Inigo Jones, Queen's Chapel, Ralph Allen, Lindsey House from *Vitruvius Britannicus*.
Realaewuk CC SA 4.0 International: Queen Square, Bristol.
Rijksmuseum: *The Golden Bend, The Market on the Dam, The Syndics of the Cloth Guild, The Little Street*
Russell, Julie Coldwell Banker Preferred: Good small American row houses.
Sones, Robin CC SA 2.0 Generic: Lincoln's Inn Fields.
seier+seier CC SA 2.0 Generic: Royal Crescent, Bath.
Taks, Public Domain: Coymans house.
Thacker, Jonathan SA 2.0 Generic: Oxmantown Mall.
Thierry – CC SA 2.5: Pissarro, Avenue de l'Opera.
Turner, Dennis SA 2.0: Birr, O'Connell Street.
Visit Bath: Bath from the air, Prior Park.
Walker Art Gallery, Liverpool: *Queen Elizabeth I.*
Warwick Visitor Information Centre: Warwick rebuilt after the Fire.
Wilkinson, Colin: The Old Dock, Liverpool; The Custom House, Liverpool; Rodney Street, Liverpool.